REFORMATIVE SPIRIT IN THE FICTION OF BHABANI BHATTACHARYA

REFORMATIVE SPIRIT IN THE FICTION OF BHABANI BHATTACHARYA

By

Dr. C.N. Latha

Lecturer in English
Govt. Degree College
Rayachoty, Kadapa (Dist.)
Andhra Pradesh
(INDIA)

DPH

DISCOVERY PUBLISHING HOUSE PVT. LTD.
NEW DELHI-110 002

Published by:
Tilak Wasan

DISCOVERY PUBLISHING HOUSE PVT. LTD.
4383/4B, Ansari Road, Darya Ganj
New Delhi-110 002 (India)
Phone : +91-11-23279245, 43596064-65
Fax : +91-11-23253475
E-mail : discoverypublishinghouse@gmail.com
sales@discoverypublishinggroup.com
parul.wasan@gmail.com
web : www.discoverypublishinggroup.com

***First Edition:* 2015**

ISBN: 978-93-5056-695-4

Reformative Spirit in the Fiction of Bhabani Bhattacharya

Printed at:
Infinity Images Systems
Delhi

Dedicated to
My Beloved Husband,
A. Chandra Sekhar Raju,
Lecturer in Zoology,
for his
Co-operation, Motivation
& Inspiration

Preface

Dr. Bhabani Bhattacharya is one of the few Indian English writers who belongs to first-rate novelists of the world. He is a much-translated Indo-Anglian writer who has won global fame. It is my endeavour to bring out the thematic concerns in all his six novels and fifteen short-stories. In addition to this, his work on Gandhi is also taken up for a chapter-wise analysis. This dissertation is divided into seven chapters.

In the first chapter, the history of Indian writing in English with special reference to Bhabani Bhattacharya is dealt with. The influence of Rabindranath Tagore, Mahatma Gandhi and some Western writers is studied with reference to his novels.

The second chapter deals with the thematic concerns in the first two novels of Bhabani Bhattacharya. The novels *So Many Hungers !* and *Music for Mohini* are taken up for intensive study. It analyses the theme of various forms of hunger and the theme of synthesis of tradition and modernity. The third chapter is concerned with the thematic concerns of third and fourth novels, *He Who Rides a Tiger* and *A Goddess Named Gold.* It deals with the theme of hunger for magic, power and possessions and the hunger for miracles and spiritual experience.

The fourth chapter presents the critical analysis of the last two novels of Bhattacharya. The novels *Shadow from*

Ladakh and *A Dream in Hawaii* deal with the clash of values represented by the East and the West. The theme of interculturation is artistically portrayed.

The fifth chapter is a detailed study of Bhattachaya's collection of fifteen short-stories titled *Steel Hawk And Other Stories*. Each story is taken up for detailed study to analyse the theme and treatment. The sixth chapter deals with his work on Mahatma Gandhi, *Gandhi the Writer. The Image As It Grew,* to commemorate the centenary of Gandhiji's birth. A chapter wise analysis is taken up to present the author's view about Gandhi the man and the writer.

The seventh chapter sums of Bhabani Bhattacharya's literary talents and careful handling of various literary devices. As an artist of social realism he identifies the evils of contemporary society and suggests solutions to overcome them. As Bhattacharya believes in the possibility of universal brotherhood, he pleads for integration of values and interculturation. A summing up of such a belief is made in a modest way. A comprehensive bibliography is provided at the end to help the above study.

Author

Acknowledgements

I would like to express my indebtedness and unbounded gratitude to my Guide and Research Supervisor *Dr. M. A. K. Sukumar,* Professor of English, S. V. University, Tirupati, for his guidance and valuable suggestions. Without his timely guidance, I would not have completed this task.

I also thank *Dr. M. R. Ashok,* Head of the Department of English, S. V. University, Tirupati for his encouragement. I extend my gratitude to *Dr. G. M. Sundaravalli* and *Dr. M. Narendra* whose guidance helped me a lot in the preparation of my thesis and also *Dr. A. Hariprasanna, Dr. P. Yerrama Reddy* and *Dr. P. Usha Rani* for their counsel.

My thanks are due to Late Prof. *C. D. Narasimhaiah* the great critic, for his guidance and his library in Dwanyaloka which is the main source for my research material. I am grateful to the librarians of S. V. University, SCILET, CIEFL, Presidency College, Madras University, Regional College, Mysore who were a source of help and encouragement.

In this endeavour, it is my pleasure to express my deep gratitude to my husband, *A. Chandra Sekhar Raju,* for his valuable and timely suggestions and needful help throughout my education. I also thank my daughters *A. Yurekha* and *A. Mouni* for their affection and cooperation. I would like to acknowledge my thanks to my parents and my well wishers for their assistance.

Above all, I bow down for ever to *God Almighty* with whose grace and blessings I was able to complete this Research work successfully.

C.N. Latha

Contents

1 Introduction
Focus on a Committed Writer

Indo-Anglian Literature or Indian English Literature forms an integral part of English literature and has attained a distinct place in the literary landscape of India. In the nineteenth century eminent Indians started to write and express their thoughts in a foreign language, English, due to the western impact. As Prof. K. R. Srinivasa Iyengar remarks, "Indo-Anglian literature... the creation too of certain gifted individuals from Ram Mohan Roy to Dom Moreas who have been able to triumph over many limitations and achieve impressive results in a foreign medium".[1]

The nineteenth century is the golden period in the history of Indo-Anglian literature. Many Indian writers made an attempt to prove their creative ability. The rapid changes throughout the country touched the genius of the Indian people. The result is the emergence of a new approach for easy communication with the whole world. Dr. K. R. Srinivasa Iyengar rightly points out, "Indians have written – and are writing – in English for communicating with one another and with the outside world, for achieving self-expression too artistically, using English, if necessary, or necessarily in an Indian way".[2]

The critics of literature began to appreciate the skill of Indian writers in expressing the life and soul of India very effectively. Commenting on the Indianness in Indian Writing in English in his General Introduction to K. R. Chandrasekaran's *Bhabani Bhattacharya,* C. D. Narasimhaiah remarks, "It can present the life of a village like, Bulashah or Kanthapura, a small town like Malgudi or Kedaram or sweep through continents and eternity itself and so long as the operative sensibility of the writer is essentially Indian it will be Indian literature".[3]

Indo-Anglian writers present the culture, customs, and contemporary issues in their works with the help of the foreign language, English. They present the typical Indian scenario and convey this literally to the world. As the sensibility of the writers is native or Indian, the writings carry and convey this sensibility. So according to C. D. Narasimhaiah, Indo-Anglian Writing is a part of Indian literature and not different from other literature of regional languages like Gujarati, Kannada, Bengali, etc. The medium of expression, language, does not make the contents of literature differ from one another.

Many critics of Indian Writing in English have asserted the use of Indian epics as the source for Indian Writing in English. The creative writers can make the Puranas as the background for their works or writings. The epics like *The Ramayana* and *The Mahabharatha* are the main sources and background for a number of writers to reveal Indian traditional values. As Syed Mujeebuddin points out, "K. R. S. Iyengar, C. D. Narasimhaiah and M. K. Naik, the doyens of English literary studies in India, have helped in establishing this search for authenticity in Indian Writing in English as a justifying discourse that authorises the native canon".[4]

'Indianness' in other words, is interpreted as bearing a distinct Hindu quality. As the Indian Writing in English is a part of Indian literature, it has the influence of regional and native setting. Not only setting but the thought is typically that of local or Hindu culture. Even eminent critics like C. D. Narasimhaiah hold similar views, "... the mainstream of Indian thought is Hindu and the mainstream of (it) literary sensibility is Sanskrit....."[5]

As most of the Indo-Anglian writers are Hindus, the literature they produce is Hindu literature, though the language is foreign, that is English. In this view Hindu literature cannot be realistic without the use of Hindu tradition. In order to appreciate this writing one has to acquaint one-self with Hindu view of life. The following comment, for example, by an Indian researcher is appreciable because the realistic art is the medium to convey the value of culture. The comment is, "It must be clear from the beginning that....Indo-Anglian literature is a Hindu literature and it is the Hindu literature composed in the English language. It is Hindu because most of the authors including all major Indo-Anglians are Hindus: and it operates in the context of the Hindu cultural ethos".[6]

The language, the writers use necessarily in Indo-Anglian literature is Indian English. The Indian English reflects the thoughts and emotions of Indian people with a regional flavor. Though the language is foreign, the life is Indian in all aspects. The best definition of Indian English is the one given by Prof. V. K. Gokak. According to him Indian English represents, "the evolution of a distinct standard-a-standard the body of which is correct English usage, but whose soul is Indian in colour, thought and imagery, and, now and then even in the evolution of an idiom which is expressive of the unique quality of the Indian mind while conforming to the 'correctness' of English usage".[7]

Most of the Indo-Anglian writers have attained special skill in the art of writing English. The notion that Indo-Anglians should also write like the English men is to misread the definition and purpose of Indo-Anglian literature. Mrs. Meenakshi Mukherjee rightly comments, "There seems to be an increasing awareness that English is a plaint language which each writer has to fashion a new to serve his particular purpose, that for an Indian writer this fashioning will have to be different from what a British or American writer does, and that the definition of good English varies not only from century to century but also from place to place".[8]

Literature is the expression of life in various angles, about different societies from East to West. As a universal language, English is a link for the flow of thought and for integration of nations. Dr. K. R. Srinivasa Iyengar rightly remarks, "English is the veritable Suez canal for intellectual intercourse between the West and the East – between England and India especially; and the traffic is by no means altogether one-sided (K. R. Srinivasa Iyengar, *Indian Writing in English*, p. 15).

The Indian Philosophy from ancient to modern times spread to various countries and attained glory due to the mastery of English language. Eminent Indian philosophers like Sri Aurobindo, Rabindranath Tagore, Vivekananda, Dr. Radhakrishnan and Mahatma Gandhi have attracted the Western People through English language.

Indian Writing in English has started with the translation of Western writings by Indian scholars. The next step was the composition of original works under the inspiration of Western models. Dr. K. R. Srinivasa Iyengar rightly points out, "Indian Writing in English is but one of the voices in which India speaks. It is a new voice, no doubt, but it is as much Indian as the others". (K. R. Srinivasa Iyengar, Indian Writing in English, p. 3).

In Indo-Anglian literature, the novel occupies the most important place. In quality and quantity its output is more than that of poetry or drama. A careful study of all the novels written by Indians in English since 1864 reveals those Indian writers have successfully achieved their desired results. As K. S. Ramamurthi remarks, "The earliest writers in the field like Bankim Chandra, Toru Dutt and Ramesh Chandra Dutt were by no means 'imitators' but conscious experimenters who adapted an alien form and medium to a socio-cultural situations and sensibility which were specifically Indian".[9]

The rise of the novel as an art form was not an imitation but an evolution and a growth brought by changing socio-economic conditions of the society. The early novelists made an attempt to prove their individuality in one form or other. This new art form developed after passing through several innovations. Dr. T. Prabhakar observes, "In short the rise of the novel in India marked the emancipation from the older literary traditions and conventions, the emergence of a new form of writing where the writer had absolute freedom to experiment, innovate and produce something new or novel".[10]

While lyrics, dramas, short stories, prose works emerged in English in early 19th century, the 'novel' as a literary phenomenon in India emerged only in the later nineteenth century. The real beginning was with the work of the great Bankim Chandra Chatterjee's first novel *Rajmohan's Wife* (1864). Rabindranath Tagore and Sarat Chandra Chatterjee followed him.

In the early decades of the twentieth century, Indian English Fiction attained its glory with the emergence of the trio-Mulk Raj Anand, R. K. Narayan and Raja Rao. But two more important names in the field of Indian English fiction after the trio are: *(i)* Manohar Malgonkar and *(ii)* Bhabani Bhattacharya.

An attempt is made in this dissertation to analyse the thematic concerns in the oeuvre of Bhabani Bhattacharya.

Bhabani Bhattacharya was born on 10th of November 1906 in Bhagalpur, Bihar in an educated family of Bengali Brahmins. He was educated at Patna University and took his B. A. (Hons) degree in 1927. University of London awarded him Ph.D degree on historical research in 1934. He married Salila Mukherji in 1935 and was blessed with three children, a son and two daughters.

The name and fame of Bhabani Bhattacharya was not only limited to India but also reached to other places of the world. In Indo-Anglian fiction Bhabani Bhattacharya is a first rank novelist. Malta Grover writes about his global reputation as, "Bhabani Bhattacharya is a much translated Indo-Anglian writer who has won global fame. Though his literary output is scanty, just six novels and a collection of short stories, his novels have been translated into twenty six languages including fourteen European languages".[11]

Bhabani Bhattacharya is a man of multitudinous interests like Mulk Raj Anand. He has made his mark as a translator, creative historian, biographer, story-teller and novelist. In terms of achievement he stands next to that of Mulk Raj Anand and R. K. Narayan. His achievement does not lie in the portrayal of life alone, it lies in the vision of life, which he conveys through it. This achievement is no less great than the achievement of any other-world-class novelist. As Harcharn Singh Boparai remarks, "Bhabani Bhattacharya's achievement as a novelist can best be assessed on the basis of his whole work. On this account, he has emerged as a world-class novelist who has presented the birth-pangs of a nation's freedom, and its agonies and aspirations in a historical perspective; who has shown concern for man's physical, mental and spiritual needs; and who has depicted the human drama at micro-cosmic as well as epic scale".[12]

Among the Indo-Anglian novelists of past and present times Bhabani Bhattacharya has a very prominent place. His works include Tagore's translations entitled *The Golden Boat, Towards Universal Man*, a commemoration Volume published on the eve of the birth centenary of Tagore; *Some Memorable Yesterdays, Indian Cavalcade, Steel Hawk and Other Stories*, a collection of fifteen short stories; *Gandhi The Writer: The Image As It Grew*, a highly stimulating and provocative study released on the occasion of the birth centenary of Mahatma Gandhi and six novels: *(i) So Many Hungers*! (1947); *(ii) Music for Mohini* (1952); *(iii) He Who Rides a Tiger* (1954); *(iv) A Goddess Named Gold* (1960); *(v) Shadow from Ladakh* (1967) and *(vi) A Dream in Hawaii* (1978).

The place of Bhabani Bhattacharya in the artistic creation is next only to the great three Indian novelists. Commenting on the art of Bhabani Bhattacharya K. K. Sharma writes,

"Though not, a prolific writer with abundant humanism and leftist leanings like Mulk Raj Anand, nor a comic genius with artistic detachment and commitment to human values like R. K. Narayan nor a creative artist with astonishing philosophical depth like Raja Rao, Bhabani Bhattacharya – one of the major novelists of the older generation of living Indo-English fictionists – is endowed with a transparently positive vision of life, explored and expressed artistically in all the five novels he has published so far".[13]

For his creative works, Bhabani Bhattacharya won international fame. In the year 1949, he was offered the prestigious post of Press Attache in the Embassy of India, Washington D. C. He was appointed consultant in the Ministry of Education, New Delhi in 1961. In 1967, he won the much-coveted 'Sahitya Akademy Award' for his novel *Shadow from Ladakh*. In 1973, he joined the University of Washington, Seattle, as Walker-Ames Professor.

Like Conrad, James and Poe, Bhabani Bhattacharya considers fiction as one of the highest forms of art. He holds that art should be firmly based on reality – social, economical, historical or political. Like Mulk Raj Anand and Raja Rao, he contributed to the development of political novel. According to Morris E. Speare the political novel as a genre is, "A work of fiction which leans rather to 'ideas' than to 'emotions' where the main purpose of the writer is party. The main purpose of the writer is party-propaganda, public reform or exposition of the lives of personages who maintain Government or of forces which constitute Government".[14]

In a political novel, the characters and events are interwoven in a political milieu. A few Indo-Anglian novelists have set their narratives in the recent political and historical milieu with significant political happenings. M. K. Bhatnagar rightly points out, "We find that, for Bhabani Bhattacharya the ethic of 'political art' is a compulsive experience, a living image, a dominant emotion and a meaningful expression. Anything, contemporary is not denied artistic value purely for the reason of its being contemporary".[15]

During Pre and Post Independence period, political novels were based on Gandhian ideology. Indo-Anglian novelists inspired by the political ethics of Mahatma Gandhi, based their novels on Gandhi's role in the political and moral awakening of the masses. In this context, A. V. Krishna Rao writes, "Almost all the Indo-Anglian novels have one or more of the following nuclear ideas predominant in them; the Evil of partition; the cult of 'Quit India; and the Gandhian Myth..... It is significant that the image of Gandhi is present in all the three types of novels though the details and emphasis may vary".[16]

In his novels, Bhabani Bhattacharya artistically presents another important facet of Gandhian political ideology, regarding the status of women. Women are considered as equal citizens of a state and hence they should come out of that sheltered existence and play their essential political role in a fearless manner. The women-characters such as Mohini in *Music for Mohini,* Meera in *The Goddess Named Gold*, Kajoli in *So Many Hungers*!, Sumita and Suruchi in *Shadow from Ladakh* are typical examples for this.

The preachings of Gandhiji made the novelist the follower of his philosophy. Regarding Bhabani Bhattacharya's application of Gandhian ideology in the modern political scene, M. K. Bhatnagar remarks, "Bhabani Bhattacharya's is a strong plea for rediscovering the true essence of ways rooted in our tradition and employing them in a constructive manner, moulding the method, if need be, to sharpen its efficacy. A genuine application of the all-encompassing political philosophy of Gandhi would seem, the most suitable in the present times as much as it had been in the past". (M. K. Bhatnagar, *Political Consciousness in Indian English Writing*, p. 152).

As a young artist Bhabani Bhattacharya was influenced by a number of factors. The works of William Shakespeare inspired him most. He used his father's library for complete analysis of William Shakespeare's plays. This helped him a lot to understand the basic human nature. As Malta Grover observes, “It is difficult to say how much he grasped of the plays that he read but the very fact that he drank deep at the fountain of humanity contained in those plays must have developed, to some extent, his insight into human nature”. (Malta Grover, *Bhabani Bhattacharya as a Novelist of Social Conscience*, p. 3).

During his college education, he found the plays of Henrick Ibsen and Bernard Shaw particularly stimulating. Among the writers who influenced him, Bhabani Bhattacharya prominently mentions Tagore and Steinbeck. Bhabani Bhattacharya’s translation of Tagore’s stories in *The Golden Boat* and his association with the preparation of *Towards Universal Man* providing ample evidence of his admiration for Tagore.

Bhabani Bhattacharya acknowledges his indebtedness to both Tagore and Steinbeck in these words, “Tagore appealed to me from my school days and my writer’s career also began from those days. It was, therefore, quite unlikely that I would miss the impact of Gurudev all-pervading personality. Later I read many English and American authors. Among those John Steinbeck attracted me most”.[17]

Under the influence of Tagore, Bhabani Bhattacharya began writing poems and prose sketches in Bengali. His articles were published in *Vichitra*, a Bengali magazine, with which Tagore was associated. Tagore encouraged Bhabani Bhattacharya to go ahead with his writing and blessed him. Bhabani Bhattacharya admits the great influence of Tagore in these words, “Whoever came in contact with the personality of Rabindranath Tagore, even for a brief space, received one predominating impression – that of richness. It was a richness of the spirit and was not limited to genius. There was the supercharm softening the intellectual blaze, the innate simpleness belying the sophistication; but above all, the never failing humanity with which the poet made his forceful impact on all levels of consciousness”.[18]

After Tagore, Mahatma Gandhi is the second great influence on Bhabani Bhattacharya. He first met Gandhi in England in 1931 when Gandhi had been there in order to attend the Round Table Conference. In an interview with D. B. Shimer, Bhabani Bhattacharya accepts the influence of Gandhi, "India's struggle for freedom had reached one of its peak points. I had been close to that struggle, though not an activist. In India, I had attended many meetings in which Gandhi spoke. But this was my first encounter with the great man, it was only a little less overwhelming than the one with Tagore".[19]

One can find the influence of Gandhiji on him by the choice of themes and the portrayal of characters. Bhabani Bhattacharya deals with the theme of Freedom Movement in all his novels except in *A Dream in Hawaii*. The central focus in the novel, *A Goddess Named Gold* (1960) is the political independence from Britain and the challenges of democratic governance. The novel, *Shadow from Ladakh* is deeply saturated with Gandhian references, thought and imagery. The novel *So Many Hungers*!, has Gandhian characters and ends on a Gandhian note. The novel, *He Who Rides a Tiger*, deals with the problems of the lower castes of society.

Both Gandhi and Bhabani Bhattacharya are deeply concerned with the moral and social uplift of the people and are against all forms of exploitation of man by man. Bhabani Bhattacharya's dream of an ideal society is derived from Gandhi's vision of *Ram Rajya* (an ideal state).

In addition to the native influences, Bhabani Bhattacharya was also exposed to the influence of Western writers and culture during his stay in London and later on in the course of his wide travels. During his study under the famous political philosopher and author Harold Laski, he was influenced by the Marxist principles. Though Bhabani Bhattacharya is not a Marxist, Dorothy Shimer points out, "a strong undercurrent of the early Marxist respect for the liberal humanitarianism and the effects of economic pressures on history runs through all Bhattacharya's novels".[20]

There are some American writers such as Dos Possos, John Steinbeck, Sinclair Lewis and Upton Sinclair, who appealed to Bhabani Bhattacharya and influenced him. Infact, Bhabani Bhattacharya's first novel, *So Many Hungers*! resembles Steinbeck's *The Grapes of Wrath* in many respects. Both of these works deal with the inhuman exploitation of man by man in contemporary society.

Bhabani Bhattacharya's marriage with Salila Mukherji in 1935, was a boon to his literary career. Salila Mukherji, had considerable influence on him. She used to contribute all her energies to the enrichment of her husband's work. She was his mental companion for more than four decades. About Salila's contribution Malta Grover writes, "She brought ideas, scenarios and her artistic imagination in the character formation of those unforgettable women who occupy such important roles in all his novels. To this Bhabani Bhattacharya adds the gifts and graces so richly found in his 'inspiring angel'. We can feel the vibrations of her mind and soul in Bhabani Bhattacharya's artistic performance".[21]

Along with so many factors, the contemporary events and situations of the Indian scene inspired this great artist. The impact of Second World War of India was very severe. The result was the Bengal Famine, which proved to be a traumatic experience of Bhabani Bhattacharya. He said in an interview, "My creative writing had its true genesis in the hunger-hit streets of Calcutta where the great famine raged. I had an intense need of release from the agony of traumatic experience. Apparent trivial like a pair of dying eyes wide-open and unblinking in misery-filled sockets could be immensely persuasive".[22]

Each of his novels tackles some pressing problems of contemporary life of typical Indians of all strata of society. *So Many Hungers*! and *He Who Rides a Tiger* are inspired by the famine in Bengal and the Quit India Movement. *Music for Mohini* is concerned with the reconciliation of old and new values in Indian life. *A Goddess Named Gold* is fully preoccupied with the meaning and significance of freedom. *Shadow from Ladakh* focuses attention on problems arising from the Chinese aggression of 1962. The experience in the University of Hawaii made the author expand the national to international understanding and the intercultural horizons. This is reflected in his last novel, *A Dream in Hawaii.*

According to Bhabani Bhattacharya creative writing ought to be spontaneous. His views can be gathered from his own statements to interviewers and articles written by him. He asserts, "I have not believed in writing for the sake of writing. I seldom planned a story structure. Each story grew in my sub-conscious mind as it were. When it had grown enough, I had to give it physical form. The characters even when I had decided how they were going to behave moved by their own violation, often defeating my purpose".[23]

As a novelist he writes with a social purpose. In his opinion, a novel should be concerned with social reality. He expressed his opinion in the following words, "I hold that a novel must have a social purpose. It must place before reader something from the society's point of view. "Art is not necessarily for art's sake. Purposeless art and literature which is much in vogue does not appear to me a sound judgement". (R. K. Srivastava, *Bhattacharya at Work: An Interview*, p. 18).

For Bhabani Bhattacharya social realism means the perception of the essential truth of a situation or incident. He expects a novelist to give true descriptions with keen observation. He has made the following observations in an interview, "Unless a writer has keen observation and an eye for noting the details of general behaviour of folks, he cannot write a social novel. I have developed this habit and I have not missed a single opportunity of observing incidents, happenings, where I can gain something for the writer in me. Most of my characters have, shaped themselves from the real earth". (Sudhakar Joshi, *An Evening with Bhabani*, p. vii).

He believes, creative literature should be instructive to humanity. There should be a fusion of the ethical values in literature. According to him, art must be for life's sake. He observes, "Art must teach but unobtrusively, by its vivid interpretation of life. Art must preach, but only by virtue of its being a vehicle of truth. If that is propaganda, there is no need to eschew the world".[24]

Regarding the characters in his fiction, Bhabani Bhattacharya may or may not pre-conceive them. His duty is to invent characters and events and then to start writing that never ends the way he planned at the start. The entire original fabric of the book is changed because characters and situations govern his narrative. He remarks about his method of writing as, "When I feel like writing upon a theme, and the characters and events fit in the pattern, I start putting it down on paper. But once I start writing, it is not I but the characters that compel me to be led by them. It is they who decide the way they should end.... The end of the story, in my case, is never the one which I had in my mind in the beginning". (Sudhakar Joshi, *An Evening with Bhabani*, p. 42).

Bhabani Bhattacharya is a committed writer like Mulk Raj Anand. He has evinced enough interest in the political, economic and social problems of India. As Stephen Hemenway rightly points out, "Bhabani Bhattacharya inherits Foster's sharp eye for East-West dichotomies, Anand's concern with social, economic and political problems and Narayan's playfulness and exaggerations".[25]

Like Mulk Raj Anand, Bhattacharya tried to expose the suffering and humiliation inflicted on the lower strata of society. Humanism literally means devotion to human interests and concern for the welfare of society. It proposes to improve the conditions of human beings. Bhabani Bhattacharya is a humanist, a novelist with a message for his countrymen. G. Rai rightly points out, "The novels of Bhabani Bhattacharya embody a positive vision of life which is obviously humanistic. He is seriously concerned with the plight of the destitutes and the low-caste people.... In his novels, Bhabani Bhattacharya explores the causes of human sufferings and suggests their possible remedies".[26]

Bhabani Bhattacharya's first novel, *So Many Hungers*!, mainly focuses on man's great hunger for food and other types of hunger like: hunger for freedom, wealth, power, sex, ethical values, prosperity and hunger for self-respect. Apart from this, the novel deals with the freedom struggle and the British administration in India. K. R. Chandrasekharan puts his view about the novel as, "Among the three novels of Bhabani Bhattacharya which deal with the pre-Independence period, *So Many Hungers*! (1947) is the one most concerned with the freedom struggle with its tensions and conflicts. Consequently this novel has comments to make on the alien government and the British people. (K. R. Chandrasekharan, *Bhabani Bhattacharya*, p. 25).

In this novel, the author portrays a pathetic human story against the setting of a historical situation. The novel is a severe attack on both the foreign government and some unprincipled Indians who exploit the situation for their own benefit. The novelist's sincerity, compassion, commitment are evident all through the novel.

The philosophy of Bhabani Bhattacharya is vividly expressed in the novel *Music for Mohini* (1952). This novel is a protest against the deep rooted social evils of our country. He emphasises that India must re-orient herself on a new social order. In his opinion political freedom has no meaning without social freedom. Syed Ameeruddin remarks, "His second novel *Music for Mohini* is a very interesting novel, which once again depicts vividly Bhabani Bhattacharya's view on our social system. He expresses his views on creating a new India, which is free from all social evils – like economic bondage, hunger, inequality, misguided faith, superstitions, rituals and above all ignorance. In this novel he vehemently criticises the cruelty and hypocrisy of Indian social life. Bhabani Bhattacharya as a socially conscious writer, stresses the need for reform from the old traditional views".[27]

In addition to social freedom, this novel brings out the eternal conflict between the two cultures of the East and of the West. The novelist resolves this conflict between tradition and modernity by mingling them and accepting the best of both sides. The result comprises synthesis of opposing ideologies and cultures by way of mutual understanding.

In the novel, *He Who Rides a Tiger*, which is developed on the background of Bengal famine, the main character Kalo moves to the city, due to lack of food in his village. He is concerned with the hunger of his dear daughter Lekha, more than his hunger. It is this hunger which has put Kalo in prison and later made him a pseudo guru. The novel also attempts at removing caste and class barriers, superstitions and false religious beliefs. The novelist attacks the wicked practices of Hindu society in the guise of religion.

The orthodoxy and superstition of the people of India is condemned. The exploitation of human beings in the name of religion is a major factor in the novel. K. H. Kunjo Singh aptly remarks, "In *He Who Rides a Tiger*, the novelist discusses the religious aspect of the Hindu society. There are certain references to Hindu religion as practised by the people of the country like the people's eager expectation of Kalo's promised miracle, offering of money and materials for the construction of false temple, etc. Infact, the novelist exposes the wicked practices of the hollow religion".[28]

The next novel *A Goddess Named Gold* deals with the happenings in a village during the period immediately preceding India's attainment of freedom. In this novel, Bhabani Bhattacharya shows the way in which a country should use freedom and the benefits may be derived from it. The story runs between the hardened hoarder and black-marketers Samsunder Sethji on one hand and the young and energetic village girl Meera. It deals with the theme of economic freedom of the hungry masses.

Regarding the theme of the novel, as Balram S. Sorot points out, "In his next novel, *A Goddess Named Gold*, Bhabani Bhattacharya deals with the theme of economic freedom of hungry masses and warns against the evils of profiteering and poverty which, if not completely eradicated, may defeat the very purpose of freedom and lead to many more hungers. With the freedom in sight, people have to work with solidarity and faith to ameliorate their lot and make their country prosperous".[29] The novel presents the clash between personal ambition and public welfare. While the character Sethji represents selfishness and exploitation, the character Meera represents the modern women who fight for their rights and against social injustice.

Shadow from Ladakh is the famous novel of Bhabani Bhattacharya which won Sahitya Akademy award for 1967. This novel is set against the menacing background of the Chinese aggression against India starting in October, 1962. Based on the incident, the novel presents the conflicting ideas of non-violent principles of Gandhi on the one hand and the forces of science and technology on the other. Bhabani Bhattacharya brings the philosophy of synthesis not only at national level but also at international level.

This novel may be considered Bhabani Bhattacharya's greatest achievement. It has greater range and scope than the other novels. In this novel, he presents the hearts of millions of people in India during the critical situation. K. R. Chandrasekharan rightly observes, "In *Shadow from Ladakh*, the novelist takes a significant step in the direction of immensity and depth. What is presented is the spectacle of a new state with an ancient culture facing a massive physical threat to its existence and at the same time struggling for a way of life that will enable it to take its place in the new world order without losing its mornings and its distinctive identity". (K. R. Chandrasekharan, *Bhabani Bhattacharya*, p. 126).

In the novel *A Dream in Hawaii*, Bhabani Bhattacharya projects the Western way of life and Eastern life. In the West, science and technology help men only in the material progress. The moral or spiritual values cannot be derived from the progress. The central character of the novel, Swami Yogananda, is a Professor turned Yogi. He preaches the spiritualism of the East and also understands the Western value-pattern. His character signifies a fusion of diverse cultures. K. H. Kunjo Singh observes,..."... Bhattacharya is a man of inter-culturation. The East-West centre helps in growing up this interculturation. The University of Hawaii with its motto; 'Above all nations is humanity' influences in expanding his inter-cultural ideas. Bhattacharya is a multi-cultural person mediating between several groups in a culturally diverse world. He is a mediating man bridging the East and West and concerning with the synthesis of old and new". (K. H. Kunjo Singh, *The Fiction of Bhabani Bhattacharya*, p. 126).

As mentioned above, Bhabani Bhattacharya pleads for inter-cultural ideas. He is in favour of synthesis of different cultures of East and West. He had a broad outlook towards the humanity and pleads for integration of traditional and modern values.

Apart from novels, Bhabani Bhattacharya has fifteen short-stories to his credit. *Steel Hawk and Other Stories* is an anthology of short stories. In his short stories he projects the social set up of India. The emotional feelings of not only humans but also animals are vividly portrayed in the stories. His theme of synthesis of traditional and the modern values occupies the prominent place in the short stories also. Regarding his short stories, Balram S. Sorot points out, "Collected in *Steel Hawk and Other Stories*, they project a cross-section of life in India and abroad, and are concerned with a deeper emotional meaning, conveyed through their widely individual dramas. Since Bhattacharya is pre-occupied with certain other issues in these sketches, the theme of blending is not in evidence in all of them. In some of the stories, however, the writer does present a synthesis of the traditional and the modern values as well as the idealism and the realism". (Balram S. Sorot, *The Novels of Bhabani Bhattacharya*, p. 101).

In the short stories, the author presents the human relationships in a realistic way. He has tried to show hidden human desires in his stories. The father and son relationship is artistically successful in his story *Acrobats*. Bhabani Bhattacharya believes even the animals have human feelings. In *Mere Monkeys*, the feelings of a female monkey are related to human beings. *A Moment of Eternity* portrays the lower middle class Indian family. In *Public Figure*, he presents a post-colonial male protagonist, a rich business man hungry for name and fame.

The fiction of Bhabani Bhattacharya has universal appeal for its wide range of motifs. All his novels have certain central ideas around which the action takes place. As Harcharn Singh Boparai points out, "The reason for this universal appeal lies in the archetypal motifs that Bhabani Bhattacharya has objectified in his fiction. The most dominant of these motifs is the quest motif which lies at the centre of all great literatures. The main configurations of this motif in Bhabani Bhattacharya's fiction may be termed as quest for food, Indian Dream of Edenic Possibilities, and Man-Woman Relationship. These quests operate at different levels of consciousness".[30]

The quest of Swarajya is prominent in *So Many Hungers*!. In *Music for Mohini*, it is the quest for Ram Rajya and this continues in *Shadow from Ladakh*. In *He Who Rides a Tiger*, the motif is the Quest for caste-ridden welfare society. In *Goddess Named Gold*, it is the quest for righteous actions of free country. In *A Dream in Hawaii*, Bhabani Bhattacharya portrays the quest for international and intercultural understanding.

Regarding the other writings of Bhabani Bhattacharya, *The Golden Boat* is a collection of Tagore's stories, allegories and other short pieces translated into English by Bhabani Bhattacharya. *Indian Cavalcade* is a sequence of several articles dealing with episodes from Indian History published in newspapers and periodicals. *Gandhi The Writer* is the only work of Bhabani Bhattacharya in which he attempts a survey and assessment of another person's writings. It was specially written to commemorate the birth centenary of Gandhi in 1969. *Towards Universal Man* is a selection of Tagore's important essays translated into English.

The vision of Bhattacharya is the establishment of Ram Rajya, a welfare society in India. According to him, only political issues are not the ultimate aim but in all other aspects, the Indian society should be enlightened. Dr. Paul Verghese states, "Bhabani Bhattacharya has the vision of a welfare society at heart. His concerns are clear and unambiguous; they are political, economic and social. In other words the dignity of man both in national and international contexts is uppermost in his mind. In this he follows the traditions of European social realism as does Mulk Raj".[31]

Bhabani Bhattacharya aims at change in all aspects of life. The transformation of society is the central motif in his fiction. The change is not confined to one aspect, but to all aspects of life, which leads to the attainment of goals. Marlene Fisher remarks, "The novels deal with the efforts of human beings to forge and to fulfil workable and communal ideals and perforce, with the struggle to reconcile individuals and social goals. Inner change then and both the transformations in a society and the fulfillment of individuals ideals to which it is directed are a central motif in Bhattacharya's novels".[32]

In his novels, Bhabani Bhattacharya holds a mirror to the Indian society. He deals with the social, religious, economic, political and even psychological aspects of Indian life. He also shows concern for the future of his country for its regeneration.

Bhabani Bhattacharya combines the traditional method of story telling and the modern method of objective narration in his novels. He uses the 'stream of consciousness technique' rarely to explore the depths of his character's mind. Regarding his style of writing, he expressed in an interview "A writer chooses a style that suits his theme and genius most. Personally, I have always felt like writing in a way I write now. I cannot give my opinion on Narayan or Malgonkar. Since it is for them to decide what way they should write." (Sudhakar Joshi, *An Evening with Bhabani*, p. vii).

It is by means of gentle irony, humour, symbolism, allegory and rhetorical questions, he presents the social ills realistically. He never comments openly on the social evils of his times, and tries to be as objective as possible. He frames a number of questions to make the reader think for himself. P. P. Sharma calls Bhabani Bhattacharya a 'Thinker – artist'. The novelist provokes the reader to think by putting a series of questions.

To make the story dramatic and interesting, Bhabani Bhattacharya uses 'Flash back Technique'. He keeps skipping between the present and the past. But the chronological order is disturbed very rarely, that too, to give some additional and necessary information to the reader. R. K. Srivastava rightly observes, "The omniscient third person narration is in a straight chronological order with occasional flashback or time-shift, but, he unlike R. K. Narayan in *The Guide* does not make major changes in the chronological method of a story".[33]

Symbolism is a major device which is used by the novelist to perceive a hidden meaning in it. In the novel *Shadow from Ladakh*, Steeltown and Gandhigram are the symbols of material and spiritual values. In *Goddess Named Gold* taveej is the symbol of political freedom.

Bhabani Bhattacharya employs irony as a device to portray the characters and present the situations in his novels. Along with this there is a comic touch in his fiction. His novels differ in tone from serious to comic depends on the theme. The themes of his novels reveal that he shows concern for man's physical, mental, social and spiritual needs in a wider aspect. These are the tools that the novelist used to grasp the reader's mind and thoughts. As Malta Grover observes, "The tools that Bhattacharya has employed – the various literary devices to render his experiences in the English language have enables the reader to get an accurate picture of Indian Society, the birth pangs of a nation's political freedom, and its agonies and aspirations in a historical perspective." (Malta Grover, *Bhabani Bhattacharya as a Novelist of Social Conscience*, p. 122).

As a realistic novelist, Bhabani Bhattacharya has a keen eye for situations and characters. He takes up varied aspects and themes in his novels and presents them realistically. He is not just satisfied with presenting a superficial view of life, but he goes into the depths of realities of life. He is not confined with the history of one man but he is concerned with the destiny of the whole society and the relationship among the individuals in the society. He has a broader outlook towards the issues in the society.

About Bhabani Bhattacharya's varied themes in his novels, Sudhakar Joshi rightly remarks, "Bhattacharya's novels have a penetrating and sympathetic analysis of the simple but unsurmountable problems of Indian life. His themes generally revolve around poverty, hunger, pestilence, traditionalism, caste, India's struggle against poverty, industrialisation and the resulting controversy of Gandhian panacea versus rapid industrialisation".[34]

The scope of this dissertation is to exhibit and explore the thematic concerns in the writings of Bhabani Bhattacharya.

REFERENCES

1. K. R. Srinivasa Iyengar, *Indian Writing in English,* Sterling Publishers Private Limited, 1985, p. 20.
2. *Ibid.*, p. 4.
3. K. R. Chandrasekaran, *Bhabani Bhattacharya*, Arnold Heinemann, Delhi, 1974, p. vii.
4. Syed Mujeebuddin, *Indo-Anglian Fiction and the Question of Indianness: A General Assessment,* Kakatiya Journal of English Studies Kakatiya University, Volume 20/2000, p. 61.
5. C. D. Narasimaiah, *Towards the Formulation of a Common Poetic for Indian Literatures*, The Literary Criterion Rao and Raghavan Publishers, Mysore, 1984, 19.1: 2.
6. Ganeshwar Mishra, *Form, Language, Context: A Study of Indo-Anglian Fiction*, Ph.D Thesis, University of Kent, 1978, p. 25.
7. V. K. Gokak, *The Poetic Approach to Language* Edited by John Press, London, 1952, pp. 93-94.

8. Mrs. Meenakshi Mukherjee: *The Twice Born Fiction* Arnold-Heinemann, New Delhi, 1974, p. 170.
9. K. S. Ramamurthi, *The Rise of the Indian Novel in English,* Doctoral Thesis, Madurai University, 1975, p. 61.
10. T. Prabhakar, *The Indian Novel in English*, Phoenix Publishing House Pvt. Ltd., 1982, p. 13.
11. Malta Grover, *Bhabani Bhattacharya as a Novelist of Social Conscience*, Shalabh Prakasan, Meerut, 1991, p. 1.
12. Harcharn Singh Boparai, *The Achievement of Bhabani Bhattacharya,* Perspectives of Bhabani Bhattacharya, Vimal Prakashan, Ghaziabad, 1982, p. 201.
13. K. K. Sharma, *Bhabani Bhattacharya: His Vision and Themes*, Abhinav Publications, New Delhi, 1979, p. 13.
14. Morris E. Speare, *The Political Novel – Its Development in England and America*, Oxford University Press, New York, 1966, p. IX.
15. M. K. Bhatnagar, *Political Consciousness in Indian English Writing*, Bahri Publications, New Delhi, 1991, p. 28.
16. A. V. Krishna Rao, *The Indo-Anglian Novel and the Changing Tradition*, Rao and Raghavan, Mysore, 1972, p. 21.
17. Sudhakar Joshi, *An Evening with Bhabani, The Sunday Standard*, April 27, 1969.
18. Bhabani Bhattacharya, *Rabindranath Tagore: A Profile*, The Golden Boat, Bombay, 1955, p. 10.
19. Dorothy Blair Shimer, *Bhabani Bhattacharya,* Twayne Publishers, Boston, 1975, p. 12.
20. *Ibid.*, p. 22.
21. *Op. Cit.*, 13, p. 15.
22. R. K. Srivastava, *Bhattacharya at Work: An Interview, Perspectives on Bhabani Bhattacharya*, Vimal Prakashan, Ghaziabad, 1982, p. 220.
23. Bhabani Bhattacharya, *Contemporary Novelists in the English Language*, St. Martin's Press, New York, 197, p. 64.
24. Bhabani Bhattacharya, *Literature and Social Reality*, The Aryan Path, XXVI, IX Sept., 1955, p. 395.
25. Stephen Hemenway, *The Novel of India*, Writers Workshop, Calcutta, 1975, Vol. 2, p. 36.
26. G. Rai, *Bhabani Bhattacharya: A Study of his Novels,* B. R. Publishing Corporation, Delhi, 1995, p. 59.

27. Syed Ameeruddin, *Social Commitment in Bhattacharya's Novels*, Littcrit, Vol. 4, No. 2, Dec. 1978, p. 23.
28. K. H. Kunjo Singh, *The Fiction of Bhabani Bhattacharya*, Atlantic Publishers and Distributors, 2002, p. 101.
29. Balram S. Sorot, *The Novels of Bhabani Bhattacharya,* Prestige, New Delhi, 1991, p. 78.
30. *Op. Cit.*, 14, p. 205.
31. Dr. C. Paul Verghese, Problems of the Indian Creative Writer in English *Indian Writing Today*, Bombay, Vol. VIII, p. 75.
32. Marlene Fisher, *Personal and Social Change in Bhattacharya's Novels*, World Literature Written in English, Vol. II, p. 24.
33. *Op. Cit.,* 22, p. 24.
34. Sudhakar Joshi, *An Evening with Bhabani, The Sunday Standard*, April 27, 1969, p. 17.

2

Unquenchable Hungers

An intense study of all the novels of Bhabani Bhattacharya reveals him dealing with the contemporary human problems with a human heart. The pre-independence period was a pathetic time in the history of India. The contemporary historical events mainly the Quit India Movement and the Bengal famine of 1942-43 had made deep impression on the mind of Bhabani Bhattacharya. This is the great inspiration to his first novel, *So Many Hungers*! published in 1947.

As to how he became a novelist, Bhabani Bhattacharya recalls, "The great famine swept down upon Bengal, The emotional stirrings I felt (more than two million men, women and children died of slow starvation amid a man-made scarcity) where a sheer compulsion to creativity. The result was the novel *So Many Hungers*!"[1]

With a remarkable sensitivity and accuracy Bhattacharya witnessed the harrowing scene around him and portrayed the same in his novel. Moved by traumatic events due to war and famine he wrote the novel *So Many Hungers*! but did not feel like publishing it till his wife Salila, persuaded him to do so. To his great surprise the novel got quick success and was translated into many languages. Regarding the novel Mahendra N. Pandia writes, "This runaway success of his first novel was due to the very human approach to a national tragedy where what man had made of man was seen in its bare nakedness!"[2]

The story opens with the declaration of war against Germany by the British. India was forced to join the war on some conditions. The result was the shortage of foodgrains and this led to the worst Bengal famine. Bengal had never witnessed such kind of hideous famine till then. As Harish Raizada observes, "Bhabani Bhattacharya's first novel, *So Many Hungers*! (1947) is one of the first pieces of creative writing born out of the agonised torment of body and spirit endured by the sacred soil of Bengal during the hideous famine years and the early stages of the Second World War".[3]

In this novel, the author analyses the real cause for the famine. According to him, natural conditions are not the reason for this, but it is the failure and inefficiency of administration. In addition to this, there were selfish hoarders who wanted to make personal gain from the critical situation. So the Bengal famine is more than the natural calamity. It is treated as man-made famine. K. Venkata Reddy remarks, "*So Many Hungers*! unfolds the tragic story of a largely man-made famine in which over a million people died. The novelist has taken one of the most stirring periods and one of the most tragic calamities in Indian history: the Bengal famine of 1943, which was so horrible and harrowing"....[4]

The poor people and the peasants of Bengal take for granted that the famine is imposed on them by God. It is their fate that has made them repent for their past sins. But the fact is that hoarders and black marketers stored the food grains for a huge profit. This fact is made clear through the character of Samarendra Basu in the novel. Though he is a lawyer by profession, he belongs to the vicious circle that causes the mass human tragedy in the story. His evil thoughts are revealed in the following words, "The grain supply from

Burma was now lost. If a fraction of time, Bengal's rice-yield could be cornered-stupendous task! Any how, huge stocks could be purchased at the next harvest, laid up frozen, till demand exceeded supply and the price level rose (one must eat, whatever the price); then the stocks could be slowly released at a huge profit".[5] (*So Many Hungers*! p. 40)

Rahoul, Samarendra Basu's elder son is the opposite pole of his father. He is a great intellectual and a D. Sc. of Cambridge. He is a staunch nationalist like his grandfather Devender Basu and is willing to make a do or die struggle for the cause of Indian Independence. Being an intellectual, Rahoul rightly finds the root cause for the famine. Through Rahoul, the novelist expresses, "The empty stomach was due to no blight of nature, no failure of crops Rahoul knew. It was man-made scarcity, for the harvest had been fair, and even if the Army bought up big stocks, with rationing at the right level there could be food for all. But there was no rationing". (SMH, p. 105)

The families in the villages suffered a lot due to the famine. They had no work to do and no food to eat. Bhabani Bhattacharya portrayed the desperate condition of people through the story of Kajoli and her family. According to him the selfish businessmen like Samarendra Basu and the indifferent attitude of the government are responsible for the situation. As K. R. Chandrasekharan states, "..... the sad tale of Kajoli is a pathetic record of what happened to more than two million men and women who became victims of a famine which was not an act of God, but which was brought about by the rapacity and selfishness of profiteers and the indifference of an alien Government".[6]

So Many Hungers! is the story of two families, one in the village of Baruni and the other one living in Calcutta. Samarendra Basu is the head of the rich family in Calcutta. Rahoul and Kunal are his sons who are quite opposite to their selfish father. The other family in Baruni consists of Kajoli, her mother and her two brothers. As G. S. Balarama Gupta points out, "*So Many Hungers*! is woven around the happenings in the lives of Rahoul and Kajoli and their families and these are meant to highlight and vivify the crushing effects of the cataclysmic consequences of the horrendous famine stalking the length and breadth of the country".[7]

Kajoli is an innocent girl of fourteen when the novel begins. She lives in a thatched house with her family. Her father and her elder brother Kanu, are imprisoned for having taken part in the Civil Disobedience Movement. She gets married to Kishore, a patriot. But her happiness is short-lived. Devesh Basu, who is called as Devata by the villagers is the bridge between the two families in this story.

When Rahoul comes to Baruni, to meet his grandfather Devesh Basu, he wonders at the affection and respect of innocent villagers. Devesh Basu takes him to Kajoli's house for meals. Kajoli respectfully removes Rahoul's shoes and washes his feet. As Rahoul is unaware of village manners, he feels reluctant. The character of Kajoli is highlighted through the following words of Devesh Basu, "She is a well-bred peasant girl. She has a legacy of manners as old as India. How could she give up her manners and proprieties to suit your new-fangled city ideas? You are a respected visitor in the house". (SMH, p. 28).

The novel, *So Many Hungers*! mainly focuses on man's great hunger for food. Bhabani Bhattacharya artistically portrays this hunger as a major theme in two of his novels. As Dr. C. Paul Verghese rightly remarks, "Food is the primary requisite of human dignity; hunger debases and dehumanises man. That is why hunger is the theme of a large number of Indo-Anglian novels. Bhattacharya has dealt quite forcefully with the theme of hunger and the concomitant theme of human degradation in his novels *So Many Hungers*! and *He Who rides a Tiger*".[8]

Bhabani Bhattacharya gives a vivid picture of hunger both in the villages and in the great city of Bengal. In the villages, people have nothing to eat, not even the roots of a plant. So thousands of people abandon their homes and start flowing to the big city of Calcutta, with lots of hope. The innocent villagers are in the wrong notion that the people of city are generous that they will feed the village folk. Their journey is described as, "Streams of desperate men ventured out of their ancestral homes in search of food hanging on the foot boards of railway trains, riding on the sun-baked roofs. The police threw up barrier. Then the men trekked the meadows and roads ten thousand village streams flowing citywards". (SMH, p. 111)

The irony is that the city, where these people migrate, has been fully dependent on the countryside for foodgrains. The city has only consumed the food products of the villagers. Bhattacharya remarks, "The city had never grown a blade of corn. The city had eaten out of the green bowl of the peasant's fields. The city, having taken the harvests, would spare a little for the peasant folk who had ever filled the bowls?" (SMH, p. 111)

The city itself was affected by the scarcity of foodgrains. The second world war had brought a calamity over the land. The following description in the novel shows hunger in the big city, "He had died for lack of food, so it was reported, and the brief news flashed past almost unnoticed. A mere beggar. No one of them felt that he was a premonition, a symbolic shape of things to come other men sank down and died. Then women. Finally, children husbands and sons had tried to shield with their blood and bones the dear ones at home, and failed. All were decaying together". (SMH, pp. 104-105).

Bhabani Bhattacharya portrays the realistic picture of hunger by collecting the details from the newspapers. In the city, the horrible scenes are common place things: the mothers kill their own children for want of milk and food; the hungry infants are seen sucking the breast of their dead mothers; the mothers sell their daughters and even send to brothels for the sake of food and pregnant women die before they give birth to their babies. As Malta Grover observes, "Bhattacharya has portrayed the image of hunger on an epic scale in his first novel, *So Many Hungers*!, by focusing our attention on the story of a peasant family, and comparing and contrasting it with the story of an urban family living in Calcutta".[9]

Regarding the condition of common Indian Peasants, Bhattacharya was moved by their miserable plight. They had been reduced to utter poverty by the exploitative policies of the alien Government. He gives a realistic picture of Indian peasants in the novel as, "On his petty income the landless peasant can have just enough of his own rice to eat, no reserve for lean days. And the kisans – they must always be hungry save for a spell of two or three months in the year, when they earn meals and a wage for field work. The hundred million kisans of India must always be hungry. It is a rare gracious day to have the stomach full". (SMH, p. 22).

The living condition of these peasants worsens during the period of famine. They are reduced to the level of mere destitute searching for food in the city. As K. R. Chandrasekharan rightly points out, "Bhattacharya is in his best when he depicts the plight of the ruined peasants, their exodus to the city and their object misery and degradation".[10]

The poor people of countryside had to face horrible scenes throughout their journey. They had to die of fear by witnessing horrowful sights. Bhattacharya portrays the horrible picture of hunger in the novel, "A myriad vultures gazed down upon the countryside.....corpses lay by the road, huddling together. Picked to the bone; only the hair uneaten-fluffy baby's hair, man's hair, the waist-long hair of women. A family group had sunk into sleep, and beyond the sleep was – vultures". (SMH, p. 137)

Vulture-eaten corpses keep company of famished humanity, who move towards Calcutta in the hope of getting food. They see jackals eating hungry people lying unconscious, because of hunger. While giving a general picture of hunger all over Bengal, Bhattacharya particularizes it by showing the flight of Kajoli, Onu and their mother. Kajoli, pregnant and hungry would go out with her mother to hunt for roots which are boiled, salted and eaten, being difficult to digest. It is described thus, "Some roots tortured the stomach, and you learnt to discard them; but those that only made you uneasy, resting in your stomach like a stone load, had to be retained in your daily fare... When you had to choose between the ache of hunger and the ache of indigestion, you would often choose the latter, so in her heart the mother knew". (SMH, p. 119).

It is this unbearable hunger, that drives Kajoli to eat the entire bread which the soldier gives her, without thinking for a minute about her mother and brother. She eats eagerly unaware of the indecent behaviour of the soldier; the result is her painful abortion. Like Kajoli, there are millions of peasants who groan due to unbearable hunger.

There are free kitchens run by public charity, yet thousands of poor folk die everyday. Due to prolonged starvation, many people are not fit to eat solid food and need a special diet and glucose. So when they take the ordinary food, they die. Bhattacharya narrates, "Wave after wave of hunger stricken masses surging from the country side. A great many were in no fit state to consume solid food. They ate and died. To give them rice was to kill them. They needed a special diet". (SMH, p. 153). The irony is that many die of the excitement, which they cannot bear, at the sight of food at free kitchens in Calcutta. In this novel there is a pathetic incident of an old man, who died while watching food being served in the free kitchen.

The destitutes in the city have to find out banana skins in the pile to eat. They eagerly approach the garbage or rubbish for food. The peels of vegetables, rotten vegetables are the food for these folk. Some of them catch and eat even rats. They have to face heavy competition even for the dustbins. Often they fight among themselves like animals. Kajoli's brother Onu describes the awkward situation to his mother, "Those garbage cans they are our food-bowls, Mother we pickout of them before the city's Scavenger folk come with their vans. Sometimes we pick at night – less competition. I saw two men fighting like animals over a dust-bin-it happened yesterday". (SMH, p. 162).

The unhealthy food habits result in Dysentery, among the destitutes. The destitutes feel that it is good for them. Because they will be taken to sick hospital, nursed and given food. The sick-hospitals are already full with patients, hence many of them cannot be taken, and are left to their fate, "A blue motor-wagon with one thick red stripe down and another across paused at the alley-mouth. Men with a stretched picked up the destitute who had dysentery and put him in the wagon. Lucky one! For some time he would live like a king!" (SMH, p. 161).

People, hurt by bombs during those days, are promptly taken to hospitals, but nobody bothers about those who are hurt terribly by hunger. When a soldier gave half a rupee to Onu, he was exited and thought of buying cheap meals. But later he changes his mind and buys flowers for the Goddess. He prays, "Mother I only ask this much: let a Japanese bomb hurt me, Mother. Then the motor-wagon with one red stripe down and another across will come and pick me up and take me to sick hospital. They will give me an iron bed to lie on Mother, and a clean piece of cloth to put on, and may be a blanket to wrap myself in against cold, and food – all the rice I can eat, Mother". (SMH, p. 190).

Thus the poignancy of hunger is reflected more in the cry of a destitute boy who, wishes to be hurt in a Japanese bomb attack. Hunger makes human beings inhuman. Destitutes often fought with animals for the leavings in the garbage dumps. It is a painful and desperate situation, "Destitutes and dogs in those days often fought for possession of the rich city's ten-thousand rubbish-heaps, in which scraps of rotting food lay buried. It was not every time that the destitutes won, routing the dogs on the streets and the dog within themselves". (SMH, p. 171)

The theme of hunger for food is presented, not in fragments, but in its wholeness. Bhabani Bhattacharya not only describes the horrible scenes of famine in Bengal, but also reflects its physical and moral aspects. The novelist assesses the overall impact of the famine, taking into account its physical as well as moral aspect. Through Rahoul, the novelist reflects the physical side of the famine thus, "Death would claim two millions, perhaps three millions more would escape by the skin of their teeth, but they would never be strong again, especially the children and the rickety babies who had so little success, who had been exposed much to Sun and rain". (SMH, p. 181)

Bhabani Bhattacharya delineates the moral aspects of the deadly famine in depth. Hunger debases the destitutes to the lowest level. The novelist brings out the inner degradation of the human souls as a result of hunger for food. Kajoli's brother Onu has grown under the idealism of Devata. He is a noble and innocent young boy who is free from selfishness. He is in the habit of sharing even his best possessions with his friends. But hunger had degraded him. This is described by the novelist thus, "Selfishness had been alien to his nature. He had always loved to share his best gifts with his friends. But hunger had debased his warm, innocent spirit. He had become a hoarder. He hoarded for himself and his sister and mother the wild green figs on tree-tops which none but he could reach". (SMH, pp. 114-115).

Bhattacharya, in his novels describes many incidents which portray the moral implications of human hunger for food. Hunger makes the human beings put aside their affection, at the sight of food. When a soldier gives some bread to Kajoli, she forgets about her mother and brother for a moment. Only after she has finished eating, she feels very sad thinking about her mother and brother. The following picture evokes sorrow and sympathy when hunger hits people, "but as hunger bit harder, the finer feelings began to be deadened. Rahoul recalled a story in the papers. A starving mother with a child at her breast was given food at a kitchen. While she ate, the child died in her lap. But the mother ate on. She finished her meal and then left with her dead child". (SMH, p. 181)

There is another instance of depravity and degradation caused by hunger. A destitute woman, gets some handful of rice after a day's hard work. When at Sunset she lights fire and is about to take rice with her three children, a hungry man seizes rice from her and runs away. There is another pathetic picture of a woman who sat on the pavement, eating eagerly from a bowl while her famished child, sat near her and gazed.

As a realistic novelist, Bhattacharya portrays both sides of the hunger – stricken people. The one side of them is their inner degradation, while the other side is the moral uprightness. He has faith in the goodness of mankind. As Shyam M. Asnani points out, "Bhattacharya as a novelist always strives to portray the innate goodness of man. This is not so because he is a rationalist or a utopian, but because he gives an evidence of his acute awareness of the history of mankind and his unflinching faith in the essential richness and nobility of the human soul."[11]

The moral uprightness, dedications to ideals, self-sacrifice and unselfishness have been amply shown in the novel. Bhabani Bhattacharya unmistakably reveals the essential goodness and nobility of the hungry people. The old mother of Kajoli is an embodiment of compassion, unselfishness, strength and hope. Once she comes across a young mother burrying her child, though the child is alive. When she comes to know that the young mother has no milk in her breast for her dying child, she gives her cow, Mangala, which is their only asset. She not only, gives her cow to save her and her infant life but also gives encouragement and hope. The mother says, "Take my cow. Sell her. Go to the wonder city and be saved". (SMH, p. 123)

During the famine days, most mothers in the villages sell their daughters to the city brokers. But Kajoli's mother bluntly rejected the offer of a brothel woman. Her character shows the importance of chastity even at the time of trouble. She prefers death instead of living on immoral earnings. "... I ate dirt from the hand of a whore. She bent forward, a finger into her throat, trying to vomit.... She dug her fingers deeper, and shaking with the fury of her effort ribs breaking apart, she vomited". (SMH, p. 131)

Onu, Kajoli's younger brother, struggles hard to feed his mother and sister by plucking figs on the top of the tree. Though he first collected figs only for his family, he later realised the sorrow of his friends. He is determined to collect a lot of figs so as to save his and his friend's near blood relations. He is ready to share his secret treasure, which he only could reach. He says to his friend, "Everyday we'll go halves, bhai, halves that tree has plenty left". (SMH, p. 116)

There is an act of self-sacrifice, when a big boy shares the jam tin with Onu, after fighting with the hungry dog. Again, there is an old villager, who is very weak and still hands over his card of free food to Rahoul saying, "Father, there is no end to your kindness of heart. I owe you my life. I can give you no service in return. I can do no good to my brethren save this much. I can give my place to a more needy person unfed at a kitchen. Do not deny me this one joy, I beg". (SMH, p. 187)

This scene makes Rahoul to feel a signal of hope and deliverance for the hunger stricken masses of Bengal. This is the other side of the moral aspect of hunger. R. S. Singh says, "In *So Many Hungers*! no hunger is satisfied but the human spirit's sanctity, richness and beauty are fully vindicated".[12]

The title of the novel itself, reveals that there are many types of hungers apart from hunger for food. K. K. Sharma rightly points out, "*So Many Hungers*!, Bhattacharya's first novel, is primarily devoted to man's hunger for food, though it also closely analyses man's other urges. It is a story not only about hunger for food but so many types of human hunger".[13]

Though, in this novel the hunger for food and political freedom dominate, there are other hungers like hunger for money, for sex, for ethical values, hunger for social prestige, titles, riches and prosperity and hunger for self-respect. As G. S. Balarama Gupta observes, "*So Many Hungers*! has for its theme, hungers – so many of them – both benign and maleficent. First there is the hunger as it is commonly understood, the hunger for food... then, there is hunger for power which means enormous bloodshed, agony and exploitation; ... the third variety is the hunger for freedom and 1942 Quit India Movement provides the novel with yet another thread of its plot".[14]

Apart from Bengal famine of 1943 which crushed millions, the Second World War, with all its brutality forms the other important part of the novel. This Second World War symbolises the hunger for power of some wealthy nations. Britain forces India to join the war on the condition of giving freedom. Bhattacharya expresses the irony of the war as, "Indian opinion was at one with progressive forces the world over. But how could a people set out into a war said to be waged for democratic freedom, so long as that very freedom was denied them? India in bondage asked to fight for World freedom!" (SMH, p. 12)

Kunal, Rahoul's younger brother has joined the army to serve his country. He feels that the war is an opportunity to express his gratitude towards the nation. He says to his mother, "I am going to war to serve myself, to find an outlet for my spirit, as it were...." (SMH, p. 13)

Even Rahoul had an urge to join the army of liberation. But as a student of Astro-Physics he has other things to do through his research work he wants to contribute to the welfare of the Nation. Through him, the novelist reveals the dangers of war, "War was mass murder. You could commit yourself to mass murder with a clear conscience only when you were convinced that you would be ridding the world of some pest. In the name of humanity Kunal and others of his generation were called upon to fight the pest in Europe. But the champions of freedom abroad were the eaters of freedom in this land". (SMH, p. 41).

The novel, *So Many Hungers*! was published in 1947, the year India achieved freedom. The author had witnessed the entire National Movement. So he deals with the major events like the Civil Disobedience and the Quit India Movements in this novel. K.Venkata Reddy remarks about the novel, "The theme of hunger for food intertwines the theme of hunger for freedom. The Indian National Movement for freedom forms an integral part of the narrative. Though Bhattacharya highlights the Quit India Movement, the other phases of the Movement such as the Civil Disobedience and the breaking of the Salt Law are presented".[15]

The first chapter in the beginning shows the hunger for freedom of Rahoul and his brother Kunal. The theme of freedom runs throughout the novel along with hunger for food. As K. Venkata Reddy point out, "The central theme of *So Many Hungers*! is the twin hunger for food and for freedom. The plot of novel is woven out of two main strands: the story of the young scientist, Rahoul and his family, and the story of the peasant girl, Kajoli and her family; the former exemplifying the theme of hunger for freedom and the latter illustrating the theme of hunger for food".[16]

Rahoul always craves for freedom for not only his country but for the world freedom. He even longs to lead and organise the freedom fighters of the world. He tells his wife Manju, how he feels sad for missed opportunities to fight for freedom. In a dilemma he says, "A greater war of liberation has started, the greatest ever. What am I to do this time." (SMH, p. 16) The younger brother of Rahoul, Kunal also exhibits his hunger for freedom. When his mother persists him to stay at home he says, "Why at this very moment a million mothers the world over must be sending their sons to war". (SMH, p. 13)

The important character in the novel Devesh Basu, Rahoul's grand father exhibits hunger for freedom throughout the novel. He is a freedom fighter in Gandhian way, *i.e.*, Ahimsa. He went to prison several times and spent a number of years there. He is the man of ideals who has sacrificed his life of luxury for freedom movement. In his old age, he leaves his family and lives in the village and educates the villagers about the national movements. The villagers treat him as their living god calling him Devata.

Devata's broad outlook towards the freedom struggle is obvious through his advice to Rahoul, "Why should you fight the people of England? They are good people. The people are good everywhere. Our fight is with the rulers of England, who hold us in subjection for their narrow interests." (SMH, p. 21) The character of Devata is modelled after Gandhi. His simple living, dedication to the service of humanity, the principle of non-violence in the story is dealt with great care. As Rama Jha remarks, "Entry of Devesh Basu in the novel is like Gandhi's phenomenal advent on the Indian political scene. Bhattacharya's characterization of Devata shows the meticulous care he has taken to model this character after Gandhi".[17]

In the village of Baruni, Devata organises flag saluting ceremonies. He is the inspiration for many families in the village. In Kajoli's family, Kajoli's father and elder brother Kanu, were deeply inspired by him. Devata's words to his followers, when he is arrested and leaving for jail, remind one of Gandhiji, "Friends and comrades do not betray the flag. Do not betray yourselves, there is violence in your thoughts; that is evil enough. Do not make it worse by violence in action". (SMH, p. 72) Even in the prison, his spirit did not weaken, he undergoes hunger strike till death. His hunger for freedom remained till the end of the novel.

At the end of the novel, Rahoul could not overcome his hunger for freedom. He left his research work and got arrested to play his part in the freedom struggle. Like Rahoul so many intellectuals, flow to prison houses singing songs of freedom with no sign of defeat in their voices. The novel ends with the singing of Tagore's immortal lines, "The more their eyes redden with rage, the more our eyes open" The more they tighten the chains, the more the chains loosen". (SMH, p. 205)

So Many Hungers! focuses on man's hunger for money and titles. This is illustrated by the life of Samarendra Basu and Abalabandhu. Samarendra Basu is an embodiment of man's quest for money and titles. He has accumulated wealth and land by his blackmarket business. He never minds feeding on the sufferings of human beings – "Rich, he hungered to be still richer". (SMH, p. 176) Ashok K. R. Bachchan points out, "Bhabani Bhattacharya uses the device of contrast to highlight the problem of hunger. He presents the contrasting scenes of hunger for food and hunger for wealth simultaneously. Kajoli, Onu, mother and the dispossessed suffer from hunger for food. On the otherhand, Sri Abalabandhu and Samarendra Basu suffer from unquenching lust for wealth".[18]

World War II is a favourable opportunity for Samarendra Basu to make money. His hunger for money does not weaken even with the advent of old age. In the period of World War II, while Rahoul and Kunal worry about the country, their father Samarendra Basu is calculating how to make huge profits in stock market. He asks his son, Rahoul, "Tomorrow there will be a storm in the share market. The bulls will carry all before them, the bears will be nowhere. Steels will rise steeply, so will gold – which to choose? The chance of a life-time". (SMH, p. 9)

Sri Abalabandhu, the Prince of the blackmarket is the Senior Director of Cheap Rice Ltd. He is the main person behind the storing of foodgrains. He was honoured by the British government, "... it was this man's hand that had spread well the grease of corruption to win the company great privileges more, it was his organising genius that had solved the intricate problem of storing the vast accumulated foodgrains – secret dumps that lay in the heart of famine areas". (SMH, p. 173).

The novelist portrays another type of hunger, the hunger for sex in the novel. This hunger, spoils the life of Kajoli in the image of a soldier. The soldier who lives away from his family craves for sex in a moment of weakness. The result is he rapes the pregnant girl Kajoli and causes a painful abortion. He satisfies his hunger for sex after satisfying Kajoli's hunger for food.

In the great city, this hunger for sex is the cause for brothel business. During the famine, many young girls from the countryside move to city to satisfy their hunger for food by satisfying the hunger for sex of the rich people. Sri Abalabandhu, a curious character is obsessed by sex. He reveals his thoughts, "The famished ones must feed well before they go into business – feed on rice and ghee and milk, so that their bones may put on meat. Hair to be rid of like, smoothed. A hundred other details. It pays. No better investment in the whole money market". (SMH, p. 176).

He took an odd pleasure in relating the sex adventures of a person he called 'my friend'. Under the disguise of a friend he expressed his own thoughts. Though he is fifty years of age, he spends money extravagantly to satisfy his hunger for sexual pleasure. He suggests that a new post of controller of Brothels, otherwise named a controller of social sickness should be created and that his friend is the most suitable for that. There are many people like him in the city who suffer from the hunger for sex-life.

Apart from this, there are many basic hungers which govern the lives of men and women. Bhattacharya throws light on these through the character of Kishore and Kajoli in this novel. Kishore expresses his view to Kajoli that in this life man has innumerable hungers, which cannot be satisfied till the end of his life. He hums, "I know, I know, beloved, Not in the life will hungers be sated – I know, I know, beloved". (SMH, p. 90)

From the masculine point of view, Kishore points out the man has several hungers like hunger for food, social status and hunger for family life, while Kajoli expresses her views from the feminine point of view as, "Women, wed, has one big hunger for home – no other. Little hungers make part of the big home hunger; they belong to it as the spokes belong to the cart-wheel. Woman, she has one big wheel of hunger. Man is a single spoke in that cart-wheel-nah may be he is the axle". (SMH, p. 93)

This clearly shows Kajoli's hunger for home. Kajoli strives to have a home for herself and her family. But throughout her life this hunger is not fulfilled. That remains a dream in her life. Till the end of the novel the hunger for home remains unfulfilled. Bhattacharya analyses the theme of hunger not only from a general point of view, but also from gender point of view.

The hunger-strike the self-imposed hunger, is another type of hunger stated in the novel. Under the impact of Gandhi, many freedom fighters use 'hunger strike' as a powerful weapon to achieve freedom. While millions of people face starvation in Bengal, patriots resort to hunger strike, fast unto death. This news creates sensation throughout the country through newspapers. It is this news that has changed Kajoli's mind at the last moment, and saves her from an immoral act.

The imaginary picture of Devata in prison comes to her mind. She decides to face the hunger bravely rather than debase herself, she visualises, "She saw him in jail house in the garb of a convict, wielding, his body's hunger like a sword strong as ever, and true and deathless". (SMH, p. 195) Here the hunger as a weapon is used for political purpose by the freedom fighters. On the whole, Bhabani Bhattacharya has analysed his favourite theme of hunger from all angles, in *So Many Hungers*! more deeper than his other novels.

During the British rule, English education has widely spread in India. As a result people faced the East-West encounter. This is also the cause of conflict between tradition and modernity in India. As Balram S. Sorot points out, "The East-West encounter highlights the polarities of these two distinct and separate cultures – spiritualism of the East and technological and material values of the West. Almost every educated Indian today is the product of the conflicts and reconciliations of these two cultures, although the consciousness of this tension varies from individual to individual".[19]

As Literature is the mirror of the age, Indian creative writers treated the theme of conflict between tradition and modernity in their creative writings. Sarath Kumar Ghose is the earliest of Indian English writers to deal with the theme of conflict between tradition and modernity. In his novel *The Prince of Destiny*, he portrays Barath, the hero of the novel, as the harbinger of the synthesis between East and West, *i.e.,* tradition and modernity.

In the literary context, tradition becomes a body of customs; beliefs, skills or sayings, handed down from generation to generation or age to age. In the general sense, tradition is a continuous process of handing down from generation to generation, conventions, beliefs, habits and even superstitions through oral and written practice. Tradition plays a significant role in the advancement of humanity. As S. N. Ganguly cogently remarks, "Tradition, and this is one of the most important functions, helps man in this selective behaviour. The human potential is realised significantly in a changing world and civilization only through the help of tradition."[20]

Society is the base for tradition. As society is dynamic, it undergoes changes in the length of time. As a result tradition is also modified. The development in humanity causes change in tradition by way of creating new ideas. The spirit of reform and revolt gives way to modernity. In the literal sense, modernity pertains to the present and more recent times. It is about the current age or period. It is wider in scope. According to Balram S. Sorot, "... modernity is that spirit of newness and uniqueness, be it in the field of literature, art or sculpture, which forces a conscious questioning – a break from the set patterns, established theories and beliefs or all sorts of influences".[21]

The Indian English novel has been a vivid portrayal of different attitudes which pleaded for the balance of tradition and modernity. In Mulk Raj Anand's *The Big Heart*, Ananth, the hero of the novel emphasises the values of modern technology and the traditional human values. In R. K. Narayan's novels, the conflict takes the form of clash between the older generation and his son Balu in *The Financial Expert*, Raju and his mother in *The Guide*, Jagan and his son Mali in *The Sweet Vendor*. There is the blend of tradition and modernity in the novels of Raja Rao like *Kanthapura* and *The Serpent and the Rope*.

Bhabani Bhattacharya has treated the theme of tradition and modernity very well in his novels. He analyses the impact of both tradition and modernity on the human society in a wider aspect. Balram S. Sorot writes, "While in the novels of the Indian – English writers in general, the problem of conflict or synthesis between tradition and modernity figures as a secondary theme, in the writings of Bhabani Bhattacharya it assumes the significance of the dominating issue in contemporary Indian life. The author analyses the political, religious, social and economic problems of modern India through the perspective of this basic conflict in our ethos".[22]

In his first novel *So Many Hungers*! Bhabani Bhattacharya, dealt with the old and new values through Basu's family in Calcutta and Kajoli's family in Baruni. In *He Who Rides a Tiger*, the author presents the blending of the traditional and the modern values through the story of Kalo and his daughter Chandra Lekha. The theme of confrontation of the old and the new values acquires a new dimension in his novel *The Goddess Named Gold*. In *Shadow from Ladakh* the central theme is the synthesis of Indian spiritual values and the Western modernism. The novelist projects the view of integration in his last novel *A Dream in Hawaii* through the principle character, Swami Yogananda.

Music for Mohini, Bhabani Bhattacharya's second novel has the conflict of tradition and modernity as its main theme. As Malta Grover remarks, "He has not only responded to this theme, the conflict of tradition – modernity in its varied aspects but has transcended it."[23]

Music for Mohini is a novel which deals with both rural and urban areas. The first part of the novel is set in the city and the rest in Behula village. Regarding the theme of the novel G. Rai points out, "The central theme of the novel is the tie or tussle between orthodoxy and modernity which remains a glaring problem in Indian Society even today. The rural-urban clash is an important feature of the novel. The traditional ways of life stand in sharp conflict with those of modern ways".[24]

As the title of the novel indicates, Mohini is the central character in his novel. She is the principle character who faces the conflict from the beginning of the novel. The conflict intensified after her marriage with Jayadev and her stay in a remote village of Bengal, Behula. There are many other characters in this novel who also face the clash between tradition and modernity in their lives.

Mohini lives in city with her father, grandmother and brother at the beginning of the novel. She is married to Jayadev, an erudite scholar of Behula, an orthodox village of Bengal. Jayadev's mother is deeply steeped in tradition and she expects her daughter-in-law to carry on the traditional ways. Though Mohini suffers initially she attunes herself, in course of time, to the new atmosphere. She undergoes many hardships in the village to adjust herself and at last comes to compromise with her life in village.

Thus the conflict and compromise between the rural and urban values, tradition and modernity become the crucial issue of the novels. As C. Tamilarasan says, "*Music for Mohini*, as already stated, hinges mainly on the theme of the conflict between tradition and modernity. This conflict goes on in both rural and urban areas. Traditional elements are not limited to village nor the modern spirit to the city. There is a mingling of these elements in both rural and urban areas. Bhattacharya deals with the interaction of the two sets of values with exquisite deftness".[25]

The story begins at Mohini's parental home in city. Mohini's father, professor is a man of modern views, while his old mother is conservative and rigid in outlook. She does not like her son's ideas, whenever her son does not hear her, she threatens to renounce the world. The conflict arises between the old mother and her son regarding Mohini's school education. The Professor wants to send Mohini to an English convent, but the old mother sternly opposes her son and says, "...let Mohini be trained at home; let her learn classical Sanskrit, the language of the gods, the precious vase that holds the essence of true knowledge and wisdom".[26] (*Music for Mohini*, p. 20) But her son would not back down. He would mould the girl in a modern way, which was his way. For the old mother, convent education is meaningless and harmful to her grand daughter. But atlast, she compromises herself.

There ensures a fierce alteration between the old mother and her son by the incident of Mohini's having a contract to sing for All India Radio once a week. The Professor is very happy and he proudly remarks that as Mohini's father, he will soon be a celebrity himself. But to the old mother, that is shameful for the family. She feels it a disgrace for the family tradition. She expresses her conventional view as, "A fellow, good or bad, saint or lout, can go to the gramophone shop and buy a shiny black disc for three rupees, and it is as though he buys a little of our girl, for her voice is truly a part of herself. Terrible! even her name is printed, there, on the disc, for every eye to feel". (MFM, p. 19)

Regarding horoscope, mother and son have different opinions. The old mother believes in horoscope and wants her son to make it for Mohini. But the Professor has no belief in the Horoscope. He regards it a joke. He remarks, "Horoscope, Mother? In this age of microscope, who needs a horoscope? Eight Stellar beings controlling the life story of every man, woman and child! Everything worked out in advance. And a good astrologer sees it all in the position of the stars at your birth hour. Our ancestors who devised this amazing joke on their pigheaded progeny-all credit to them". (MFM, p. 22)

Though he mocked many of the old beliefs, he wears amulet for his mother's satisfaction, Bhattacharya remarks that clashes like these are frequent between them, but they can compromise. "Over Mohini developed a clash between mother and son, even though on many points of orthodox living they had reached a fair adjustment". (MFM, p. 20)

Confrontation between the old and the new ideas, the traditional Indian and the modern Western ways of life is brilliantly brought out in the novel, when a suitable husband for Mohini is being searched out. Bhabani Bhattacharaya reveals the attitudes of old – fashioned elders and modern youngster in the ceremony of bride-showing. The first one was an old – fashioned party of elders, who came at dusk, the traditional bride showing hour. They didn't bring the bridegroom with them. They asked questions in ancient culture and yoga and demanded more dowry.

In this novel, Bhabani Bhattacharya points out the ill-manners of some people in bride-showing of society. Regarding the second party, the novelist observes, "Four pairs of eyes surveyed the girl from foot to head. She had to walk a few steps at the mother's bidding to prove she did not lack grace of movement. They fumbled with her prettily arranged hair and unloosed it down her back to know its length. They rubbed her face with their thumbs to make sure the fair complexion was natural, not of paint". (MFM, p. 49)

This indecent behaviour made Mohini shameful. Mohini's father couldn't bear this so he asked them to quit. The third party comprised only youngsters. The bridegroom came with his friends, to make his own choice. As they were all modern young men they joked and appreciated Mohini's voice on the radio. Bhabani Bhattacharya points out the contrast between traditional elders and modern youngsters through this bride showing. The third party asked in the following questions, "You play tennis? You dance? Who is your favorite film star? What novels have you read? Do you think Free India should remain in the Commonwealth?" (MFM, p. 51)

The third party approves the girl. Her father was happy that he has found the right match for her. But the old mother is greatly annoyed by their modern way of questioning, Mohini also wishes that the marriage should be settled. On the contrary, the old mother rejects the proposal by saying that the groom has no tradition and culture. This leads to the conflict between tradition and modernity. However all the clashes disappear soon, and they are on harmonious terms again adjusting themselves with one another. Balram S. Sorot writes, "The novelist synthesizes the old values with the new ones in the persons of the Professor and the old mother, showing that on many points of orthodox living they had reached a fair adjustment".[27]

Even the old mother is not very rigid in her attitude towards modern values. Though she upholds values and orthodox ways, she is often ready to compromise with the spirit of the new items. With all her orthodox heart, she enjoyed English pictures. Bhattacharya observes that, The old mother had compromised with modernity and her struggle to uphold the orthodox way was without passion". (MFM, p. 154)

The issue of marriage is left unsettled due to the difference between the mother when Jayadev appears on the scene and is found to be the most suitable groom for Mohini. Initially the Professor does not like her daughter to live in the remote village of Behula, because Mohini is a city-bread girl. When Mohini whole-hearted by approves the match, he joyfully accepts it. He says, "The old customs and conventions are not too unsound. They seem to suit our mental climate. It's as though in Hindu social life there was no room for big business!" (MFM, p. 66)

The attitude of Mohini towards Jayadev provides interesting insight into the novelist's attitude towards traditional Indian women. Though Mohini has education of a new kind and is dare enough to reveal her mind, her sensibility is coloured by her traditional inheritance. The thought of marrying Jayadev, fills her with a desire to offer her body as a gift, fit for offering. Bhabani Bhattacharya observes, "The Hindu maiden, born and bred in the ancient starlight of vedic civilization washed by the running stream of the centuries sheathing her limbs and her thoughts in a conventional dress to suit the needs of each passing age was innately unchanged: She had retained all her ancient hunger to offer worship". (MFM, p. 65)

Mohini, a girl of 17 years old is seen to indulge in romantic fancies. Soon after her school education, she is married to a handsome well-educated and affluent young man. Jayadev is the head of the aristocratic family called the Big House in Behula village. He is both a great scholar and master of Behula village. As a scholar he is sensitive to modern progressive ideas, while as the master of the Big house he symbolizes the old traditions in his personality. He dreams about a fusion of the past with the present. As a master of Big house he is well aware of its traditions and beliefs. So, he warns her about this, "The Big House, will make heavy demands on its young mistress. Demands that you find. Universonable. Some of them will have to be met with patience and a spirit of give and take. Other foolish demands must be resisted". (MFM, pp. 92-93)

Mohini, a city bread girl is full of emotions. She dreams of a glamorous life. But the Big house is contrary to her expectations. She has to adjust herself to the new environment, which is full of traditions. As K. H. Kunjo Singh rightly remarks, "*Music for Mohini* dwells on the intellectual and emotional development of the heroine, Mohini, from care-free and sheltered girlhood to the position of wife and the mistress of a prominent and influential house with great traditions and orthodoxy".[28]

Jayadev, who is a visionary and an idealist, expects. Mohini to be different from an ordinary young woman. He looks at Mohini as the vedic women like Gargi and Maitreyi. He expresses his view on vedic woman as, "She was no household drudge, no decorative being, but an intellectual, striding beside man in a tireless quest for knowledge. Her contribution to Aryan thought, lived still, shining as ever. There was Gargi. There was Maitreyi". (MFM, p. 84)

In the Big House, Jayadev is idealistic even in his feelings towards her and expects that she should sympathise and share his scholarly pursuits. But Mohini believes in the warmth of love and compassion. But Jayadev assumes that love on the spiritual and love on the physical plane should be kept apart. So, Mohini, the believer of romantic ideals is surprised by her husband's indifference. Though frustrated in the beginning she does not give vent to her dejection.

To adjust herself to the wishes of her husband, Mohini endeavours to rise expectation of Jayadev and starts learning Sanskrit from him. She shares his ideals and renders him help in the social reconstruction programme. She identifies herself with the women of the village and establishes communication with her husband. In this way the conflict between herself and her husband is resolved. She began to share his responsibility and became one with him. The novelist writes, "He belonged to the people what right had she to claim him for herself alone? She had the power to destroy his work-what higher compliment could he pay her? And in paying it had he not vested her with high responsibility, lifted her to a pedestal? She, too, appeared to be an idealist... She would be his true partner in feeling, in faith and in dream". (MFM, p. 152).

Mohini comes to Behula as the new mistress of the Big House. The village of Behula is a typical backward village of India. Its people are superstitious and conservative. They have blind faith in obscurantist religious beliefs, horoscopes and irrational religious rites and ceremonies. The beautiful Sudha's life is ruined by her uncle due to horoscope and she – is nick named as 'Saturn's Eyesore' and she remains unwed.

In the Big House, the conflict starts between Mohini and her mother-in-law. As Mohini has been brought up in an altogether different type of environment, convent education and a radio-star, she finds life at the Big House unbearable.

She has to struggle hard to adjust herself. Her mother-in-law is stern and puts a number of restraints upon Mohini. For Mohini, the Big House is in the shadow of the family tree. Bhattacharya writes, "An old proud house of an old proud family. A tradition within a tradition. And here she was, sprung out of shallow soil, forced by circumstance to be mistress of the ancient house and trustee of an alien tradition. The struggle to retouch her mental values, readjust her expectations, hurt fiercely". (MFM, p. 128)

Her mother-in-law advises her not to use powder, not to wear sleeveless blouses, not to wear glass bangles. She tells her to sing only religious songs and to wear a plain cotton saree. The widowed mother-in-law has kept a pair of wooden sandals of her late husband in the family prayer room and offers worship to them daily. Many taboos like this make life-colourless and monotonous for Mohini. Balaram S. Sorot writes "Besides Jayadev, Mohini has to adjust herself to the obsolete ideas and superstitions beliefs of her stubborn mother-in-law too. Known as 'Mother' in the village, this old lady is in a way the ruthless past reincarnated she is all for the family tradition".[29]

Mohini's sister-in-law Rooplekha combines in her character the traditional and modern values. When Mohini doubts the fusion of the city and the village representing the modern and the traditional value – patterns respectively, Rooplekha being village-bred and city-bred girl, remarks that such an union is necessary. Through the character of Rooplekha, Bhattacharya asserts his vision of India, "we connect culture with culture. Mohini, our old Eastern view of life with the new semi-Western out look. The city absorbs a little of the barbaric village, the village absorbs a little of the 'West-polluted' city. Both change, unaware. They are angry with each other. This is more urgent today than ever before. Our new India must rest on this foundation". (MFM, p. 111)

There is another conflict between the old and the new values in the story of Harindra's family. Harindra's father the old Kaviraj is a practitioner of Ayurvedic system of medicine, while his son Harindra is a Surgeon, educated and trained in a Western-style medical college. The old father often argues with his son about the supremacy of Ayurveda, that had prevailed for the millennium. The old man gives her Ayurvedic medicine and never allows his son to treat her. Through Harindra, the novelist asserts the efficacy of the modern Allopathic system. Harindra says, "There are many good drugs in our Ayurveda system. We know them, we use them, not the home products but those made in modern laboratories. What's wrong in using in the fight against disease the best that East and West have to offer?. Medicine knows no race or nationality, Father! No greater blessing for our people than the sulpha drugs". (MFM, p. 166) Through this story of Harindra, Bhattacharya reconciles the old values and systems with the new values and systems.

The reconciliation starts in Mohini's family also. For Mohini, the Big House is in the Shadow of the family tree. She came to know that her mother-in-law has dedicated her right hand to Lord Shiva. She eats with her left hand, for her son's longevity. She also tells Mohini about the horoscope of her son that he should have a child within two years after his marriage. Only a child can save his life. Mohini strives hard to adjust to the old ways and modes of life in the rural society and in his process she too, changes unawares. Bhattacharya affirms, "Yes, the young mistress of the Big House took deeper colour from her new life every day. Slowly she fitted herself to the several design. Her sprightliness, her quick girlish laugh, she easily subdued. The mother was a ruthless teacher". (MFM, p. 154).

Though Mohini does not believe superstitions and old beliefs, she begins to fear about her husband. She begins to realise that the mother is not completely devoid of the basic qualities of compassion and sacrifice. She develops a great love and sympathy for the old lady. So she becomes ready to give her skin from her bosom to satisfy the Devi in the temple. Mohini views, "Perhaps she saw the wrong side of this old tapestry of tradition and missed the design of duty and compassion were not at odds in the mother; the key to the design was sacrifice which was a right and privilege, not a duty alone". (MFM, p. 204)

The struggle between the contrasting values, resolves finally into a happy compromise. Both Mohini and her mother-in-law representing the modern and the traditional values respectively being to understand each other. As Shashikala Singh says, "Even though, Bhattacharya reveals the conflict between the old and the new cultures, there is more of a compromise than a violent confirmation".[30]

Bhattacharya makes his older and younger characters struggle between their views and atlast arrives at mutual adjustment. In his novel, Mohini's father and his mother, Jayadev and his mother, Harindra and his father are in continuous conflict with each other. The conflict arises due to their different ideas and faiths.

The conflict between Jayadev and his mother is regarding blind beliefs, horoscope and superstitions. The conflict turns serious when his mother attempts to make Mohini offer her heart's blood to the virgin Goddess to get rid of her barrenness. Jayadev sternly opposes the act and says, "We are not slaves of the stars. There is no room in the Big house for crazy beliefs. The village looks to us for ideals and a way of living. The pattern we set is not our private affair; it carries the strongest social sanction". (MFM, p. 211) The infuriated mother scolds her son for displeasing the Goddess. She curses her Karma for her son's deeds. She struggles hard to control herself and she decides to leave the matter to her fate.

As soon as the mother comes to know from Harindra of Mohini's pregnancy, she is reconciled to her son and Mohini. She realises that it is the age of the young men and women with their new ideals and aspirations. She starts changing her ideas to cope with the new age. Bhabani Bhattacharya points out that the mother agrees that her son's path is the right one, ".... for the first time, she could see her son clearly. His ideas, his point of view, moulded by the new spirit in the land, were different from hers and opposed to them, but they were, none the less, true ideals.... In that moment of insight the mother almost understood her son and, through him, the new revolt, the restless spirit of the new dawn". (MFM, pp. 219-220)

Bhattacharya in *Music for Mohini* depicts the two contraries, *(i)* tradition and *(ii)* modernity, old and the new and arrives at compromise between them. He resolves the conflict between mother and son, father and son, husband and wife, daughter-in-law and mother-in-law and ends in compromise.

There are two sets of characters in the novel *Music for Mohini*, the first set of characters uphold the old, conventional, values of the past like old mother, Mohini's mother-in-law, Harindra's father. The second type, plead for a change and unconventional values of modern age like Jayadev, Mohini's father, Mohini and Harindra. As Balram S. Sorot says, "The novelist juxtaposes different antagonistic characters in order to bring out their ideological conflict and then finally leads them towards a reconciliation so as to create a harmony of life".[31]

Bhabani Bhattacharya perceives the conflict of old and new values both in rural and urban societies. Hence he projects the same in this novel in the city and in the remote village of Bahula. As T. Vasudeva Reddy remarks, "Being a true son of the soil, he has gauged the pulse of the society, both rural and urban, and perceives the open confrontation between the old and the new values. This struggle between tradition and modernity is nowhere better presented than in this entire novel, *Music for Mohini* which perspectivizes the conflict in all its phases, ideological and sociological, ethnological and psychological".[32]

Regarding the urban side, Mohini's family in the city, represents both traditional and modern values. Mohini and her father represent modern values but the old mother represents traditional values. At the rural side, Jayadev and Harindra represent modern values but Jayadev's mother and

Harindra's father represent traditional values. So the conflict is not limited to village but it extends to the city also.

Regarding the theme of conflict of tradition and modernity C. Tamilarasan points out, "*Music for Mohini*, as already stated, hinges mainly on the theme of the conflict between tradition and modernity. This conflict goes on in both rural and urban areas. Traditional elements are not limited to village nor the modern spirit to the city. There is a mingling of these elements in both rural and urban areas. Bhattacharya deals with the interaction of the two sets of values with exquisite deftness".[33]

The novel *Music for Mohini*, was published in 1952. After independence there was a great concern for country's stability and the steps to be taken in order to ensure the country's greatness. So Bhabani Bhattacharya reflects the benefit of political freedom in this novel. For the development of nation, political freedom should lead to healthy social changes. The social evils of pre-independence time should be eliminated. Certain major social reforms like prevention of child marriages, widow remarriage, elimination of caste system, and untouchability are mentioned in this novel. Dr. K. R. Chandra sekharan rightly points out, "*Music for Mohini* is a forward-looking novel in which the author dwells on certain sociological aspects of Indian life and suggests the direction in which we have to move if we are to fully benefit by our political freedom".[34]

Jayadev in this novel fights superstitious beliefs and blind belief in astrological predictions. He educates the villagers about the new social changes. Harindra, the young medical man, takes up social work with other interested people and fights against the social evils. K. H. Kunjo Singh observes, "Viewed on the social plane, the novel concentrates upon social freedom, which is all important for the real progress of the orthodox and superstitions people of India. Hence the hero of the novel, Jayadev is shown to be dedicated to social reform and freedom".[35]

In this novel social reformation and reconstruction programmes are being taken up by a few youngmen with the help of Jayadev and Mohini. A village moneylender's plan to marry a very young girl as a fourth wife is overthrown. Jayadev prefers an old man's second marriage only with a widow. He intends to abolish the evil system of early marriages and the bondage of caste and creed. He also teaches people not to believe in false astrology.

The words and deeds of the hero, Jayadev, reflect Gandhian views on social reconstruction. Dr. P. N. Bhatt rightly remarks, "Jayadev in *Music for Mohini*, reveals Gandhian views on social reform. It is the story of a fight against old superstitions, taboos and religious orthodoxy. Jaydev believes that political freedom without social and economic freedom has no value. The rural society is sick with the set taboos of caste, untouchability and the blind belief in superstitions. He wants to reorient the set values of rural folk".[36]

In the village of Behula, Jayadev and his friend Doctor Harindra take active part to bring positive change in the attitude of the villagers. Jayadev insists Mohini to take part in the social work and teach women folk about the social evils. Jayadev forms a group of active young men to carry on the constructive works in the village. His involvement in the reformative activities is the symbol for modern values in the post-independence India, which is the dream of Gandhiji. Rama Jha observes, "*Music for Mohini* deals with the protagonist Jayadev's passionate involvement with the Gandhian constructive programmes in the village Behula. As a practical idealist Jayadev is trying to turn Behula into a model village rid of superstitions, caste-system and exploitation of women".[37]

Bhabani Bhattacharya, in this brief study of his novel *Music for Mohini* fully vindicates his social purpose. His outlook towards the society is constructive and reformative.

REFERENCES

1. Bhabani Bhattacharya, *Contemporary Novelists in the English Language*, St. Martin's Press, New York, 1972, p. 71.
2. Mahendra N. Pandia, *Relevance of Bhattacharya's Fiction*, The Indian P. E. N., Vol. 50, No. 10-12, Oct-Dec., 1989, p. 6.
3. Harish Raizada, *Bhabani Bhattacharya: Novelist of Social Ferment,* Explorations in Modern Indo- English Fiction. Ed. Dr. R. K. Dhawan, Bahri Publications New Delhi, 1982, p. 158.
4. K. Venkata Reddy, *An Approach to Bhabani Bhattacharya's So Many Hungers*!, Journal of South Asian Literature, East Lansing, Michingan, 1970, p. 43.
5. Bhabani Bhattacharya, *So Many Hungers*!, Orient Paperbacks, New Delhi, 1978, p. 40.

   All Sub-sequent References from his Edition Ref. to as SMH with page No. in Parentheses.
6. K. R. Chandrasekharan, *Bhabani Bhattacharya*, Arnold - Heinemann Publishers, New Delhi, 1947, p. 11.
7. G. S. Balarama Gupta, *Bhabani Bhattacharya's So Many Hungers*!*: A Study*, Aspects of Indian Writing in English, Ed. M. K. Naik, The Macmillan Company of India Ltd., Madras, p. 210.
8. C. Paul Verghese, *Article in Indian Writing To-day*, Vol.VII, *Studies in Indo-Anglian Literature,* Ed. Dr. K. N. Joshi, Bareilly, 1971, pp. 120-21.
9. Malta Grover, *Bhabani Bhattacharya as a Novelist of Social Conscience* (Shalabh Prakashan, Meerut, 1991, p. 34.
10. *Op.Cit*, 6, pp. 31-32.
11. Shyam, M. Asnani, *Form, Technique and Style in Bhabani Bhattacharya's Novels*, Littcrit, Vol. 5, No. 1, June 1979, pp. 23.
12. Ram Sewak Singh, *Bhabani Bhattacharya, A Novelist of Dreamy Wisdom*, Banasthali Patrika, Banasthali Vidyapeeth, Twayne Publishers, Boston, 1975, p. 33.
13. K. K. Sharma, *Bhabani Bhattacharya. His Vision and Themes*, Abinav Publications, New Delhi, 1979, p. 41.
14. *Op.Cit.*, 7, p. 210.
15. K. Venkata Reddy, *Major Indian Novelists*, Prestige Books, New Delhi, 1990, p. 64.
16. *Op.Cit.*, 4, p. 44.

17. Rama Jha, *Gandhian Thought and Indo-Anglian Novelists*, Chanukya, New Delhi, 1983, p. 164.
18. Ashok. K. R. Bachchan, *The Theme of Hunger in Bhabani Bhattacharya's Novels*, The Literary Voice, No.1. December 1994, p. 31.
19. Balaram. S. Sorot, *The Novels of Bhabani Bhattacharya*, Prestige Books, New Delhi, 1991, p. 53.
20. S. N. Ganguly, *Tradition, Modernity and Development,* The Macmillan, Delhi, 1977, pp. 44-45.
21. *Op.Cit.*, 19, p. 51.
22. *Ibid*, p. 58.
23. *Op.Cit.*, 9, p. 45.
24. G. Rai, *Bhabani Bhattacharya: A Study*, B. R. Publishing Corporation, Delhi, 1995, p. 29.
25. C. Tamilarasan, *Bhattacharya's Music for Mohini: A Study*, The Literary Endeavour, Vol. 2. No. 2, The Mysore Printing and Publishing House, p. 36.
26. Bhabani Bhattacharya, *Music for Mohini*, Orient Paperbacks, New Delhi, 1952, p. 20.

    All sub-sequent References from his Edition Ref. to as *MFM* with page No. in Parentheses.
27. *Op.Cit.*, 19, p. 68.
28. KH. Kunjo Singh, *The Fiction of Bhabani Bhattacharya*, Atlantic Publishers and Distributors, New Delhi, 2002, p. 85.
29. *Op.Cit.*, 19, p. 69.
30. MS. Shashikala Singh, *The Image of Modern Indian Women in Bhattacharya's Music for Mohini*, The Journal of Indian Writing in English, Vol. 28, No. 1, Jan. 2000, p. 39.
31. *Op.Cit.*, 19, p. 65.
32. T. Vasudeva Reddy, *Tradition versus modernity in Bhattacharya's Music for Mohini.* The Rajasthan Journal of English Studies, Vol. 9,1988, p. 21.
33. C. Tamilarasan, *Bhattacharya's Music for Mohini: A Study*, The Literary Endeavour, Vol. 2. No. 4, p. 36.
34. *Op.Cit.*, 6, p. 36.
35. *Op.Cit.*, 28, p. 88.
36. Dr. P. N. Bhatt, *The Impact of Gandhi on Dr. Bhabani Bhattacharya's Novels*, Triveni, Vol. 54, No. 3, Oct-Dec., 1985, p. 84.
37. *Op.Cit.,* 17, p. 170.

3

Magic and Miracles

The Bengal famine of 1943 obsessed the mind of Bhabani Bhattacharya, resulting in his first novel *So Many Hungers*!. Though his third novel *He Who Rides a Tiger* was published in 1955 after a twelve years gap, still the famine become a haunting memory for him. As the mentioned it in his third novel. "It was almost the darkest in the history of Bengal. A plague took the land in its grip, the plague of hunger, in the wake of war, 1943".[1] (*He Who Rides a Tiger*, p. 15)

The Indian freedom struggle especially the Quit India Movement is the background for his both the novels *So Many Hungers*! and *He Who Rides a Tiger*. But the treatment of the theme varies in the two novels. As Dr. K. R. Chandrasekharan observes, "In *He Who Rides a Tiger*, the Quit India Movement is mentioned and lies in the background, but the spectre of the famine looms large on the horizon. The two novels are in way twins and owe their inspiration to the same sources. There is, however, great difference between them with respect to the treatment of the theme and the final effect aimed at and produced".[2]

While focussing on the effect of freedom struggle on the character of these two novels, Bhabani Bhattacharya presents his own artistic talent. Regarding the difference between the novels Dr. K. R. Chandrasekharan rightly points out, "While the earlier novel focuses attention on the national movement and Bengal's travail and their cataclysmic effect on the teeming millions of people the later novel is more concerned with the history of one mind or at the most of two or three minds".[3]

Both the novels differ in another aspect also. In *So Many Hungers*! The characters are the silent and passive observers of the effects of famine. They yield to the situation without any revolt or protest, where as in *He Who Rides a Tiger*, the characters are not mere spectators of sufferings but they revolt against the human injustice. As Malta Grover Points out, " The novel *He Who Rides a Tiger* is also written with the famine for the background and deals with the same theme, the only difference being that whereas, So Many Hungers! is a silent sage of human miseries and sufferings, this novel is their vocal protest".[4]

As a result of the Bengal famine, poor people are deprived of food. The middle class and rich people are managed to get through the situation by their savings and reserve supplies. Poor people are the sufferers, as they depend on their day-to-day earnings. The result is the massive hunger deaths. Bhabani Bhattacharya portrays the picture of poor people during the time of famine as, "Weavers sold these looms to traders from big cities who scoured the country side for bargains. Artisans sold their food. Fishermen's boats were chopped up for firewood to sell. The plague washed up in fierce tides. Bengal was dying. Jharna was dying". (HWRT, p. 15)

In his first novel *So Many Hungers*! the novelist vividly portrayed the effects of famine and the life of poor peasants in the remote village of Bengal, called Baruni. In his third novel he again mentioned the evils of famine in Jharna, a remote town of Bengal. The village of Baruni is the symbol of Poverty.

The conditions of poor people and the exploitation of selfish traders are same in both the places. The village of Baruni, and the Jharna Town are the symbols of whole Bengal during the famine period.

The hunger makes the people behave like animals without any human elements. The theme of hunger is very elaborately dealt in his first novel *So Many Hungers*! This theme forms the basics for his third novel, *He Who Rides a tiger* though it is not as deep as in his first novel. Dr. C. Paul Verghese rightly remarks that, "Food is the primary requisite of human dignity; hunger debases and dehumanises man. Bhattacharya has dealt quite forcefully with the theme of hunger and the concomitant theme of human degradation in his novels *So Many Hungers*! and *He Who Rides a Tiger*".[5]

In *So Many Hungers*! the human degradation is at the lowest level. The hunger stricken masses behave like beasts. The hunger turns Kalo, the main character into a thief in *He Who Rides a Tiger*. Kalo could not resist hunger, at the sight of bananas in the high-class compartment in the train. The hunger drives him and he steals the bananas in an aggressive mood.

The novel, *He Who Rides a Tiger* is based on an ancient saying "He who rides a tiger cannot dismount". But Bhabani Bhattacharya, through the character of Kalo, makes it possible to dismount the tiger if the necessity arises. The character of Kalo is one of the best creations of Bhattacharya. Kalo, is a blacksmith in a small town Jharna where he lives with his only daughter Chandra Lekha. The novelist describes the appearance of his hero "But Kalo, Black, was true to his complexion, which had the color quality of ink and people said that when he sweated, you could collect the oozing fluid for your inkwell". (HWRT, p. 1)

Kalo's wife died in her youth after giving birth to a child. He did not marry again only due to his affection towards his daughter Chandra Lekha. Chandra Lekha is very beautiful like her mother and in colour she is just opposite to her father.

People comment, " He is iron all over, three maunds of the metal, with one tender spot at his top, and that spot is Lekha, his daughter". (HWRT, p. 1)

The name Chandra Lekha had a history. When Kalo's wife was pregnant, he was thinking over the names for his unborn child. One day a brahmin customer suggested him two names, Obhijit and Chandra Lekha. Kalo was impressed by these names and he decided to give them for his children. Kalo expressed his gratitude to the brahmin in the following words, "you have paid me with the names. I bow at your feet ... Let the soldering come off in a year and I shall do it newly for you at no cost. At no cost. You have paid me with the two names son Obhijit-daughter Chandra Lekha. This shows the innocence of Kalo in the beginning of the novel.

Kalo joined her in a mission school, inspite of the financial constraints. He worked hard and earned enough to pay for Lekha's school fees. Lekha is not only beautiful but also intelligent. Kalo has no limits to his joy, when Lekha stood first at the annual test and got double promotion. Kalo was very proud of his daughter's intelligence and wanted to help her in her studies. As Kalo could just read and write he could not answer her questions in her subjects. So, he started to learn from her books – "All day he was busy with his work but late at night, when Lekha lay asleep, he took her books from her green school bag and pored over them for hours by the light of a Kerosene lamp". (HWRT, p. 9)

This shows his eagerness to help his daughter and his determination to face any difficulty for her sake. He feels sad when, anybody calls his lovely daughter, as Kamar's daughter. For Lekha, Kalo is everything. She could not tolerate when anybody illtreated her father. One day when her classmate comments at her father's work, she feels hurt and fights with her. She even does not want to hurt her father by telling the incident. She prefers to suffer alone than make her father sad. Even in her fancy she could not bear to see him mocked or insulted.

Bhabani Bhattacharya beautifully portrays the father-daughter relationship, in this novel. It is because of his daughter's sake, Kalo dares to ride on a tiger's back. It is this love that forces him to take revenge against the society. Lekha also prepares to sacrifice her life for her father's sake. Above all, this affection leads them to kill the tiger to reveal the truth at the end of the novel.

When Lekha was sixteen she participated in an essay competition for the students all over Bengal. She stood first and got the Ashoka Memorial medal. She was the first girl in Bengal to get the medal. Kalo was very proud of her cleverness. He bought three copies of the paper, which praised Lekha's achievement and preserved them safely. He values the medal more than his life. The novelist comments, "In the next few days he sat expectantly on his veranda, waiting for the great ones of town to visit his house and pay compliments to the girl who had put to, shame even the great Calcutta city!" (HWRT, p. 13)

But no one in the Jharna town responded to the incident because, the medal was won by a Kamar's daughter. Jharna town remains silent, as though nothing has happened. Through this incident the novelist picturises the discrimination between the higher and lower castes, that prevails in the society. This incident sowed the seeds of hatred towards higher caste people in kalo.

The lower caste people are scorned by higher castes during the time of famine. The traders, who come to the town for their selfish gains make fun of the poor people, who still suffer due to self-respect. When Kalo rejects the offer of a trader, the trader remarks, "The lowborn people won't bend but they will crack. God has sent this mighty hunger to teach the lowborn people a true lesson". (HWRT, p. 16) This shows how the low class people are ill-treated and mocked because of their poverty, during the time of independence.

The plague of hunger strikes the people of Jharna and many have already died due to starvation. Kalo could not see his daughter suffer like others. In those lean days he could not do any work to get money. The thought of pathetic condition of Lekha, due to lack of food, haunts him. He worries, that she might have to roam the fields with hundreds of others like a hungry animal, digging out soft wild roots for a meal". (HWRT, p. 18) So he decides to go to the capital city. He leaves Lekha to the care of her old aunt and starts his journey. This journey for the sake of his daughter takes many turns in the novel.

The thought of leaving Lekha pains him, but he must earn for her and for her better future. He hopes" He must find work soon. He must save all he could. When he had a hundred rupees in his waistcloth, he would rush back home – the day of rejoining – and take Lekha with him to the city. Never again would Chandra Lekha have to fear hunger." (HWRT, p. 21) The irony is the city itself is the source of hunger in addition to many evils.

The pathetic condition of hungry destitutes and their struggle to reach the great city Calcutta, by train. For thousands of hungry destitutes, it is difficult to find place in the train in those days. Bhabani Bhattacharya picturises the cries of helpless destitutes as, "Hungry, we die – give us a few grains of food, Bab Give us a side to the great city. Food enough in the great city, food even for dogs and cats. Take mercy on the dying ones, Baba, permit us to leave". (HWRT, p. 23) Many have died on the way, during their long tedious journey. Some have fallen and died fast, while many stay back and die day-by-day.

Kalo has to wait for many hours. The Red Turbans have no pity towards the destitute. They do not allow the hungry masses to board the rain. So, Kalo began to walk for miles so that he could find safe place to board the train. At last he could manage to stand on the foot board of a train. He could not relax till next train, as he was in a hurry. His affection towards Chandra Lekha, his daughter, forces him to take risk at any cost. The novelist narrates" His hours and minutes were not his own. They were all Chandra Lekha's for the sooner he made good and earned a living, the sooner his girl would come to him in the great city". (HWRT, p. 26)

After a long walk for hours, Kalo had nothing to eat. He has eaten nothing for the past few days. So, he was hungry and lost his sense. In a fit of madness he has stolen three ripened bananas from the first class compartment and is caught red-handed by the police. For this petty offence, he was handed over to the court for punishment.

The cruelty and the inhumanity of higher people are depicted clearly by Bhabani Bhattacharya in the court scene. Kalo pleaded with the Magistrate in the following words, "I was hungry sir. Madness came upon me. It was because I thought I had to eat or I would die. Madness came upon me. I had to live". (HWRT, p. 31) This indicates that people degrade to the lowest position during the time of hunger.

The Magistrate after hearing Kalo's misery, instead of showing pity questioned harshly, "Why did you have to live?" (HWRT, p. 31) This question made him a rebel afterwards. Hunger has debased a man to a thief and a rebel. K. K. Sharma points out "Hunger not only alienates him from his family, profession and native place, but also sends him to jail for stealing fruit at a time, when hordes of hunger-mad folks are moving about throughout Bengal. He is sent to prison as a common thief by a magistrate who knows nothing of the meaning of hunger because he has never experienced it".[6]

The words of Magistrate completely changed the attitude of Kalo, the blacksmith of Jharna town. Kalo knows fully that he wants to live not for himself but for his daughter. He was not afraid of punishment but he was afraid of wastage of time. It was not his time but Chandra Lekha's. He has to live because Chandra Lekha has to live. He was ordered to undergo three months imprisonment. This is the turning point in his life.

He came to know the life of a destitute downtrodden person, is not worthy enough to live, in view of high-class people like the Magistrate. He has lost his innocence and sowed the seeds of revenge, "His bulky figure, the face beard

– stubbled and lined with shock, shuffled away slowly from the prisoner's bar. But a part of him stayed there, never to be regained. Some thing was gone and Kalo, blacksmith of Jharna town, could never be whole again". (HWRT, p. 32)

In his first novel, Bhabani Bhattacharya makes his characters suffer and undergo hardships and miseries. But in his third novel *He Who Rides a Tiger* the novelist makes his characters revolt against the injustice and hitting back the people who are the cause of sufferings. In this novel, Biten gives the idea of hitting back the people to Kalo in jail. Kalo becomes friendly with another prisoner, B-10. Biten, as he was called later, imprisonment for inciting hungry destitute to loot a food shop.

From Biten, Kalo comes to know about the horrible situation in the city that he always dreams of a saviour. To face the society, the only way according to Biten is "hitting back". He remarks bitterly, "We are scum of the earth. The boss people scorn us because they fear us. They hit us where it hurts badly in the pit of the belly. We have got to hit back". (HWRT, p. 37)

Through the character of Biten, Bhabani Bhattacharya analyses the idea of honour of women in those days of hunger. Most of the poor women prefer death instead of living an immoral life. Only few women sacrifice their honour to lead their family and feed the dependents. Though their bodies are polluted, their souls remain purified. Biten supports the idea of selling their bodies instead of ending their lives. He comments, "Must a woman die rather than herself'? Why must she die? Only her body, which seemed to be of no account, was involved, a body that, unsold, had less value than a seer of goat's meat. Why must she die for her honor, die for a dead idea?" (HWRT, p. 41)

Regarding the status of women, Bhabani Bhattacharya makes them equal to men in all aspects. Even during famine times, women maintain their nobility. On some occasions they appear to become victims to the circumstances. But they stand firm and ready to struggle instead of surrendering themselves.

In his opinion they need not be victimized at the expense of the other. In this aspect he looks forward to social change. Dr. Shantha Krishnaswamy remarks, "He affirms again and again that the woman need not be a victim. He can play a positive role in the development of society. He presents an optimistic, affirmative picture".[7]

Being a realistic novelist, Bhabani Bhattacharya reveals the conditions of prisoners in the jail during the British period. In those days the prisoners were forced to do hard work and it was looted by the officials. In this novel, he point out the misuse of mustard oil produced in the prison. "It was sold to officials and a favored few at a cut-rate. The oil press was worked by convict labour that carried a yoke on their shoulders and ground the mustard seed by walking endlessly round". (HWRT, p. 33)

When the principal character, Kalo was sent to prison for his petty theft, he works hard and bears the insults by the warders. He becomes P-14 and never complains like his fellow convicts. While making oil the other prisoners wipe their sweat and cast it into oil they produce. While doing this they address the unseen consumers as, "Eat this, the oil of our bones, eat. Take this to fry thy fish with....that, for the egg – apple curry thou fancy...and this to rub thyself with. Eat this, the oil of our bones, eat". (HWRT, p. 33)

The treatment of the prisoners was also harsh before independence. The guards beat the prisoners with whatever weapons they have at hand by getting orders from the Deputy Jailer. The attack of the prisoners by the guards was very often in their cells. In this way, they not only break the heads of the prisoners but also their spirits, which fast remains in their minds throughout their lives.

In prison, Kalo was friendly with Biten who was imprisoned for inciting hungry men in the great city to loot a food shop. While Kalo was thinking of finding an honourable job after his release from prison. Biten explains him the condition of present society and the easy way to make a living in the great city.

"Can you wear a Saffron loincloth, smear your body with ashes, and mark a red-paste trident of Shiva on your forehead? Then, as you walk the streets, your alms bowl will fill up in no time; and may be, if you have luck, someone with money enough to squander will see in you a yogi with great spiritual power". (HWRT, p. 40)

Through the character of Biten, Bhabani Bhattacharya puts forth his views about the pseudo priests and money mongerers by creating false temples. While thousands of people suffer due to hunger for food there are some rich people, who suffer due to hunger for soul. The hunger for soul is well cashed by some pseudo sadhus at all times. The innocent people are always the victims for this. As Biten says, "Food for the soul is produced and sold like food for the stomach, and though the ways of the two trades are different, you pay for both with hard cash. The temple is a market and the priest a dealer. People are always ready, to pay well for feeding the inner man!" (HWRT, p. 41)

Biten stresses on the way to feed the inner souls of innocent lives. It needs a trick to achieve the way to serve this spirit food. As the Brahmin alone has right in this business, one has to become a Brahmin by having a sacred thread on his chest. To achieve this idea of spirit or soul business there is a need for the trick of magic". K. H. Kunjo Singh observes, "Biten disillusions Kalo about his honest living in the cruel city. He advises him to retaliate against society by faking a miracle and by befooling people making them worship his bogus image".[8]

Through this novel Bhattacharya exposes the evil of pseudo-sadhus, who deceive people of their faith in their religion. Spirituality has become a business for those who deceive people by the blind beliefs and encash their devotion. He also attacks the high-class people, who use spirituality to meet their personal gains. K. H. Kunjo Singh points out, "In the story religion seems to have lost its pristine glory and forgotten its ethical values. It is turned into spiritual trade where people try to buy spiritual merit in exchange for merchandise".[9]

After three months of hard labour in the jail, Kalo enters into the big city to find work. 'He could not find any decent job, as there are thousands of men like him on the streets to do any kind of work to escape from hungry deaths. Kalo becomes a stretcher-bearer piling the corpses of destitute people in the truck and dropping them at the cremation ground. As there are many hands to work in the city, he loses his early job and seeks the help of Rajani. Though he never likes to do the loath some work of a pimp he is helpless. He earns enough money in this filthy job. All this he bears only for his daughter "If she was dead, he himself would not want to live because, Chandra Lekha was the very spark of his being. She was the sole reason for his existence". (HWRT, p. 47)

The only aim in life for Kalo is to earn money and to bring Lekha to the city, where both of them can lead a happy life. He earns enough money in his new job and sends some money to Lekha. But the irony is, before the first letter reached, Chandra Lekha had sold her memorial medal. As nothing is left to sell, Lekha has no other way except her medal, which is dear to her father. She recalls her father's words about the medal, "The medal was not money. The medal was your self-respect. It was you. Selling it, you lost a part of yourself which you could never get back". (HWRT, p. 55) But hunger forces her to part with the medal.

Bhabani Bhattacharya dramatically portrays the incident where Lekha and her father meet in the brothel house of Rajani. Lekha is trapped by a city woman and forced into the filthy profession. It is the irony of life that both father and daughter are in the same house without knowing each other. Fortunately, he rescues her from that filthy place and takes her to his residence. That horrible night has changed his life altogether. Kalo starts thinking, "Society, red-eyed with rage, had branded him as evil when he had done nothing truly wrong. But now that he was engaged in work truly evil he was smiled at and paid handsomely." (HWRT, p. 76)

That whole night, Kalo was restless, thinking about the past and the struggle for future. The words of Biten gave him enough strength. For his daughter's sake, he wants to fight the battle against the society. He has the weapon of 'Trick of Magic' with that he can settle the accounts. He finds the way, "yes, yes, there was a way, a way not simply to make a living but a way to settle accounts with them". (HWRT, p. 77)

Kalo wants to avenge the society that prevents him from doing any honest work. AS K. K. Sharma points out, "Kalo wants to fight, not with an individual, but with the entire upper class that dominates society".[10] For that he plans a trick to deceive the people steeped in religious feelings. In the big city, he chooses a spot under a banyan tree. A vast crowd has assembled to witness a promised miracle. Kalo sits cross-legged with the sacred thread around his waist. Bhabani Bhattacharya through his description, brings the picture before our eyes, "Shiva's coming that was the occasion. He sat with his legs crossed on a striped tiger skin spread under the banyan, and tirelessly, in a sonorous tone, he spoke the charmed words 'Namo Shivaya' which his listeners solemnly echoed". (HWRT, p. 78)

The promised miracle takes place and a stone image of Shiva slowly emerges from the ground. The people present there, are thrilled and happy because Lord Shiva has chosen this spot in the city as a habitation. Bhabani Bhattacharya comments the foolishness of the common people, "The fools; How he had tricked them! He could have laughed. He had created a god. He had created a legend. The legend would pass from generation to generation". (HWRT, p. 85)

Playing the Brahmin's role to cheat the people, in the name of God, had a great moral struggle in Kalo. Being a mere Kamar, a low caste man has to pose a man of higher caste. Though it is a terrible fraud, Kalo is prepared to take risk for his daughter's sake. The great city has made him a rebel. "The rebel had been stern and implacable. The rebel was reason and justice, and they had transformed Kalo. The Brahmin masquerade was only a step toward a basic reincarnation". (HWRT, p. 83)

With the help of Lekha, Kalo has created a false God. Lekha has suffered more than her father at the hands of the society. Her part is only to assist her father mechanically without any inner impulse. Now Kalo need not toil from dawn to midnight to earn for Lekha. A blacksmith has become a Brahmin overnight. He has created a lie and he begins to ride on it, "He rode a lie as if it were a tiger, which he could not dismount lest the tiger, pounce upon him and eat him up". (HWRT, p. 85)

Kalo is now known and respected as Mangal Adhikari. Those who have humiliated him in the past, now become his devotees. The Magistrate, who sent him to jail, touched his feet for his blessings. Kalo's thirst for revenge is satisfied. He expresses his feelings to Lekha as, "They're paying. They touch our low caste feet. They pray to a god who is no god. What expiation could ever cleanse their souls? They're polluted, fallen. They're doomed for many lives to come". (HWRT, p. 93)

The existing social inequalities and the indifferent treatment towards the lower strata of society made an innocent blacksmith to protest against the social evils. He started his fight against the society. Kalo himself satisfied when he could get the land from a merchant for the temple. He agrees, "Yes, the fight was going well indeed". (HWRT, p. 90). He could get the land free of cost to erect a false God, by cheating the high-class people of society.

Regarding the theme of novel, H. G. S. Arulandram rightly points out, "Bhattacharya's third novel *He Who Rides a Tiger* (1954) is a novel of protest-protest not only against a political and economic system which degrades human beings but also against an established social order which stamps on men as superior and inferior by virtue of accidence of birth". (HWRT, p. 11)

Bhabani Bhattacharya scorns the wealthy people, who never think about the famine stricken masses but donate cash or kind to temples out of fear about their sins. In this novel there are many incidents where most of the people come forward to donate for the construction of the temple. Kalo satirically criticizes the merchant, when he hesitates to donate his land, "This is truly the age of sin. Man does not give to man out of kindness, even when hunger prowls and tens of thousands die. What wonder that man will not give to the gods out of love? Have you no fear? Do you not shake at the thought of Shiva's thunderous Wrath". (HWRT, p. 89)

The ritual of Shiva's bath reveals the blind belief of ignorant people. According to the ritual, every day litres of milk is used for Shiva's bath, and the milk after that was cast into the holy river. No one among them bothered about the hungry children in the streets. Harish Raizada rightly remarks, "The novel satirises the blind religious faith of ignorant masses who grudge to feed famished destitutes but fill whole heartedly the alms – bowls of the sadhus dressed in saffron loincloth".[12]

The same issue of the milk for Shiva's bath revealed Kalo in her purity and kindness towards the hungry children. It was observed by the pujari that milk after Shiva's bath was found missing. One day the pujari caught Viswanath red handed, while he was collecting buckets full of milk. The Pujari and the Board of members strictly condemned the issue. But Kalo felt happy, after knowing the truth from Viswanath that the milk was used to food the destitute babies. He permitted Viswanath to continue the act of kindness. He derives satisfaction, by this act of charity. Balram S. Sarot says, "Though Kalo in the Brahmanic garb moves on a new plane in society, the 'Kamar' within him remains alive and intact".[13]

By wearing the mask of a Brahmin, Kalo feels lonelier than before. Though he assumes a new role, he still remains a Blacksmith in his heart. In his leisure time his hands ached for the touch of the tools of his trade. In his attic he set up a smithy secretly. Since the smoke has created doubts in the minds of people of his neighbourhood, he had to give up his little smithy unwillingly. He identifies himself with the poor kamar, Viswanath whom he had employed in the garden.

With his new role, Kalo has to move among higher strata of society. He feels helpless about his condition, "He had hurdled class – boundaries only to find others: he must move only among high – caste people for whom he felt no warmth. It was better to avoid them, to eschew all social contact because the kamar might peer through the Brahmin mask". (HWRT, p. 96)

Inspite of his high status in the society Kalo leads a simple life. Daily he goes to the market by walk to bring vegetables. He still feels for the poor and the sick people. Once a man came to Kalo to request him to fix his date of Shiva's milk bath within a week, so that his aged father will die in peace. Kalo struggled hard to fulfil that man's wish but no one was ready to delay his chance. Atlast the old man died without fulfilling his last wish. Kalo was very much hurt by this incident. He scorns at the selfish people with his daughter "It's better far to be in hell than share heaven with such selfish people". (HWRT, p. 118)

In this novel Bhabani Bhattacharya has made his principal character, Kalo, a rebel. But the story of Kalo reveals the birth of a rebel not suddenly out of a single moment, but a gradual development from many situations. Bhattacharya gives us a clear idea of the development of Kalo as a rebel. "A small rebel was born when he sold his tools and set off for the big city. The rebel grew eyes and ears in court and prison, with the help of Biten gave it a mouth and protest. Out of that protest he has acted mutinously, challenging man and God". (HWRT, pp. 120-121)

The novelist drew the character of Chandra Lekha most sensibly. She is one of the major characters in the novel *He Who Rides a Tiger*. Bhabani Bhattacharya vividly portrays the inner beauty of Lekha from childhood to the mother of Seven fold Bliss. Though she does not like deceiving the people, it is because of her father's sake, she decides to ride on the tiger's back, with her father.

From her childhood, Lekha was calm and her only hope in life was her father. While he was studying in missionary school she faced shabby treatment from her friends – "Smith girl, tell your father not to cheat his customers. He mended one of our buckets and it was leaking again in two months". (HWRT, p. 8) But Lekha had firm faith in her father's goodness. She couldn't tolerate the ill treatment towards her father. She was vexed with her caste affiliation. Her own caste men do not spare her from passing teasing comments: "A Kamar girl puts on the feathers of learning. A sparrow preens as a parrot". (HWRT, p. 11) Still she does not lose her confidence and performs well by getting first prize in the Annual All Bengal Essay competition.

It is because of her innocence that she was deceived by the city woman and has suffered in the harlot-house. The past always haunts her even after acquiring a high social status. She feels herself a thief when she recollects the incident of stealing pumpkin from a poor old woman's garden during those famine days. She praises the poor old woman, who has sacrificed her meagre food in those lean days. Lekha says to her father "It's only the poor who help the needy poor. Just the same; the fact remains that I have been a thief". (HWRT, p. 147)

After the narrow escape from the harlot house by her father, Lekha was mentally depressed. She could not come out from that fearful shameful incident. It was difficult for Kalo to bring her daughter out of that depression. The thought of their survival made him to face any risk. His only wish is to provide a safe and secure life for his daughter. The thought of Chandra Lekha gave Kalo sufficient strength and energy to take necessary action. Marlene Fisher rightly remarks, "In Dr. Bhattacharya's third novel, *He Who Rides a Tiger* (1954), that energy, both symbolic and real in Chandra Lekha provides the impetus and force behind her father's actions to assure the survival of both himself and his daughter".[14]

Lekha tried hard to forget her past, and live in the present. She expresses her feelings only to her father. The pseudo life has become her shadow. She reveals to her father, "our new life is unreal to me. The house. The temple. The great city itself. The prison is real". To overcome this feeling, Lekha adopts a little waif Obhijit, whom she has picked up from the street during famine. She has a motherly love for him. Shantha Krishnaswamy remarks, "Her physicality as the natural woman rebels against this bogus sanctity and tries to reassert itself. One natural consequence is her outpouring of motherly love towards Obhijit, the low caste street waif she adopts".[15]

When Kalo poses as the Brahmin Mangal Adhikari and becomes the Chief Priest of Siva temple, Lekha is forced to perform the role of the mother of the sevenfold bliss. Many people come to her from far and near expecting her to perform miracles. The incident of the death of a sick boy, whom Lekha has touched its brow with her bare toe, brought her back to the crude reality of life. The curses of the dead child's mother revealed the absence of any mystic power within her, which the innocent devotees don't know. Even Lekha feels herself responsible for that death "This is what I deserve. I have killed a child. I deserve to be hanged". (HWRT, p. 224)

Except the little boy Obhijit whom Lekha treats as her brother, she has no hope in her life. She wants to live freely with the boy, without any more, bondage of the false temple. She is vexed with the role of divinity and slowly recognises her wordly feelings, "But Lekha was not fit for a divine role. She was all too earthly, too human." (HWRT, p. 230) Both Kalo and Lekha have some mental relief by taking care of this destitute boy, whom Lekha named as Obhijit in memory of her unborn brother.

Before the arrival of Biten, Lekha was always sad and gloomy. She was untouched by the outward familiarity. Even Kalo could not make her happy by material things. Kalo was worried about the emptiness in her heart. But after Biten's arrival, Lekha was free from her inner misery. Inspired by the ideals and the individuality of Biten, Lekha was attracted towards him. Biten has awakened the faminity in her. She loved him deeply, but kept it a secret from her father. Shantha Krishnaswamy writes, "She looks forward to linking her life with Biten the noble minded reformer and working for the downtrodden men and women of the lower castes".[16]

When Biten leaves her without telling, she longs for his arrival. In order to lead a free life and to save Obhijit from the clutches of Mothichand, Lekha decides to sacrifice her love and marry Mothichand, whom she never respects. "By giving herself to Mothichand she would payoff her debt of love to her father and then atlast have the right to be free". (HWRT, p. 230) She tells her father that she would rather become the fourth wife of Motichand than get herself buried in the temple for ever as the Mother of Seven fold Bliss. As K. Venkata Reddy states, "The quest for individual freedom is presented through Lekha".[17]

Bhabani Bhattacharya portrays the character of Biten as a man of ideals. He is the person who gives the idea of riding on a tiger. Biten who is the associate of Kalo in the prison, never reveals his real caste, but identifies himself with the 'convict class'. The original name of Biten is Bikesh Mukherji, a brahmin by birth. He throws away the sacred thread after his sister's death due to caste cruelty. He revolted against his own caste by encouraging Kalo to become a Brahmin to deceive the traditional caste ridden people. He insists, "The Brahmin has sole right in this business. To take it from him you have to be a brahmin. What mark distinguishes him from others? Just one thing. A sacred thread on his chest". (HWRT, p. 41)

Biten intensely loves Lekha and wants to marry her. When Kalo insists on him to become a brahmin he rejects the idea though he is a brahmin by birth. He is not involved in the temple business. He rejects the share in the temple, offered by Kalo. Biten is the only person who could bring out the feminity hidden in Chandra Lekha. The novelist remarks, "For the first time she was self-aware. She owed this to Biten. Though the passion of his embrace had provoked horror and revulsion, it had wakened a woman". (HWRT, p. 209)

When Kalo came to know the facts about Bikesh Mukherji, he wonders at the nobility of this young man. Once Biten refused to wear the sacred thread which was his birthright at the cost of losing his beloved Chandra Lekha. This issue had great impact on Kalo. He wonders, "Whence came the strength by which a man would be prepared to suffer for an idea in his heart?" (HWRT, p. 216)

The inner conflict of Kalo attained its peak when he came to know that his beloved daughter, Chandra Lekha, for whose sake he dares to ride the tiger, prepares to ruin her life to satisfy him. He was shocked when he hears from her, "I cannot play that game with a person whom I am supposed to hold in respect". It was clear that Lekha decides to marry Motichand, to deceive the Brahmin and she has no respect to him. Marlene Fisher points out, "It is ultimately a decision of self-sacrifice on Chandra Lekha's part that restores Kalo to himself and to her".[18]

The main purpose of wearing the mask of a brahmin is to make his daughter happy throughout her life, But Kalo realises that his false life does not serve his purpose. He is on the wrong side of his life. His aim and dream of Lekha's golden future comes to ruin. So he decides to throwaway the mask and to lead the life of reality. As A. V. Krishna Rao points out, "*He Who Rides a Tiger* is an authentic attempt at revealing ironically and imaginatively the complex relationship between the mask and identity in the web of circumstance."[19]

When the identity of Biten as Bikesh Mukherji is revealed, Kalo is shocked. This truth makes him rethink about his falsehood. He is ashamed of his narrow thinking towards her daughter's marriage. Bhabani Bhattacharya comments, "And here was a blacksmith with his Brahmin posturing who had not let his daughter marry the man of her choice lest their caste be desecrated and the posturing ended". (HWRT, p. 216)

Atlast Kalo comes to a decision to end his game of false identity. He feels that the hour has come to dismount the tiger, and he has enough courage to do so. As rightly pointed out by Vasanth A. Shahane, "Kalo, conscious of Chandra Lekha's resistance as also of his own inner revulsion, summons up enough moral strength to dismount, the tiger of the lie he has been riding".[20]

After clearly understanding the heart of Lekha for leading a normal life, Kalo takes the right decision. He dares to risk his life to save Lekha from the clutches of selfish businessmen of false temple. Thus Bhattacharya makes his central character Kalo successfully dismount the tiger by killing the tiger at the right moment. "His hand had atlast attained, the power of his will. It would plunge a dagger into the tiger's heart". (HWRT, p. 238)

The right moment is the day of Yagna. On this day, Kalo reveals the truth to the audience. I who made this temple was not born a Brahmin". (HWRT, p. 237) He bravely expresses the crude realities of life. "Nothing is as true as falseness! The more false you are to yourself and to others, the more true you become! The rest of the answer is, evil is to be faced and fought with its own knives". (HWRT, p. 239) He has avenged himself by betraying the persons corrupt with caste and cash.

Among the audience, the high-class people who were sitting in the front could not tolerate the deception by a mere Kamar. They are filled with anger to punish him. They curse him for his evil deed. But the common folk who are at the back, identify themselves with Kalo. Their indignation from many generations made themselves feel avenged by the act of Kalo. They proudly accept Kalo as their brother: "He who has been master of the temple is our kin, our own brother". The hundreds of common people shout "Victory to our brother". (HWRT, p. 243)

There are Biten and Viswanath, Among the audiences, who appreciate Kalo's decision. The presence and support of these two men gives more strength to Kalo. Biten responds,

"You have chosen my friend. You have triumphed over the others – and over yourself. What you have done just now will steal the spirit of hundreds and thousands of us. Your story will be a legend for freedom, a legend to inspire and awaken". (HWRT, pp. 244-245)

Kalo, with his daughter Chandra Lekha, is going to start a new life. Lekha is there to give Kalo, the moral support to lead the rest of his life without any misery. She is optimistic about their new life. "Babu, after this, whatever happens to us, where ever we go, we can never again be unhappy or defeated". (HWRT, p. 244)

As a realistic novelist, Bhabani Bhattacharya has successfully resolved the crisis in the novel. As K. Venkata Reddy remarks, "Its beauty lies in that Bhattacharya employs a lie to expose truth about caste and religion as they obtain in the present day society".[21]

Bhabani Bhattacharya's fourth novel, *A Goddess Named Gold* was published in 1960. But it deals with happenings in an Indian village during the period immediately preceding India's attainment of freedom. The novel opens exactly a hundred days before 15th August, 1947. Dr. K. R. Chandrasekharan rightly remarks, "The preoccupation of Bhattacharya in this novel is with the way in which a country should use freedom and what benefits may be derived from it".[22] Bhabani Bhattacharya analyses the achievements of freedom in a decade after the attainment of Independence.

The Indian village life during the time of Independence is depicted very realistically. The freedom Movement in the Indian villages those days attained significance. In the beginning of this novel *A Goddess Named Gold* the Quit India Movement of 1942 is mentioned. The village mentioned in this novel is Sonamitti. Both men and women participated in the freedom struggle. The women of Sonamitti fought against the British like lions. The two women of the village, Shoagi and Lakshmi, recall their active participation in the struggle, "Proud, chins up, we marched in a column of our own, across the meadow of Pipli, onward of Kanhan. 'Quit India! We shouted to Engrez alines in one big voice." (*A Goddess Named Gold*, p. 12) This shows the unity in the villages in their fight for their country. Women took equal part along with men during those hard days.

Apart from young people, many aged persons also took part in the freedom movement. The central character in this novel is teenaged girl, Meera. Along with her, aged grand mother also plays major role in the novel. Lakshmi describes the heroism of Meera's grandmother. These aged women marched with the lovers of freedom in hot Sun. Lakshmi had gone to prison with this grand old woman, while she was pregnant. She says, "She made us forget the fear we had in our bones and we faced lorry loads of Red turbans as if they were mere goats". (GNG, p. 13)

Bhabani Bhattacharya dealt with the theme of freedom in a broader aspect. The freedom includes not only political aspect by also economic and social aspects. In this novel, the central character Meera and other women of cowhouse five launch a movement against the Seth of their village for economic relief. The irony is the wife of the Seth is against her husband's exploitation. K. K. Sharma points out, "Surprisingly enough, Lakshmi, the wife of the Seth, is one of the leaders of the movement because she is wedded to the lofty ideal of economic freedom and prosperity for all".[24]

The Seth in this novel is represented as an economic offender, who has made the people to suffer. The people could not bear the economic slavery by him. So the women leaders decide to fight against him with the support of his wife, Lakshmi. The Seth is the main dealer of cloth in Sonamitti and nearby villages. As there was countrywide sari shortage, he wants to exploit the people. So he corners the supply and raises the prices to gain profit. As a result, "the clothes the women of Sonamitti wore-saris patched over and over, jackets cut from caste-off gunny sack-that was why price of old bags was going up". (GNG, p. 14) Condition prevails in a village of rich black earth yielding large quality of good fibre cotton that is enough to supply clothes to the entire district.

To save their honour, the women of Sonamitti demanded one free sari for every woman. But the greedy Seth did not yield. So the women planned to make a threat to strip themselves bare, including his wife. The creator of the idea, Meera, putsforth her view. That taking the rags off their bodies, will shake him to the roots of his honour and he will see sense. Though at first the Seth did not care, later he yields to his wife's threat for his honour sake and for his future political purpose.

While referring to the profit motive of the Seth, the novelist once again recalls the evils of Bengal famine in this novel also. The trick of hoarding cloth was learnt by watching the exploitation during rice famine. "At that time three million men and women had to die so that there could be thirty new millionaries, and none condemned the profiteers". (GNG, p. 33) Bhattacharya hints at the inefficiency of the government to stop the exploitation of the poor by the rich.

The Seth is not only a cloth merchant but also lends out money to the villagers at a high rate of interest. As a result, the villagers are deep upto the neck in debt to him. At a crucial period immediately after independence, India needs economic freedom, which can be attained only through a successful struggle against the exploiters like the Seth. As Ashutosh Roy points out, "In this novel Bhattacharya is occupied with the theme of economic freedom of the hungry masses and warns against the evils of the profiteering greedy rich men who may exploit the freedom to serve their vested interest".[25]

The life and career of Seth Samsunderji presents a true picture of modern corrupt politicians and hard-hearted moneylenders. Neither pity nor prayer can move him. He cannot be shaken with threats or tears. His character portrayal reminds one of noted villains like Shylock. B. Syamala Rao Remarks, "Bhattacharya shows skill in drawing the portrait of Seth Samsunder, who reminds us of Shakespeare's Shylock and Martone's Barakas. At times even Shylock pales into insignificance before the Sethji".[26]

The protagonoist in this novel is, Meera Bai, a simple peasant girl. She is portrayed as pure, brave, unselfish and adventurous girl. The novel begins with the episode of Meera's Brave conduct of saving Lakshmi's child, Nago, who has slipped into the well. Once she has saved a peasant lad from snakebite by sucking their poisoned blood. For her courage "Each woman held up folded palms as if mock-seriously, yet each in her heart paid silent homage to the girl of sixteen, bowing to her strength of spirit". (GNG, p. 26)

Many critics comment on the female characters of Bhabani Bhattacharya. While compared to male characters, his women characters are maturer and carefully developed. He treated them equal to their male partners and sometimes more active than them. It is true with all major women characters of his novels. Neelam Singh and Rashmi G. rightly remarks, "Bhattacharya creates the woman protagonist as a finer human instrument than the male. They are always intune with their instinctual needs are filled with noble ideas".[27]

As Bhabani Bhattacharya allots significance to women characters in the beginning of the novel itself, a group of women are introduced. These six women are of different age and represent different strata of rural society. They call themselves, the cow house Five because they daily meet in the unused cow-shed in the house of one of them called Lakshmi. They are all ardent nationalists and participated in the Quit India Movement. The youngest of the cow house five is the heroine, Meera.

By depicting the female characters Bhabani Bhattacharya putsforth the meaning of freedom from feminine point of view. Those were the days, the women, especially in countryside are not allowed to participate in public gatherings. But by Gandhiji's inspiration the womenfolk freed them from the bondage. They equally participated with men in the freedom movement. Lakshmi reminds her friend, "Those days-Sohagi, remember? Gandhiji touched our spirit as it slept. Wakened, we became the equals of our menfolk." (GNG, p. 12)

Apart from Meera, another significant female character in this novel is Lakshmi, wife of Seth Samsunderji. In those days in patriarchal Indian village, the lot of a woman is to keep quiet and submit to suffer. While portraying the character of Lakshmi, the novelist at some times symbolizes as typical Indian Women. But at most of the times, during crucial period, Lakshmi is portrayed as a woman of new India. K. K. Sharma points out, "In the gallery of female characters created by Bhattacharya, Lakshmi distinguishes herself with a strong consistent character".[28]

The novel takes a new turn only after Lakshmi replaces Meera's copper ring with gold ring without the knowledge of Meera. She did this as an act of gratitude for saving her only son Nago, in the presence of Meera's grand father. Through Seth, Bhabani Bhattacharya echoes the conventional attitude towards women by the incident of cinema-show in the village "Children and women are alike in a way. Spare them and they get spoilt. It is for their own good that, now and again, they should be taught a hard lesson". (GNG, p. 42) He planned to deny, womenfolk the pleasure of watching the show. The women could not tolerate this ban against the womenfolk. They planned a trick to drive away the men during the right time. This shows awareness of women in the modern society. The women are ready to defy the unfair male superiority.

The inspiring character in this novel is the Minstrel, who is the mouthpiece of Bhabani Bhattacharya. It is through this character the novelist putsforth the true meaning of freedom and the effective use of freedom for the development of the country. Minstrel is the symbol for Indian's progress in future. Though his physical presence is limited in this novel, his ideas are present throughout, from beginning to the end. The power of the Minstrel is portrayed as "Owning nothing, he had the dignity of a king. He had more power than a king, for he could take the hearts of people in his fist, he could make them laugh and cry at his will". (GNG, p. 59)

Bhabani Bhattacharya believes that the progress of free India rests on the people. For that Democracy is the most suitable. He reveals his thoughts through the Minstrel, "Since India was to be free, the wheels of life would from hence forth under the power of the people is vote. Wheels of many kinds, big and small...." (GNG, p. 67)

The Minstrel is moulded on the principles of the father of our nation, Gandhiji. Most of the Bhattacharya's novels convey Gandhism as the basic idea. In addition to Minstrel, major characters like Devata in *So Many Hungers,* Jayadev in *Music for Mohini,* Sathyajit in *Shadow from Ladakh* are Gandhian characters. Though Gandhiji as a character is not included, his presence is felt on many occasions. There is a focus to Gandhiji's wish in this novel, "An old man whose voice has filled this country for thirty years has a curious wish in his heart. It is to wipe every tear from every eye". (GNG, p. 70) The assurance to fulfil Gandhiji's wish is given by the Minstrel to his grand daughter Meera. "Every one of us could wipe a few tears from eyes of misery if we tried". (GNG, p. 71)

Sohanlal is the one more character used by the novelist to represent Gandhiji's views. Sohanal is an young man who worked in the army. Later he joined as a motor cycle driver to assist Seth Samsunderji Sohanala is eagerly awaiting the day of Independence to our country. He visualizes a golden future for India after freedom. He explains to Meera's grand mother, "The people are going to be the masters. It is they who will own everything. The land, the rivers, the railways". (GNG, p. 105)

Regarding the character of the Minstrel, Dr. K. K. Sharma rightly points out, "The novel express the author's lofty concept of freedom. The Minstrel is the month piece of the writer; his actions and words embody an ideal concept of freedom".[29]

Bhabani Bhattacharya symbolically analyses the theme of freedom through a touchstone, a taveez. The minstrel ties an amulet to Meera's right arm and insists on the power of it as, "Wearing it on your person you will do an act of kindness.

Real kindness. Then all copper on your body will turn to gold.... Gold with which to do good". (GNG, p. 80)

The villagers believe that the taveez is a wonderful gift given to Meera and it has a magical power of converting base metal into gold. Seth has a thirst for the taveez for his personal gain. So he makes a business deal with Meera, expecting a miracle. Dr. Narasingh Srivastava observes, "The touchstone symbolises the hopes of Meera as well as of the poverty – stricken people of her village, on hand, and the selfish designs of the greedy Seth, on the other".[30]

The Minstrel warns Meera about the hardly won freedom. His observation on freedom are as follows, "Freedom is the beginning of the road where there was no road. But the new road swarms with robbers. There were the robbers of many kinds. The Seths of many kinds are common in free India. The Seth believes in the survival of the fittest' theory. Making money is his duty. That alone gives a meaning and value to his life. Like the spider, he thinks he should trap the fools and fatten on their meat. Business is business with him and there is no place for soft sentiment. Bhattacharya warns about this type of men, "There was the money-Seth, of course, to whom freedom meant a chance to seize fields of trade vacated by the aliens". (GNG, p. 110)

There are Seths in the Politics, where they use their power to meet their personal gains. They don't miss any opportunity to gain power and will fight with every means, fair or foul. In this novel, the Seth competes to be elected to the board. He is confident about his victory by bribing the people to vote for him. He remarks, "People in general will keep away from the voting booth. But a few sons of vizen will come out of good incentive. All the bad people, drunks and the like, will vote for me". (GNG, p. 119)

The modern cheap politics is viewed by the novelist nearly a half century ago. The hypocritic man cheat the people with their false promises. Then the Seth of politics ready to dupe the people with the power of his glib tongue, "...The Seth of religion with gods for sale. The Seth with a Gandhji cap on his head and the cap itself a deceit". (GNG, p. 110)

The battle against the British was won by the people. But it gives place to other battle against the native selfish politicians. By wearing a mask of leaders; they list the wealth of the nation. This is the time to fight against them, thought it is difficult. As Sohanlal worries, "Freedom's new battle would be more difficult in a way than the battle that had been won". (GNG, p. 114) Sohanlal draws the picture of free India, how it will turn out to be if uncontrolled.

Like Gandhiji, the Minstrel in this novel is not content with the mere attainment of freedom. Through him, Bhabani Bhattacharya focuses that the political freedom is only the beginning and it is the first step towards the nation's strength.

As the title indicates, the whole novel centres around the two dominant symbols, gold and goddess. Gold stands for wealth and property. It has become the most venerated goddess, worshipped mostly by the greedy and selfish people in the society. Gold has both material and spiritual implication. On the material plane it means power and possessions. On the spiritual plane it stands for purity and dignity. K. R. Chandrasekharan aptly remarks, "Gold in the popular connotation is material wealth, but gold may also symbolise richness of mind or spirit".[31] Even the name of the village called Sonamitti is symbolic, means the land of gold.

Bhabani Bhattacharya comments on the value attached to mere metal. A man's worth and status was determined by the gold. "Such madness about gold! A mystic value was set on the yellow metal, so that there could be a game for men to play". (GNG, p. 41)

Seth mistakes Meera's gold ring as miracle by the amulet given by Minstrel. The condition for the touchstone is that it will act only when an act of Kindness is done. So the Seth makes experiments for making the amulet function. Some situations created to motivate Meera's act of kindness, combined by the Seth one after another. These are parodies of those spontaneous acts of compassion performed by Meera earlier. The irony is the, kindness should be spontaneous; but here its a planned action. The act that has made the touchstone work, the key to the great mystery. That key has to be found and used with care. Planned approach. Cautious Calculation". (GNG, p. 131)

The two opposite poles are the two partners in the gold business deal. The people of Sonamitti wonder how Meera can work with a person and work against that person at the same time. But Meera is confident, "With all of myself I will work with the Seth in one field where our motives meet. With all of myself. It will work against him in another field where our motives are in conflict". (GNG, p. 150)

According to the business deal with Sethji, Meera's body is wrapped with copper ornaments. She is asked to wear them in such a way as to touch her body so that the amulet can work. Along with this, Meera's friends also compel her to wear their copper coins, expecting a miracle. Though her body is encumbered with ornaments her soul is untouched by the value of gold. She needs gold only for others sake but not for herself. Gold has no value for her. For Meera, "Gold is a strip of field released from bonds. Gold is a new straw thatch on the walls of mud hut. It is the rag-woman's escape from hunger and the old father's wish for pilgrimage to Holy Benaras". (GNG, p. 162)

Through this novel, Bhabani Bhattacharya putsforth the value of Gold and money in different aspects. The gold and money which can be attained through miracles without hard labour will only harm the society, instead of doing good. He conveys through Sohanlal that unearned money do no good in the long run, "All the people must earn it by their own effort, not one individual on behalf of the community. Or else the benefits will not be real". (GNG, p. 162)

In free India the innocent dedicated people believe that people can be saved with a lot of wealth. This idea is symbolically revealed through the mind of Meera. Sohanlal argues with Meera that the gold, she desires can save only a few people. But it can not save the whole nation. The actual fact is, "It is the fight with the Seths that will save India, not a miracle, not armfuls of gold. You did have your share in the fight, a big share". (GNG, p. 181) Through these words, the novelist calls the people to drive away the evil through fight in order to develop the country.

Bhabani Bhattacharya symbolically presents money both as a beginning for Meera and an end to the greedy Seth. This is presented through the clash of motives between Meera and Seth, "Here was her inherent clash of purpose with the Seth....Making money was his duty as which alone gave his life its meaning and value. Money, an end in itself. For her, however, this end was to be the point of a new beginning". (GNG, p. 179) The purpose of Meera is to make her village, Sonamitti, a bright jewel.

The theme of hunger once again occupied the novelist's mind as in his first novel where Bhattacharya has portrayed many types of hunger. In this novel, one more type, the hunger for miracle has attained prominence. As Ramesh Kumar Gupta remarks, "The novelist portrays two more forms of hunger in the novel–hunger for miracles and hunger for spiritual experience".[32] It is evident through the comment of the people of Sonamitti, "We hunger for the miracle, whatever else may follow, good or bad". (GNG, p. 190) Through the villagers the novelist putsforth this type of hunger not only in India but also throughout the world. He refers to the old legends, which describes the philosopher's stone of the West.

The elders in Sonamitti wait eagerly for the miracle, even after the failure of some attempts. They remark, "We must pray for the miracle, but let us do so with hearts undeceived....The pice game had lost some of its bright promise; yet no one was prepared to give it up. We have a hunger in us, dear brother". (GNG, p. 191)

The hunger for gold, which has started from the beginning of the novel, has taken many turns. This hunger leads to the hunger for miracles. This in turn paves the way for preplanned acts of kindness. Meera has become a puppet in the hands of Seth. The people misunderstand her selfless acts of kindness. Her own friends comment, "Like old father we all must hide our bone marrow from thine hunger, dear daughter". (GNG, p. 203)

Meera's hunger for miracle is not for herself, but for people of the village. Sohanlal could only understand her heart fully, as he whole-heartedly loves her. As he feels, for Meera the miracle is just the means to achieve the right purpose, to eradicate poverty in her village. But the villagers including her friends began to scorn at her. Meera could not bear this. She worries, "It is my fate to wear the taveez for one purpose. To be scorned; to be deposited; to be the scourge of Sonamitti". (GNG, p. 206) The Seth polluted her ideals. Unaware of this, she was chasing the shadow with the tyrant Seth. People began to see her in the Seth's world. The novelist reveals her true self through Sohanlal, "She wants nothing for herself. I know her mind. She has less hunger for riches than every one else in this village". (GNG, p. 210)

The worshippers of Meera turned her villains. They even planned to bury her effigy. The goddess appeared as demoness to the villagers. The girl whom everyone in the village admired has to face a horrible situation. Meera's grand mother could not tolerate the ill treatment of her grand daughter. Holding the effigy of Meera, the grandma shouts in a troubled voice at the villagers, "You try to make a saviour out of her. You bid her fulfill an inner most wish of your heart. Your stern voice says, Do or die. She has no value for you apart from the gold she must be made to produce". (GNG, p. 247)

The people of the village watched Meera with contrary feelings after she became the symbol of gold. They view her with love, hate, and expectation anger and atlast vengeance, which led to the idea of burning of her effigy. Meera could realise that her aim leads to wrong concept of generosity and kindness, through the arrangements of marriage of drunkard and a brothel woman. She tripped the ornaments off her body. But she could not come out of her taveez.

Still there is a ray of hope in her heart. It is evident from the words of her grandma, "At midnight, when she was asleep, I felt under her jacket. Alas, the taveez was still on her arm. I felt under her sari and, alas, the nugget was still there and the waist-chain also. The gold game was not over". (GNG, p. 267) After the arrival of Minstrel towards the end of the novel, Meera rids herself of her fancy as soon as she becomes aware of its ill consequences. She discards the amulet and throws it into the river.

Bhattahcarya makes the Minstrel his mouthpiece in conveying his own message and ideas on freedom. He is an indirect representation of the father of the Nation. He feels that freedom will be the greatest boon to mankind and will be the means to a higher end and to enable the people to become strong and worthy. The minstrel speaks to the inhabitants of Sonamitti on Independence day, "Freedom was the touchstone....It was a touchstone for everyone. To possess this touchstone was not enough, for it could make to life and work its miracle only when acts of faith were done". (GNG, p. 277)

In the last chapter of the novel, Bhattacharya reveals the real meaning of the touchstone, the taveez. He symbolically presents the freedom as the touchstone and the acts of kindness as the acts of faith of people. "Without acts of faith freedom is a dead pebble tied to the arm with a bit of string, fit only to be cast into the river." (GNG, p. 277) Regarding the miracle, the novelist speaks through the Minstrel, "The miracle will not drop upon us. It is we who have to create it with love and with sweat. Freedom is the means to that end". (GNG, p. 278)

The address of Nehru from the Constituent Assembly is given by Bhattacharya to express the concept of freedom more effectively, "At the stroke of midnight hour India will awake to life and freedom. A moment comes, which comes but rarely in history, when we step out from the old to the new, when an age ends, and when the soul of a nation, long suppressed finds utterance". (GNG, p. 278)

Bhabani Bhattacharya deals the treatment of the theme of freedom in all aspects in this novel. Commenting on the presentation of Nehru's speech in this novel, M. K. Bhatnagar remarks, "Inextricably woven within the texture of the novel is the famous speech of the Indian Prime Minister, Jawaharlal Nehru, delivered at the time of India Independence".[33] It is suggestive of the political consciousness of the people at that time.

Bhabani Bhattacharya successfully handled this theme of freedom from his point of view in all aspects. In addition to this he included many points for the proper utilisation of the freedom for the welfare of the society. This indicates his commitment to the country and for the all round development of the people of India. As Harcharn Singh Boparai rightly remarks, "In *A Goddess Named Gold* the quest for righteous actions, which a free nation must perform in order to fulfil its destiny, continues at a microcosmic level".[34]

REFERENCES

1. Bhabani Bhattacharya, *He Who Rides a Tiger,* Arnold-Heinemann, New Delhi, 1977, p. 15.

   All Sub-sequent References from this Edition ref. to as HWRT with page number in Parentheses.
2. Dr. K. R. Chandrsekharan, *Bhabani Bhattacharya*, Arnold-Heinemann Publishers Pvt. Ltd., New Delhi, 1974, p. 58.
3. *Ibid,* p. 58.
4. Maltha Grover, *Bhabani Bhattacharya as a Novelist of Social Conscience,* Shalabh Prakashan, Meerut, 1991, p. 79.
5. C. Paul Verghese, *Problems of the Indian Creative Writer in English*, Somaiya Publications, Bombay, 1971, p. 71.
6. Dr. K. K. Sharma, *Bhabani Bhattacharya his Vision and Themes*, Abhinav Publications, New Delhi, 1979, p. 57.

7. Shantha Krishnaswamy, *The Women in Indian Fiction in English (1950-80)*, Ashish Publishing House, New Delhi, 1984, p. 81.
8. K. H. Kunjo Singh, *The Fiction of Bhabani Bhattacharya*, Atlantic Publishers and Distributors New Delhi, 2002, p. 97.
9. *Ibid*, p. 101
10. *Op. Cit.*, 6, p. 81.
11. H.G.S. Arulandram, *Bhabani Bhattacharya's Novel's TRIVENI, Journal of Indian Renaissance* Vol. 46, Oct. Dec, 1977, No. 3, Triveni Publishers, Machilipatnam, A. P., p. 71.
12. Harish Raizada, *Explorations in Modern Indo-English Fiction* Ed. R. K. Dhawan, Bahri Publications, New Delhi, 1982, p. 162.
13. Balram S. Sorot, *The Novels of Bhabani Bhattacharya,* Prestige Books, New Delhi, p. 76.
14. Marlene Fisher, The Women in Bhattacharya's Novels, *WLWE* Group 12, M. L. A. V. 11: 1, University of Texas at Arlington, Apr., 1972 p. 95.
15. *Op.Cit.*, 7, p. 69.
16. *Ibid.*, p. 69.
17. K. Venkata Reddy, *Major Indian Novelists*, Prestige Books, New Delhi, 1990, p. 75.
18. *Op.Cit.*, 14, p. 90.
19. A. V. Krishna Rao, *He Who Rides a Tiger: A Study, Ed.* T. Prabhakar, The Indian Novel in English – Evaluations, Phoenix Publishing House Pvt. Ltd., New Delhi, 1984, p. 232.
20. Saros Cowasjee, Vansant A. Shahane, *Modern Indian Fiction*, Vikas Publishing house Pvt., Ltd., 1981, p. 61.
21. *Op.Cit.*, 17, p. 69.
22. *Op.Cit.*, 2, p. 74.
23. Bhabani Bhattacharya, *A Goddess Named Gold*, Arnold Heinemann, New Delhi, 1984, p. 12.

    All Sub-sequent References from this Edition Ref. to as GNG with page number in Parentheses
24. *Op.Cit*, 6, p. 62.
25. Ashuthosh Roy, *Bhabani Bhattacharya's A Goddess Named Gold,* The Quest, Vol. 9 and 10, No. 2 and 1, Dec and June 1995-96, p. 47.
26. B. Syamala Rao, Bhabani Bhattacharya, Blackie and Son Publishers Pvt. Ltd., Bombay, 1988, p. 87.

27. Neelam Singh and Rashmi G, *Depiction of Women in the Novels of Bhabani Bhattacharya and Shobha De : A Comparative Study,* Indian Writing in English: A Critical Study, Ed. K. A. Agarwal, Atlantic Publishers and Distributors, New Delhi, 2003, p. 222.
28. K. K. Sharma, *Indian – English Literature A Perspective,* Vimal Prakashan, Ghaziabad, 1982, p. 86.
29. *Ibid*, p. 88.
30. Narsingh Srivastava, *Symbol and Allegory in A Goddess Named Gold*, Perspectives on Bhabani Bhattacharya, Ed. Ramesh Srivastava, Vimal Prakashan, Ghaziabad, 1982, p. 153.
31. *Op. Cit.*, 2, p. 86.
32. Ramesh Kumar Gupta, *A Study of Bhabani Bhattacharya's, A Goddess Named Gold*, Studies in Indian Writing in English, Ed. Mittapalli Rajeshwar, Atlantic Publishers and Distributors, New Delhi, 2000, p. 82.
33. M. K. Bhatnagar, *Political Consciousness in Indian English Writing,* Bahri Publications New Delhi, 1991, p. 35.
34. Harcharn Singh Boparai, The Achievement of Bhabani Bhattacharya, Perspectives on Bhabani Bhattacharya, Ed. Ramesh K. Srivastava, Vimal Prakashan, Ghaziabad, 1982. p. 208.

4 The Inner Consciousness of Interculturation

The themes of national importance dominate the novels of Bhabani Bhattacharya. His first novel *So Many Hungers*! is based on the struggle for Indian independence and the aspects of patriotism. His novels of post-Independence period also deal with the themes of national significance. His fifth novel, *Shadow from Ladakh* deals with an important national crisis, the Chinese invasion on the northern frontier in 1962. As Elena J. Kolinnikova rightly remarks, "The Indo-Chinese border dispute finds a brilliant and literary portrayal in the novel of Bhabani Bhattacharya, *Shadow from Ladakh* which received the Indian Sahitya Academy Award in 1967".[1]

The early novels of Bhabani Bhattacharya are preoccupied with the theme of freedom. Based on the contemporary events, the novels present India's struggle for freedom and the sacrifice of millions of people to achieve independence. In the later novels, Bhabani Bhattacharya projects the problems of Indians to protect their hard-on freedom.

The contemporary issue of Chinese troops entering the unguarded parts of Indian borders made a serious threat to India's freedom. As K. K. Sharma aptly points out, "While

Bhabani Bhattacharya's earlier novels concentrate upon India's urge for political and social freedom his latest masterpiece, *Shadow from Ladakh*, deals with people's concern to preserve the country's political independence at all costs".[2]

There is a reference to Ladakh and a detailed description of the place, in the beginning of the novel itself. The title of the novel, Shadow from Ladakh has a great significance. It is based on the popular proverb, 'Coming events cast their shadows before'. The shadow of the military encounter with the enemy forces at Ladakh is felt everywhere. Even the characters and places are shadows casting on the future of India. As K. H. Kunjo Singh observes, "While the whole action of the novel is based on the shadow cast by the Chinese peril, many of the characters are shadows too chasing other shadows. Satyajit and Gandhigram are shadows of Gandhi and Sevagram. Similarly, Bhashkar and Steeltown is shadows of Nehru and his dream edifies of industry".[3]

Satyajit is a devoted follower of Mahatma Gandhi and believes in the principles of Gandhiji. Educated in Cambridge, he served as a teacher, at Shantiniketan. Tagore's educational ideals and his philosophy of life influence him. He rejects his surname 'Sen' to become casteless and rootless like Yogis. At Shantiniketan, Satyajit meets Suruchi, a beautiful girl from a different caste and falls in love. Without any caste distinctions, he marries Suruchi and leads a happy life.

During his stay at Shantiniketan Gandhiji came there and selected Satyajit to form an ideal village in the model of Sevagram. This is the reason for the emergence of Gandhigram. It is depicted as, "The apparently insignificant village was building up a model for the whole of India. The new community of people was truly equal. All land belonging to the cooperative".[4] (*Shadow from Ladakh*, p. 28)

As Satyajit, Bhabani Bhattacharya was greatly influenced by both Mahatma Gandhi and Rabindranath Tagore from his youth. His earlier novels follow Gandhian ideology and at the same time Tagore's philosophy. In this novel, he vividly conveys the life and nature of Santiniketan, the World University and Tagore's part in the task of village reconstruction. According to Tagore, the village reconstruction is not only restricted to economy upliftment but also the upholding of values. This cannot be done as a whole involving the country, but it can be fulfilled by starting from a single village and later this can spread to the whole country. Tagore asserts, "Let's make a start with one village. If we succeed with one village, a model for the whole of India will be established". (SFL, p. 14)

Regarding the adherence of Gandhiji's doctrine, there is difference between Bhabani Bhattacharya's early novels and the later novels. While his early novels focus on Gandhijis views on social problems in the context of pre-independence period, his later novels focus on different contemporary issues in the changed social aspects. In the novel, *Shadow from Ladakh*, the principles of non-violence and Satyagraha are viewed in different aspect due to the threat from the neighbouring countries. As P. N. Bhatt points out, "His earlier novels follow Gandhian ideology and Gandhiji's doctrine of non-violence, Satyagraha, his views on untouchability and casteism, etc., whereas his later novels, which we call post-Gandhian novels, present Gandhi in the context of free India".[5]

The idea of brahmacharya in Gandhiji's view is, complete chasity of body and even of mind, which is a great source of spiritual strength. As a true flower, Satyajit wants to take the vow of brahmacharya after the birth of his daughter Sumita. At that time his wife Suruchi was only twenty-nine years old. He quotes Gandhijis words. "Those who perform national service...must have a celibate life, whether married or unmarried. I do not think that in our conception of marriage our lusts should enter". (SFL, p. 23)

As Satyajit does not want to impose his ideals on his wife, he asks Suruchi to marry again in order to lead a normal life. But, being a faithful partner, she wants to be his companion throughout her life. Through Suruchi, Bhabani Bhattacharya questions, "how one's dedication to national service could gain strength from the state of celibacy". (SFL, p. 23). She surrenders herself to the ideas of her husband but silently longs for her unborn sons.

The plea for a full and joyous life is one of the philosophical ideas of Tagore. Satyajit's suppression of natural instincts is against Tagore's views. Joy in the sense, the satisfaction of innerself but not in the external riches. Bhabani Bhattacharya refers to this through the words of Tagore as, "Happiness cannot compete with wealth in its list of materials. But happiness is creative, it has a source of riches within itself. It is fullness of life that makes one happy, not fullness of possessions". (SFL, p. 14)

Bhabani Bhattacharya deals the importance of industrialization in modern age very accurately through the character of Bhashkar in this novel. For country's defense purpose in the crucial moment, the utilisation of steel is essential. Apart form this the economic progress depends on the industries. Even poverty can be eradicated by creating employment for the labours in the age of machines. The theme of hunger once again captures Bhabani Bhattacharya and this leads him to find out various ways to overcome the economic crisis. Bhashkar, the Chief Engineer of Lohapur Steel Company expresses, "Steel means economic progress. Machine, tools, tractors, big industrial plants, locomotives steel to fight poverty and hunger. But steel has gained a second meaning. It stands for our country's freedom". (SFL, p. 30)

Mechanization, according to Satyajit is an evil for the country, which is based on village economy. As there are millions of people in the villages depending on small-scale industries, machines cannot afford to provide employment to all. So he wants to fight against the system of machines, which cannot feed the surplus of people. Being a follower of Gandhi, Satyajit could not fully understand the need for the existence of big industries. Though Gandhi is in favour of cottage industries, he hints at the inevitability of machines at the time of shortage of labour. Bhabani Bhattacharya views, "Gandhi was not against the kind of machine that helped an individual to add to his efficiency without turning him into its helpless slave". (SFL, p. 29)

Both Satyajit and Bhashkar are in the favour of production for the economic growth of the country. But the means they adopt to achieve their goals are different. While Bhashkar works for fast-placed production through latest technology, Satyajit has his own methods to contribute to sufficiency. For Satyajit, the means are as important as the ends while working for the national interest. He adheres to Gandhiji's philosophy of good and evil in the ways of production and asserts, "You can never attain good through evil. That was the essence of all that Gandhiji had to say". (SFL, p. 32)

Bhabani Bhattacharya analyses vice and virtue, as two sides of a coin, through his characters. Satyajit focuses virtue as creative and vice as destructive. So vice in all aspects should be eliminated. But Bhashkar views, that within its limits vice in life makes a person realise the innerself. So that the positive side of life can be appreciated and enjoyed fully. Bhashkar reveals his views to Satyajit thus, "Let me tell you, Sir: Vice is the darkness that gives values to light. No darkness and light is hurtful. Let there be some virtue, some vice. Le them are juxtaposed balanced. Virtue and vice together give life its color, savour. That's what I've experienced personally". (SFL, p. 32).

This confession of Bhashkar portryas him as a matured person. Even Satyajit wonders at this Gandhian way of expressing truth without any pretention. K. R. Chandrasekharan rightly remarks, "A basic question raised in *Shadow from Ladakh* is the extent to which industrialization on vast scale is relevant to the Indian situation".[6]

The character of Bhashkar is portrayed interestingly from the beginning to the end of the novel. As he was efficient engineer in Washington, a visiting minister from New Delhi invited him to India to be the C. E of the Steeltown. As India is facing a problem of survival, he agreed to contribute his hard work. Being a sincere officer, he spends most of his time in the office, preparing notes for the project work. The novelist observes, "So here he was in the new Steeltown, a machine among the machines, all working at top gear to make four hundred million lives a little more livable". (SFL, p. 36) He casts his mind on the maximum usage of resources to meet the challenge of China. He is noble at heart and leads a simple life. The workers of Steeltown are attracted towards him due to his helping nature. His personal Secretary Mrs. Sarojini Mehra praises his simplicity as "Twelve years in the land of fabulous wealth, and he comes back empty-handed. He is a saint". (SFL, p. 39)

The rapidly growing population is major threat for country's development, as viewed by Bhabani Bhattacharya. He questions, had production risen over to that level to meet the growing demand? He thinks that the problem of population growth can be solved only by sufficient production of required items. This is expressed in the novel as, "Each tick of the clock meant an opportunity used or lost. Each five ticks – or it could be four – signaled the birth of an Indian child. A child to be fed, clothed, reared educated; given cultural fare, given employment, given his due share of the human heritage". (SFL, p. 34) This shows how accurately Bhabani Bhattacharya observes the social issues and his concern for the fulfilment of the needs of growing population.

The needs of growing population are related to the economic progress of the country. The economic progress based on the production of steel. Steel is the means to achieve the end of prosperity. Bhabani Bhattacharya points out, "Two hundred tons of steel ingots in each round of smelting: the means of life for hundred newborn babies. The babies would not eat steel. But steel was the spine of the economy. Steel was food and clothing and dwelling. Steel was culture and art and ritual. And steel was soon to be the honor of the people, the shield of their freedom". (SFL, p. 37)

The village of Gandhigram is contrary to Steeltown in its ideology to meet the needs of rapid production for military purpose, it has to be occupied by Steeltown. Bhashkar broods over this idea, "What was Gandhigram but an idea? The idea could be transplanted to some other. Soil! The men of the village would get full compensation". (SFL, p. 41) The mud houses of the village can be exchanged for brick houses. But the values it cherished cannot be exchanged. This village is modeled on the spirit of Gandhiji. Bhabani Bhattacharya projects the value of Gandhigram through the character of Satyajit, "The village with its two hundred mud houses, seeking to build a set of values to be expressed in terms of deed, complete equality, unreserved fraternity, limitless non-violence, as much as thought as in action". (SFL, p. 49)

There are five direct disciples of Gandhi, who give guidance in the matters of Gandhigram. The novelist refers to Gandhi as the rainbow and these five men are the five colors of the rainbow. Satyajit is the intellectual aspect of the Father of Nation, Swamiji, the man of religion in Gandhi. While the social worker, Krishnamurti is dedicated to welfare work, the politician, Chittaranjan Ghose refers to public aspect. The other person is Madhab uncle, who is just the human side of Gandhiji. Satyajit leads Gandhigram as the symbol of Sevagram with the assistance of the other four persons.

Bhabani Bhattacharya advocates that the only way to solve the problem of threat from the neighbouring countries is the Gandhian way of non-violence. Satyajit in *Shadow from Ladakh* echoes the view of the novelist. During the time of Chinese aggression, he plans to form a Peace Mission to establish friendly relationship with China. As K. R. Chandrasekharan observes, "The major teaching of Gandhiji that figures in the novel is Non-violence. Satyajit's plan of forming a Shanti Sena is born of his faith in this creed".[7]

Mahatma Gandhi's weapon of passive resistance of free Indian labours in South Africa is mentioned briefly in the novel. Even during the crisis in East Bengal, Gandhiji made a peace plan using his moral force as a weapon to drive away evil. As a historian Bhabani Bhattacharya mentions the victory of non-violence both in South Africa and in the freedom-movement of India. Satyajit prepare himself to follow the path of his Master in the present crisis. He wants to be the shadow of Gandhiji to make his ideals relevant to modern age, "He is gone but the idea lives, and it must live for all time. Will it not find dramatization in the new crisis facing the country today, fifteen years after freedom was gained? Through another man of that kind? But a Gandhi is not born more than once in a century". (SFL, p. 70)

The promotion of universal brotherhood and international under standing is needed for the world for peaceful existence. India's Prime Minister, Jawaharlal Nehru already announced his friendship with China for mutual coexistence. "India believed in many paths leading to one goal – human happiness. Those many paths had to coexist. Universal brotherhood was the ultimate value". (SFL, p. 79)

To achieve the motto of human happiness, disputes should be solved in a peaceful and friendly manner through mutual exchange of ideas. Based on this, Satyajit sends his wife Suruchi to attend the World Peace Conference at Moscow. As an Indian delegate she explains India's hope and faith in establishing peace even at the time of crisis. H. G. S. Arulandram rightly remarks, "Bhabani Bhattacharya fervently advocates that all disputes however provocative may be, must be settled at the table and not at the filed of battle for such action endangers world peace. Inspired by and drawn to this idea of Gandhiji and Nehru, he pleads for meeting of minds to settle all disputes".[8]

There are many references in the novel *Shadow from Ladakh*, which advocate the principles of Jawaharlal Nehru. According to Bhabani Bhattacharya, Nehru's concept of non-alignment and neutralism are the gifts to the world. Nehru's humanistic vision makes the whole nation united and spread positive signs to provide an atmosphere of friendship. In the

Peace Conference held at Moscow, a Chinese delegate quotes Nehru's letter, "Again India and China look toward each other and past memories crowd in their minds; again pilgrims of a new kind cross or fly over the maintains that separate them, bringing message of goodwill and creating fresh bonds of friendship". (SFL, p. 10)

Bhabani Bhattacharya's faith in peace is asserted through the words of Gandhiji, "Not to believe in the possibility of permanent peace is to disbelieve in the godliness of human nature". (SFL, p. 82) In this novel, Steeltown symbolises Western modernism and Gandhigram symbolises Indian traditional values. In the beginning of the novel, Bhabani Bhattacharya deals with the conflict between the two different types of values and synthesizes the Western with the eastern ways of life. As Balram S. Sorot points out, "the synthesis of the Indian spiritual values and the Western modernism is undoubtedly the central theme of Bhabani Bhattacharya's celebrated novel, Shadow from Ladakh".[9]

The Meadow House in the novel is the symbol for synthesis of two contrary ideas. Bhashkar creates it as a centre of social communion. The villagers were invited to mingle with the men of the Steeltwon. This opportunity made the village understand the use of modern technology. Even electricity was banned in Gandhigram. But the contact with Meadow House makes Sumita the daughter of Satyajit to know the production and usage of electricity. She enjoys the programmes in the Meadow House along with the inmates of Gandhigram.

Besides social communion, there is a cultural communion between the people of Gandhigram and Steeltown. The old and the new values intermingle freely to make life meaningful. Regarding the interchange of culture, Bhabani Bhattacharya quotes Gandhiji's words, "No culture can live if it is to be exclusive. I do not want my house to be stuffed. I want all cultures to flow free about my house. Mine is not a religion of the prison-house". (SFL, p. 156)

Though Suruchi extends her assistance to Satyajit for village reconstruction, She has not fully accepted the ideals of Gandhigram. She believes in the Tagorian philosophy of integration of different element of life. She refers to his as, "Integration-that was the poet's life-long quest: integration of the simple and the sophisticated; the ancient and the modern; city and village; East and West". She takes a middle ground between the extremes of Gandhigram and the Steeltown. She encourages Bhashkar's love for her daughter, Sumita. As Neelam Singh and G. Rashmi observe. "Suruchi is really a woman of aesthetic temperament and collaborates in all reformatory activities of her husband. Suruchi though devoted to her husband and his vow of brahmacharya, is an incarnation of the aestheticism of Tagore".[10]

The character of Sumita is modeled on Gandhian ideology, like her father she holds the traditional moral values in great esteem. She wears white dress, without kumkum, are bangles. She is unaware of her physical desires at the age of twenty. Even the women of Steeltown admire her for simplicity. The Meadow House has a great impact on her innerself. Bhashkar is astonished at her interest to learn about electricity "The ease with which when could resolve all contradictions in her mind. Machines were the enemy. Yet she fascinated by the very life spark in machines-electricity. The life spark, the energy that had begotten the new century, the new civilization". (SFL, p. 142)

From her childhood, Sumita is determined to dedicate herself to her father's principles. Attracted by Satyajitism, she even risks her life and prepares herself to take part in the Peace March. She goes to New Delhi to help her father there. Her company with Nandini makes her to see life in its full splendour. She becomes aware of her womanhood while thinking about Bhashkar.

The change in Sumita is depicted symbolically by the novelist. After falling in love with Bhashkar, she discards her white garb and wears a green coloured sari. She adorns her forehead with a redmark and wears glass bangles. Her love changes Bhashkar's attitude to Satyajit and decides not to annex Gandhigram without its consent. Through the love of Bhashkar and Sumita, Bhabani Bhattacharya reveals his theme of synthesis between contrary values. As Balram S. Sorot rightly remarks, "Bhashkar's union with Sumita also illustrates a blending of the antagonistic values. In their marriage, Bhabani Bhattacharya synthesizes Western with the Eastern elements in life".[11]

As Sumita is brought up in the small house, in the atmosphere of the ashram, she is unaware of her natural physical desires. At Delhi, when she experiences the wider world, she begins to rethink her rigid ideals. She returns to Gandhigram as matured women. At last, she freed herself from her father's asceticism and accepts life's aesthetic sense. As a mother, Suruchi welcomes positive change in Sumita and encourages her. Even Satyajit realises that he had denied real happiness to his wife and daughter. Bhattacharya has artistically dealt with the theme of life's fulfilment in the family of Satyajit. As Prof. R. S. Singh remarks, "The Psychology of the maturing girls and the imperceptibly changing attitude of the parents towards them are delineated by Bhabani Bhattacharya with tenderness and care".[12]

According to Bhabani Bhattacharya, the Chinese Aggression is due to the wrong policy of the rulers but not the people of that country. The nobility of human spirit is advocated as, "The rulers were the Dragon, not the people. The people of China were the Dragon, not the people. The people of China were like people everywhere. The richness of the spirit of man knew no barriers of race and color or even of historical development. The novelist eagerly looks forward for a new young leadership in China which is peace- oriented and believed in mutual coexistence.

The episode of Chinese shoe-maker Ah To and his five children is interwoven in the novel to show the affection among the people of two countries over during the critical situation.

Ah To was doubted by the Indian Government as a spy and was arrested for investigation. As a result, his five children become homeless. His personal Secretary, Mrs. Sarojini Mehra, brings these children to Bhabani Bhattacharya's house. Bhashkar takes care of these girls very affectionately as a father and sends them to school for studies. He recalls the humanistic vision of Nehru and his attitude towards the Chinese people as, "We have nothing against the Chinese people. We must not transfer our anger or bitterness at what has been done by the Chinese Government to the Chinese people". (SFL, p. 256)

When the five girls offer prayer to Mao Tse-tung as their god, Bhashkar is shocked by their attitude. But later he realises that the innocent minds are not affected by alien feelings. They treat Bhashkar with respect as their father. As K. H. Kunjo Singh points out, "Bhabani Bhattacharya wants to show that inspite of the hostility between India and China, the hearts, as least of the younger generation, remain untouched by hatred".[13]

Bhabani Bhattacharya very subtly handles the character of Rupa. She is the daughter of an American mother and an Indian father and come from a broken home. Once she was an airhostess and then joined as a Stenographer in Bhashkar's Office. The novelist portrays her as a sexy Anglo Indian girl involved in romantic affairs with men. Bhashkar stresses those modern Indian needs women of her kind when he says, "You'll destroy the stability of our social life; You'll create chaos, but you will give us something dynamic. You will restore the youth of the nation". (SFL, p. 122)

Rupa takes care of the children of the Chinese prisoner and she teaches them at Bhashkar's house. Her affection for the girls vindicates her motherly heart. As she comes from a broken home, she is denied the love of her American mother. There is a tragedy in her life regarding her mother and she reflects her feelings in the following words, "Was there any love in her still for the child. She had left behind years ago. The child who had once been part of her body, who had lain on her milk-filled breast". (SFL, p. 135) What Rupa cannot get from her mother, she wants to give to the Chinese Children.

Bhabani Bhattacharya makes Rupa an instrument to awaken the hidden natural feelings in Satyajit. Bhashkar sends her to touch the human elements in Satyajit, So that Satyajit can realise the basic needs of human beings. In this aspect, the novelist briefly mentions Tagore's strong attainment to shown an ascetic falls from his spirituality for the sake of girl of the wood gatherers. Through her sensitivity, Rupa could make Satyajit recall his early Cambridge days of youthful pleasures.

Being a woman of Western style, Rupa attracts Bhashkar, whom she needs most. As Bhashkar is full of Indianism, she could only satisfy him physically but not mentally. Through Bhashkar, Indianess is presented by novelist in a realistic way. The contact with the West cannot make an Indian neglect his heritage. It is evident through the words of Rupa, "So many years you lived in the West, absorbing its life, becoming part of that life. Yet, back home, you were sucked at once into five thousand years of Indianism" (SFL, p. 317).

By contrasting the characters of Rupa and Sumita, the women of modern India and the ancient India are symbolically picturised. While Rupa represents the turbine, Sumita represents the spinning wheel. Though Bhashkar is impressed by Rupa's adult and uninhabited nature, he is attracted towards Sumita. When he realises that Sumita is an uncommon woman without responding to natural instincts, he wants her to be changed in a modern way. Bhabani Bhattacharya presents her as a symbol of India and needs transformation in all aspects of life, "She was India, wasn't she? The India of Satyajit. The India that had to be transformed. It wasn't enough to fight Satyajit on the economic front. The battle must touch every art of living". (SFL, p. 127)

The transformation of Sumita is brought through the temple incident. During her first visit with Bhashkar, the stone lovers at temple could not arouse any feelings in Sumita. But after her return from Delhi, the natural feelings of a woman brought some change in her attitude. As a result, during her second visit to the temple with Bhashkar, the sight of the stone lovers made her flush. Bhashkar could notice some change in her feelings. The novelist pictures as, "In the temple, to this vast surprise, she had stood defenseless and as though transformed. He had felt on her face the heat he knew". (SFL, p. 221)

According to Bhabani Bhattacharya, the modern society can be developed only through the maximum use of resources. The mobilization of resources is an important aspect for the development. By following the ideology of self-imposed poverty, a nation cannot progress. The modern civilization is the only way for rapid progress of a country. He reveals himself through the words of Bhashkar, "Voluntary poverty is no answer to our country's problems. True, as things stand we have nothing to give to the people, nothing to distribute except poverty. With industrial progress, we will attain higher standards within a short span of time. We have big resources of men, materials". (SFL, p. 90)

Though the ideologies are different, both Satyajit and Bhashkar work hard for the sake of the nation. Though the means are different the end is common. They travel in two ways to reach the same destination. Sumita could understand them and wants both of them should succeed in this service notive. She thinks, "Why was it that two men of complete dedication had to face each other with challenge, and one or the other must bear the pangs of defeat?" (SFL, p. 91)

The element of Satyajitism is found deep in the heart of Bhashkar though he is unaware of it. Even Rupa feels that his attitude towards her reflects Satyajitism. When Erh-ku brings. Spinning wheel to Bhaskhar's house, he is amused. Rupa wonders at his interest towards the wheel, "Such a big engineer could not spin thread! Bhashkar though shamed, devoted half an hour every day to the wheel. Would it simply be a mechanical gesture or would he gain from the gesture some element of spirituality with which the simple wooden implement was vested?" (SFL, p. 331)

Bireswar Basu, Satyajit's college friend at Cambridge has contrary ideas and disbelieves in self-denial of life's pleasures. Though he mocks at his friend's beliefs he assists Satyajit in his efforts. He has a clear idea of Bhashkar's phenomenon and believes though Satyajit's phenomenon is different, both are needed for the society. He compares them to day and night which represents light and darkness. For India's national interest both are needed. Satyajit without Bhashkar is futile. He analyses, "It's the hour of both dawn and twilight; the two are alike in content. So are the two flesh and blood symbols! There's Bhashkar deep within you. Satyajit! And there's you somewhere in Bhasakar, of that also I am sure". (SFL, p. 344)

Bhashkar and Satyajit symbolise the synthesis of Steeltown and Gandhigram. By pointing out the old and new civilization in India and the need for mutual understanding, Bhabani Bhattacharya aims at integration of both. As K. K. Sharma rightly points out, "Preoccupied with the theme of synthesis, the novelist shows how the clash between Gandhigram and Steeltwon embodying two contrary thoughts and modes of life, disappears gradually bringing without a true adjustment between them".[14]

The Buddhist Monk, Dalai Lama, who fights for the freedom of Tibet in the ways of Gandhiji exhibits the similarity in the freedom struggle between India and Tibet. The Chinese threat that India faces is similar to that of Tibet. When the Chinese invaded Tibet, the Tibetan people had to face too many reforms. They were slowly prepared for slow adjustment to current realities. For the cultural interchange between the nations, the novelist inserts the episode of Dalai Lama in this novel.

Regarding the cultural differences between Tibet and India, Satyajit believes in slow integration between them. When he meets Dalai Lama, he expresses his wish for a harmonious blending of the old and the new culture. For the healthy friendship between the people, there is a need for slow and everlasting adjustment. He expresses, "What was alienated us from the Tibetan way of life is the semifeudal pattern of society. A relic of the Old World cannot live within the shell of the new; under the hard pressures it's bound to be crushed into pulp". (SFL, p. 295)

As a follower of Gandhiji, Satyajith believes in the concept of cultural synthesis. So he accepts the invitation of Bhashkar to Meadow House. But he invites the mutual exchange willingly instead of forced and artificial one. Bhattacharya focuses on India's relationship with other countries in a friendly manner. He mentions Nehru's Panchsheel Treaty with China for solving the international disputes and creating friendly relationship. As G. Rai rightly observes, "The novel presents India's internal and foreign policies and affairs, East-West encounter and international politics".[15]

As a humanist, Bhattacharya feels that life should not be a burden by imposing restrictions. Life should be according to one's natural feelings and emotions. It is not a thing to be tested based on certain grades. He analyses the values of life from different angles through different characters. He putsforth his view of life as, "Life did have to be easy, anyway. You experimented, and lost. Experienced and became enriched. That was the modern age". (SFL, p. 289)

Bhattacharya believes that life depends on the friendly relationship among different types of people. Love can be generated in the minds of people, if they are ready to receive without any negative feeling. He strongly feels that hatred is the vice, which should be eliminated from the minds of people. Even enemies can be turned into friends by destroying the feeling of hatred. Satyajit in this novel expresses the novelist's view. "To give hate is only to make the evil grow stronger. To hate is to be defeated in the moral struggle". (SFL, p. 124)

Pure and gentle love can win the hearts of enemies in course of time. This is proved through the episode of Chinese children. Though Bhashkar could not tolerate the worship of Mao Tse-Tung in his own house by the Chinese girls, he bears it silently due to his love for the children. Bhabani Bhattacharya highlights the value of love in life through the words of Rupa, "They've been brought up in a certain orthodox faith. Attack that faith, and they will simply despise you. It is better that you are winning their love. Love is more potent than rout in ritual imposed by a cult. One day you will be more to the children than Mao Tse-Tung". (SFL, pp. 283-284).

The transformation in the Chinese children is portrayed symbolically by the novelist. The unselfish love of Bhashkar changed the minds of innocent Chinese girls. They started to worship him as their god. In the words of Bhabani Bhattacharya, "The five children were down on their knees in a row before Bhashkar; eyes closed, palms cupped in the gesture of a votive offering and each pair of joined palms held flowers. It was the way they used to kneel before the oleograph of Mao-Tse-Tung. With an Indian touch added flowers!" (SFL, p. 350).

After the proclamation of Chinese ceasefire, the children of Ah To were asked to return to homeland with their father. Under the care of Rupa and Bhashkar, the five Chinese girls indentify themselves as a part of India. One of the sisters Erh-Ku-Roy takes the spinning wheel with her luggage to her country. This symbolically presents the integration of different cultures of neighbour countries. Through the Chinese children Bhabani Bhattacharya wants to carry the real facts of India to China. The friendly and affectionate atmosphere in India makes the children understand the truth. It is evident through the words of the Chinese girls. "We found a sixth sister. We found a second father. All that love and joy and...All that feeling has gone into our bone and blood. When we are back in China and people ask us about India, we will tell them the truth, Rupa". (SFL, p. 334)

Bhashkar's love for the Chinese children shows his faith in moral values. Even Satyajit is aware of Bhashkar's noble nature in his frank expressing of his views. Though Bhashkar seems to be against the existence of Gandhigram, his inner image exhibits his faith in the principles of Gandhiji. His views about vice and virtue and reveal Satyajit as truly Gandhian,

"There is something Gandhian about such a confession thought Satyajit in astonishment". (SFL, p. 33)

As a talented artist, Bhabani Bhattacharya develops his characters as dynamic ones. The characters change and mould them in a modern way, according to the situations. In this novel, as a contrary to Gandhian principles, Bhashkar unknowingly follows non-violence in thought and deed. This itself shows the presence of Gandhism in the Chief Engineer of Steeltown. Bhashkar as devoted Engineer, strives hard to help the growing population by providing sufficient employment. As Pandeya Shiva M. and Dr. T. N. Dhar rightly remark, "It is Bhashkar who moves bit by bit, towards the spirit of Gandhism. His initial goodness consists in his complete dedication to the task he thinks, will do its bit to help feed the starving millions".[16]

Bhabani Bhattacharya analyses the relevance of Gandhian principles in the modern context during such a period of external threat from other countries. The concept of non-violence could not receive public support in the changed national policies. This is evident from the incident of failure of public response to Ladakh. The concept of Satyagraha, which brought wonderful results in the past, could not succeed in the present international crisis. As Harcharan Singh Boparai points out, "Bhabani Bhattacharya has further probed the value of Satyagraha as a political weapon at national and international levels. Whereas his Satyagraha against the acquisition of Gandhigram by Steeltown for the purpose of expansion evokes national indignation and succeeds his Satyagraha for liberating Ladakh from the Chinese fails at the international level".[17]

According to Bhabani Bhattacharya the younger generation can create wonders and build bridges of international understanding. As the Chinese children brought transformation in Bhashkar, they can do so in China. He expresses his view through Bhashkar as, "Slender and small, they are fighting the battle of humanity, which their vast powerful country had already lost". (SFL, p. 257) This shows that while the older generation has become biased, the younger generation remains unbiased.

Satyajit's enormous ego and his yielding to temptations and his craving for personal glory imply that he does not understand what Gandhism is as a rational subject. Though he wants to have a normal life with Suruchi after his arrival from Delhi, he fears of his loss of self-respect. He strongly feels for the pain he had inflicted in Suruchi in the past years due to his behaviour. He announces the fast unto death; though he had no wish to die. Bhabani Bhattacharya, reveals the difference between Gandhi and Satyajit in this aspect as, "He would go all the way that Gandhi would have gone. But Gandhi would have gone his way with absolute peace of mind...Satyajit would be battling hard every hour, every minute; battling against the inner man, the common man whom he wanted to be uncommon" (SFL, p. 338).

Bhabani Bhattacharya portrays love as a basic life force in his novels. Though mind gets the priority in love, the need of flesh is not neglected. It does not stop at the physical level but it goes beyond it to reach the mental level. In this novel also Bhabani Bhattacharya sketches his characters attracted towards real and natural course of love. In real love, the differences in the opinion of the lovers admits the facts and at last resolves the conflicts by mutual understanding. Shantha Krishnaswamy remarks, "In *Shadow from Ladakh*, we have Suruchi, struggling her feminity pitted against her husband's asceticism; Sumita falls in love with Bhashkar who is poles apart from her own milieu".[18]

The transformation comes to both the persons, under the influence of love. They began to absorb each other's values and come to an understanding to share their principles. In this angle Bhashkar moves towards the Gandhian principles as represented by Sumita. In her turn, Sumita began to absorb the ways of Steeltown. As Shiva M. Pandeya rightly observes, "When he has been transformed, too; the two can now meet on a common ground of shared values. They not only find self-identity but identify with each other".[19]

The male and female characters in this novel have a positive attitude towards life. Satyajit at last, throws away the mask of asceticism and finds life's fulfilment with his wife Suruchi. Bhashkar wants to share his life with Sumita for his happiness. Sumita at the end, frees herself from the asceticism to join Bhashkar and Suruchi looks for life's true fulfilment with her husband Satyajit. Rupa decides to leave Steeltown to lead a happy life according to her way of approach.

Satyajit knows the facts about himself, the fact that all the past years he was in bondage. He could not make out the right path to lead a happy life with Suruchi. He denied her the natural pleasures of life, which every woman expects from her husband. When he realises the realities he could not compensate the loss. He himself admits to his wife, Suruchi as "All these years, I have deserved nothing from you and yet my demands have been limitless. At last, it all with clears sight. And it is too late". (SFL, p. 341) Only towards the end, he experiences a release from his inhibitions leading to self-knowledge.

To solve the crisis in Gandhigram, Government allots a site for a new Gandhigram. His friend Bireswar advises Satyajit to establish a new Gandhigram based on his ideals. As Gandhigram stands for the idea and the people, both can migrate for the easy ending of the dispute. But Satyajit disagrees to solve the problem in a peaceful way, which is a signal of non-violence. He even rejects the advice of his friend to meet Bhashkar for mutual co-operation. This shows his deviation from the principles of Gandhiji. His friend, Bireswar makes the point clear, "You are yielding to violence, Satyajit, in your spirit. Gandhi always offered every possible opportunity to his adversary to win. His own personal stand was never important. It was always truth, truth and truth again. You must give truth a choice, Satyajit". (SFL, p. 345)

H. G. S. Arulandram rightly remarks, "In *Shadow from Ladakh*, Bhabani Bhattacharya suggests synthesis on three different planes-synthesis of the spinning-wheel and the spindle on the economic plane, of asceticism and aestheticism on the physical plane and of violence and non-violence on the plane of international understanding".[20] Bhabani Bhattacharya asserts the theme of synthesis and co-existence of different ways of life. According to him, India's future depends on the integration of various aspects for the development of the country.

The difference of opinions between Bhashkar and Satyajit is due to strong belief of their being in the right path, which results in mutual conflict. The only possible solution is reconciliation and readjustment. There should not be rejection of one idea in favour of the other but a synthesis of different ideologies. Bhabani Bhattacharya pleads for the type of synthesis in this novel, "Let there be a meeting ground of the two extremes; let each one shed some of its content and yet remain true to itself". (SFL, p. 274)

The idea of integration motivates the workers of Steeltown to form a procession in support of Gandhigram. They were stirred by Satyajit's dedication to protect the values at the risk of his life. The procession of workers lead by Bhashkar hails the people of Gandhigram as their brothers. Bhabani Bhattacharya describes the integration of Steeltown and Gandhigram as, "When the visitors had crossed the threshold of the homes, all barriers between city and village were gone. The slogan of brotherhood, enriched with emotional content, became real". (SFL, p. 352)

As K. S. Jha rightly remarks, "The central theme of the novel is India's crying need for an integration of divergent sets of values to cope with the challenge of the times. Industrialilzation is necessary, but not at the cost of the best elements in our own tradition".[21]

Except in his last novel, Bhabani Bhattacharya focuses on the problems of contemporary India in his novels. He dealt with the social evils like hunger, poverty, untouchability, caste prejudices and blind religious beliefs. The freedom movement and the struggle for nation's independence occupied a prominent place in his early novels. In his last novel, *A Dream in Hawaii* he comes out of his national problems and focuses on the values of the West. As K. A. Agarwal rightly remarks,

"The novelist extends his vision beyond the problems of his country to the problems of the sick Western civilization of today".[22]

The creative imagination of the Indo-Anglian writers is attracted towards the East-West theme due to the impact of British rule even after independence. The cultural differences that exist between the East and the West stimulated some of the novelists to explore and to reach an understanding. As Punim Juneja points out, "One of the reasons for the recurring East-West theme in the works of many Indo-English writers can be traced to their endeavour to address themselves to a Western audience and of their desire to define and interpret the East for its benefit and in the process rediscover their country and their own special identity".[23]

The novel *A Dream in Hawaii* is the outcome of Bhabani Bhattacharya's stay at Honolulu as a senior specialist at the East-West Centre. His growing wisdom makes his feel that mere material prosperity and economic stability is not sufficient for a man for his fulfilment of life, the spiritual aspect is also necessary to lead a full life. After the attainment of worldly riches the human soul craves for self-realisation, which is the ultimate goal in life. As he becomes more matured, he began to feel more for spiritual nourishment in life.

In his early novels, Bhabani Bhattacharya deals with the themes of hunger for food, sex, money, titles etc. In his last novel, he deals with the theme of hunger in a different aspect. The hunger for spiritual attainment is the major theme in this novel. As H. G. S. Arulandram rightly remarks "Bhabani Bhattacharya's latest novel *A Dream in Hawaii*, published in 1978, which deals with the theme of East-West encounter in its spiritual dimension is a sure pointer to the novelist's faith that man does not live by bread alone and that he needs for his hungry soul too".[24]

The advanced technology of modern age could provide all comforts in human life. But it has failed to answer the inner man. This resulted in the craving to satisfy the self and answer the questions of soul. People in advanced country also feel the need to spiritual nourishment in life. Bhabani Bhattacharya was able to grasp Western people's mind during his stay at Honolulu for a few years. This could be the reason for so much demand for the Gurus and Swamijis in Western countries. Commenting on the Americans' response to spiritual classes by Indian Gurus, Bhabani Bhattacharya remarks, "The place was packed with young people, sitting in the aisles, standing at the rear. Their faces displayed their hunger for spiritual nourishment".[25]

The Guru or Swamiji in this novel is Swami Yogananda. Before his rebirth as Swami, he was Neeloy Mukherji, a young teacher of Philosophy in an Indian University. The handsome youngman has turned a yogi at the suggestion of his student, Devjani, whom he secretly loves and his own spiritual hunger. Soon he becomes popular and sets up an ashram at Rishikesh. A large number of disciples both native and foreign are attracted towards his spiritual discourses. The image of Swami Yogananda is framed on a famous Indian Swami, who has visited Honolulu, when Bhabani Bhattacharya was a Professor at University of Hawaii.

Bhabani Bhattacharya expresses his views about a Yogi and the qualities of yogihood while describing Swami Yogananda, "He was ageless anyway. He had no race, no country, no kith and kin, no roots in his past beyond the beginning of his yogihood".[26] (*A Dream in Hawaii*, p. 1) Regarding his age, Yogananda feels though he is young, his external image is a mere myth. He has to be just as old as others make him. So he has to be hundred years old.

Yogananda is quite different from other Swamijis in the appearance. He has long hair, but he is clean – shaven, which is uncommon in a holy man. The novelist during his spiritual discourses dramatically portrays Yogananda's unique sensitivity. Normally, every speaker accepts applause as his success. But, Yogananda is quite different in this aspect also. He requests the audience as "Handclap is good for politicians, for public figures. They need it, I don't'. All I ask of you is this. Listen to what I have to say-in silence. Then rise and leave in silence". (DIH, p. 7)

Bhabani Bhattacharya very often quotes the words of great thinkers like Gurudev Tagore, Mahatma Gandhi, Pandit Nehru and Swami Vivekananda. In this novel, he quotes Swami Vivekananda's words regarding the Religion, "Hindu or Buddhist or Christian, let each assimilate the spirit of the others and yet preserve his individuality and grow according to his own law of growth. Let this be inscribed on the banner of every religion: Assimilation, not destruction. Harmony, and peace, not Dissension". (DIH, p. 62) As a humanist, Bhabani Bhattacharya pleads for universal religion that is man-centred and embraces all values related to humanity.

Religion is for the welfare of humanity in a broader aspect. It can feed the human souls if the stomach is full. For hungry people religion can not provide solace. In this aspect Bhabani Bhattacharya quotes Swami Vivekananda's words, "Religion is not for empty bellies". (DIH, p. 11) He stresses the need to feed hungry people in order to make them ready to receive the values of religion. The theme of hunger always obsesses the mind of the novelist.

The relation between religion and art is brought out by the novelist in an interesting way. He stresses the similarity between both forms when one goes deep into them. Through the words of Yogananda, Bhabani Bhattacharya observes, "Religion and art have the same intent: To go beneath the surfaces forms, to seek, to find the basic truths and ignite them". (DIH, p. 9) He advocates a broad outlook of religion and art. On the superficial level both the forms don't convey the fundamental principles. To find the truths one has to drive deep into them.

Here and there the novelist touches the philosophy of Swami Vivekananda in the novel. The central character, Yoganada himself received his initiation from his guru Vivekananda. He is the man, who has given a new meaning to Vedanta and spread the values of universal religion throughout the world. Bhabani Bhattacharya explicit the mission of Vivekananda in this novel, "Knowledge has grown but not understanding Swami Vivekananda's mission was to build human understanding rather than dispense knowledge. He was a path finder". (DIH, p. 11)

At the beginning of the novel it self-Bhabani Bhattacharya Bhattacharya refers to the inner conflict in Yogananda, "A firefly tries to be a star!" (DIH, p. 14) This single line indicates the controversy within the person who wants to attain a state, which is beyond his reach. Though Neeloy is present within him, he struggles hard to be Swami Yogananda, "An inner fury begins to drive him towards self-alternation. It is not long before he achieves this. The struggle for a new identity won, Neeloy is reborn". (DIH, p. 13)

Within his yellow garb, he hides his love for Devjani. Many times, he escapes from himself to his past, the picture of Devjani is unshaken within his mind. This is the reason why he could not accept her request to be in his ashram as a disciple. He cannot imagine her in the yellow garb. His weakness is revealed through the words, "He has no strength to endure her salutation, her hand touching the guru's bare feet. In her gestures of reverence Swami Yogananda will be destroyed!" (DIH, p. 15)

Yogananda's struggle for a new identity is carefully developed from the beginning to the end of the novel. With his strong determination he remakes himself at times of weakness. He is the central character in the novel, which feels the need for spiritual nourishment, which could give a real meaning to his life. His character is moulded on the analysis of other characters in the novel.

Stella, a Ph.D. Student in Hinduism and an American tourist becomes Yogananda's disciple. She requests him to accompany her to America to give discourse on Eastern Philosophy "to present Universal Religion in its Vedantic Concept". (DIH, p. 144) She could not adjust with her husband

Walt Gregson due to his uninhibited sex. So she feels revulsion for the kind of mechanical life and turns to Swamiji for spiritual nourishment. She is the symbol of modern American sickness, which needs some support to overcome the problems. She feels that kind of solace in Swami Yogananda. The following lines prove this, "She felt reborn-like the Yogis, like Swami Yogananda himself. He had set right her balance. Countless others in America were in need of such redress. Here was a chance for her to be the tool of a rich human purpose". (DIH, p. 23)

The other character in the novel that symbolizes the emptiness of American materialism is Jennifer. She is a rich young widow who seeks the help of Swami Yogananda to lead a meaningful life. She feels, "He could give her life a direction, a meaning. He could show her how to be free from the void she had been trying to fill; but making it worse and worse". She looks forward for the fulfilment of life other than the senses. After yielding to sensual pleasures, she could realise that life is not only for the satisfaction of senses.

The predominance of sensual pleasures in American Society and the craze for temporary happiness is revealed through different characters in the novel. Contrary to this is the aspect of spirituality, which is expressed through Yogananda and his followers. Dr. D. Ramakrishna rightly remarks, "In Bhabani Bhattacharya's A Dream in Hawaii (1978) as in Raja Rao's, The Serpent and the Rope (1960) the quest is that of an academic for spirituality despite his sensual involvement's. The binary opposition of the sensual and the spiritual determines character and action". [27]

Bhabani Bhattacharya mentions the ancient philosophy of Hindus in Bhagavad Gita, the song celestial in the novel. Through Swami Yogananda, the novelist interprets the concept of the original Sanskrit verses. It intones the Hindu thinking, "Do your work with no wish for results – that is the key command. Be totally free from the desire to gain the fruit of your work. Do not let your feelings be directed to the outcomes of your endeavour". (DIH, p. 31)

Bhabani Bhattacharya analysed in detail the Bhakti Yoga with reference to Sri Krishna Consciousness and Mahaprabhu Chaitanya's movement. Bhakti-Yoga is the way to realise the Divine by loving Him as a human being. This Chaitanya movement is casteless; equalitarian which contributes a broad approach to India's value system.

Swami Bhaktivedanta's International Society of Krishna Consciousness has great influences in the West. The novelist focuses on the movement and its impact on the Western scholars that has contributed to this movement. In Hawaii, the young devotees of this movement move far from the current patterns of American life. The basic facts of life followed by the devotees are depicted thus, "Men and women, under the same roof, lived in strict celibacy. They could marry but a woman in wedlock was pledged to renounce sex when she had two children or has passed her thirtieth year". (DIH, p. 72)

Bhabani Bhattacharya mentions Maharshi Mahesh Yogi's Transcendental Meditation and Maharishi's visit to Hawaii and its impact. It is not a philosophy but is a technique, which is called as awareness – expansion technique. Transcendental Meditation is defined as, "A simple natural technique which expands awareness, develops clear thinking and perception, and provides deep rest – resulting in more dynamic activity and full expression of creative intelligence in daily life". (DIH, p. 105).

In this novel, Bhabani Bhattacharya discusses various cults and their practices. The principle character Swami Yogananda is totally averse to the personality cult. His World Center would be well apart from all other movements. He plans to evolve it according to his thoughts. But Dr. Swift plans in a different way. Money lies at the root of establishment of the World Center. His fund raising appetite motivates him to call various types of persons like astrologer, Hatha-Yogi and Hanuman Ojha from India. His aim is to attract the audience to the Amphitheater to get profit. The novelist comments on the failure of various movements as "Fads, freakish movements have come and gone. The hunger is unappesed. Whatever holds out the promise of fulfilment is hugely accepted; then broken heartedly discarded". (DIH, p. 118).

According to Bhabani Bhattacharya, the great personalities do not get name and fame in India as they get in the West. Only after they are recognised in the West later they get recognition in their motherland. He comments, "Curiously, Indian gurus first get discovered in the West – that become an accepted norm". (DIH, p. 125). He points out Buddhism in this aspect. In India there may be hundred thousand Buddhists. But there are more than a hundred million Buddhists outside India.

Regarding Mahatma Gandhi, the father of our nation, though he has so much reputation as a dedicated leader, his principles are not followed in spirit by the people. In history, there are number of examples, whom the world accepts, while India neglects them Gandhism is wide spread throughout the world for its noble principles. As Bhabani Bhattacharya comments on this, "I know people who honestly believe that Mahatma Gandhi in his homeland has been turned into one of the numerous Gods and placed on a high pedestal, a dead image with flowers on its stone feet; while, abroad, he is more and a living presence". (DIH, p. 126)

Bhabani Bhattacharya presents the necessity of two systems, materialism and spiritualism and none of the two should be neglected. Bhabani Bhattacharya expresses his view in the following words: "One cannot exist without the other". (DIH, p. 245). At the end of the novel, Devjani feels that Yogananda needs further Sadhana to achieve his goal. The novelist indicates his firm belief that man should exclude neither the claims of body nor the spiritual claims as, "Would the spiritual accept the needs of materiality? Would the material make room for what was beyond its calculations of demand and supply?" (DIH, p. 44)

The central character Yogananda himself could not come out of the haunting memory of Devjani. Mr. Walt Gregson, who is fully interested in earthly pleasures, begins to realise the need for spiritual aspect in life. Jennifer symbolises the modern American thrust for inner satisfaction. Devjani who hates her mother due to her mother's betrayal to her father, could realise the need for satisfaction of both body and soul. As B. Syamala Rao observes, "Bhabani Bhattacharya deals, in main with the two poles of life – Kama (physical desire) and Moksha (spiritual bliss or salvation). The novel also highlights the two aspects – Tamas (darkness, referring to the bodily pleasures) and Jnana (light, enlightenment) referring to the realisation of the ultimate reality".[28]

The detachment, which Yogananda preaches during his discourses on the *Bhagavad Gita*, could not achieved by him. Even in Hawaii he looks for her arrival and fails to avoid her thoughts. As Bhabani Bhattacharya reveals mind of Yogananda, "his submerged mind could not be controlled, nature's compulsions could not be denied". (DIH, p. 44). The novelist depicts Yogananda's chastity thus "As he lay asleep, he was in the act of making love. That act possessed him". (DIH, p. 44). It is not the external conflict, but the inner conflict of his own soul that disturbs Yogananda.

The character of Yogananda is ironically presented through the thoughts of Jennifer. In America, she listens to Swami Yogananda's speech about Vedanta and wants to feed her innerself. At the same time she recollects her sexual affair in India with a New Delhi boy, who satisfies the sexual hunger of the tourist ladies without taking money. The novelist depicts the crazy thought thus, "Driving away from Waikiki, she found herself thinking again of Swami Yogananda and that New Delhi boy in the same breath!. As apart from each other as noon from midnight, they met some-where in the depths of her awareness! (DIH, p. 43).

The blending of ancient and the modern is the favourite theme of Bhabani Bhattacharya. His early novels, *Music for Mohini* and *Shadow from Ladakh* are based on mainly the same theme. In this novel, the two different societies from East and West show some similarity as Yogananda says, "That our ancient philosophy is boldly modern in its own way. The West has read that same story in our ancient temple sculptures at Konark or Khajuraha!" (DIH, p. 18).

Bhabani Bhattacharya selected 'Hawaii' as the background for his last novel to show the cultural unity. As a Professor he visited that place to deliver his lecturers. Apart from being a fantastic tourist place, Hawaii is a symbol for cultural unity. According to Bhabani Bhattacharya, "Hawaii is a multiple image. The unique East-West mix. The strong interculturation. You cannot find the like of this ethnic spectrum anywhere else on the globe". (DIH, p. 56)

The main action of the novel takes place in Honolulu in Hawaii. Swami Yogananda lands in Hawaii, on his mission to 'reorientate vedanta to the records of the American Society". The place is described as the meeting ground for East and the West. The character of Yogananda is also described as, "Within him the East and the West so, readily coalesced!" (DIH, p. 18). The title of the novel, *A Dream in Hawaii* symbolically expresses the way of life based on intercultural approach. As Harinder Sohi remarks about the novel, "In this serious work of fiction, Bhabani Bhattacharya seems to be striving towards the realisation of a vision of life based upon a synthesis of both the worlds, the East and the West".[29]

Bhabani Bhttacharya describes the beauty of the Hawaii islands, in his novel. The Sunshine beach and the scenery arouse his creativity. It is felt from the lines, "To think, to write or simply to enjoy the ocean. Our Hawaii has an explicable way of getting into one's blood and spirit". (DIH, p. 64).

The Hawaiian experience contributed a lot for the expansion of Bhabani Bhattacharya's intellectual horizons. The motto of University of Hawaii widened the intercultural ideas of the novelist. This is obvious from the usage of symbols of the novelist. The symbol of rainbow reveals the mind of the novelist. Though the colors in a rainbow stay apart from each other; on the whole they make the rainbow. As Bhabani Bhattacharya writes, "Seven brilliant colors building a symphony. Our World Center will be transcription of that rainbow, though in medium not of colors!" (DIH, p. 69).

The sickness of American society is brought out through the words of Frieda, "For the young and unmarried, dating and mating were the same. Virginity became a sin when you were over sixteen. Virgin girls and virgin boys beyond their teens were all too rare anyhow". (DIH, p. 109) The Western sickness is attached to the fulfilment of the physical desires. This is vindicated through the characters of Jennifer, Walt Gregson, Vincent swift, Syliva Koo and Frieda".[30]

The East is not free from the other kind of sickness. The Phony gurus exploit the spiritual craving of the people. Yogananda comes to know about heaven's ambrosia through Frieda's experience with a phony guru. The novelist criticises spiritual corruption through the incident of Frieda. It reveals that along with the soul, body should also be submitted to them. They mislead the innocent followers by preaching them that spirituality cannot come to a body, which is needful. Bhabani Bhattacharya comments, "All through the history of civilization every spiritual system had attracted to it an aura of corruption. An enveloping vapor which threatened to suffocate the system itself". (DIH, p. 113)

Bhabani Bhattacharya's characters like Kalo in *He Who Rides a Tiger* and Swami Yogananda wears the mask to satisfy their inner aspirations. Both the characters throw their masks at the end. For Yogananda, the aim is self-satisfaction rather than pretention. Neeloly wears the mask for his self-fulfilment but does not take revenge like Kalo. Neeloy wears the mask of Yogananda more under the influence of Devjani than his inner self. So when the time comes, he throws away the mask by revealing his inner thoughts to Devjani. In his search, Neeloy may enter into Sadhana for his perfection or attain Devjani. About the novel S. Krishna Sarma and V. Rangan remark, "It is a dissertation on the sickness of modern society, both Eastern and Western. At the same time, it presents man's search for the self or alternately his endeavour to discard the masks".[31]

The character of Dr. Vincent swift is modelled on the image of selfish and greedy people who exploit the devoted persons in the name of spirituality. He is an egotistical person who tries to make use of Swami Yogananda for his own advancement through the establishment of Yogananda's World Center. When Yogananda refuses, he becomes ready to take over the control of the centre and even to replace the Swami himself. Regarding his part in the novel, Bhagwat S. Gayal remarks, "He is critique of the bourgeois value system, which believes in naming a profitable business venture out of even personal human needs like sex and yoga".[32]

Bhabani Bhattacharya ironically portrays the character of Swami Yogananda in this novel. The main aim of the arrival of Swami in Hawaii is to cure the sickness of American society. The youth of America consider him as their future. They feel, "the curious thing is that Yogananda, an alien, is intune with the new dream of American youth. Purpose. Belief. Hopefulness". But the irony is that Swami could not fully realise his purpose in his life.

Swami's stay in Hawaii brings his hidden love for Devjani, which he himself could not recognise. When Devjani comes to Hawaii to meet and take Deeksha from him, the inner feelings touch his thoughts. He could find the same restlessness within himself, which he could find in the American society. As Malta Grover points out, "Swami Yogananda in *A Dream in Hawaii* is apparently trying to bring peace to the restless and frustrated youth of Hawaii, while his own heart is restless for his former beloved, Devjani".[33]

Bhabani Bhattacharya projects his idea of synthesis of East and West in this novel through most of the main characters. Devjani the main character in the novel is a typical Indian girl, who believes in the moral values of the East. She could not tolerate her mother's illicit love affair and leaves home for higher studies. She discovers that, "within her was a hunger for the spiritual life! A hunger of which she had been totally unaware". (DIH, p. 87) Later she joins East-West Centre at Honolulu for her research work.

Her mental attitudes are reshaped during her stay in America. She begins to fit herself into the Western life-style. She is able to comprehend the true meaning of her mother's life. The Western society makes her recognise the significance of the basic physical urges of man in addition to spiritual attributes. She could realise her inner craving for the company of Swami Yogananda. She felt, "It was in her American experience that she would find the values. She searched for all the same, she had to admit that in this hour with Swami Yogananda she was aware of an inner strength she had not felt before". (DIH, p. 186)

Devjani desires to see a complete man in Yogananda, with the blending of the Western materialism and the Eastern Spiritualism. She does not wish him to live only on the physical plane or the spiritual level. She expresses her wish to him, "Reveal yourself again as an illumined one" (DIH, p. 245). Balram S. Sorot rightly remarks, "Bhabani Bhattacharya also pleads for a synthesis of the modern materialism of the West and the traditional spiritualism of the East through the character of Devjani in *A Dream in Hawaii*".[34]

The principal character Swami Yogananda harmonizes the values of the East and the West. His ideas on the integration of diverse elements of life are expressed through the Yoga centre. Though a Yogi, he has nothing against modern science and technology. He justifies the need of Vedantic Spiritualism for the West and the scientific advancement for the East. He views, "Science could even deepen the relationship between nature and man. The Yoga centre would be of both East and West, modern and ancient, open to every value, every insight". (DIH, pp. 179-180).

Neeloy, the Professor of Philosophy turns into Swami Yogananda. Though Swami renounces the world, he finds it difficult to overcome his love for Devjani. There is an element of Neeloy in Swami. At nights his sub-conscious mind forces him to make love to Devjani in his dream. He is ashamed of himself when he discovers his mistake. He is convinced atlast that the claims of both spirit and body cannot be neglected.

He makes a confession before Devjani, "At sadhana, where I was so far away from your presence, you were in my dreams at night. Year after year. The truth is that I never got away from Neeloy". (DIH, p. 234)

Yogananda finally accepts that human life is not fulfilled more on the ascetic plane; one must respect the fundamental urges. So he decides to return from America to India. By this time Devjani could understand his dilemma and replys, "It may be that one cannot exist without the other". (DIH, p. 245). His departure from Hawaii makes the other character, Walt Gregson, to realise the claims of both body and spirit.

Walt Gregson is a typical Western man, who has faith only in the materialistic values. His marriage with Stella leads to divorce because of his sexual experiments. He distrusts Swami Yogananda and questions him about a Yogi's sexual life. He defends Western out look about sexual permissiveness in the presence of the Swami as, "The right to enjoy sex – that's normal. Abstinence – societal or self-imposed – that's abnormal. In our permissive society, abstinence has no validity whatever". (DIH, p. 59).

Gradually Walt realises that his innerself thrives for something more than more physical gratification. He feels that he is not content within despite his deep involvement in the sensual pleasures. He could feel his urge and need of Swami Yogannanda and the need of modern American society. The Western social set-up can be a complete one with the higher moral values of the East. It is made clear by these lines, "There was a new dream of youth, and Yogananda seemed some how closer to that dream than he who claimed to be today's America". (DIH, p. 243).

The dream of American youth is clearly depicted through the discussion of Professor Walt Gregson with this students about his poem, 'A dead rat stinking under the nylon rug'. Bhattacharya portrays a dead rat as a powerful symbol. According to Walt Gregson 'The Dead Rat' is the old social order with its code of personal conduct. He feels that the sexual liberation is the answer for the modern American youth. But the words of his students reveal the minds of the modern American youth. In the words of a student Mildred, "Our sexual liberation does not give us the freedom to be free".

The symbol of "The Dead Rate" is most artistically dealt by the novelist. It is viewed as a symbol of national interest by one of the students of Walt Gregson. His words echo the modern problems of violence in the name of terrorism, "Spectacular crimes committed in the name of national interest. One day nuclear bombs will be dropped somewhere on the globe in our national interest. The bombs will come flying to our country in someone else's national interest. (DIH, p. 134)

Alex, another student of Walt Gregson calls the 'dead rat' as technology. He views that upto a point, technology is good for mankind but beyond that point it turns anti-social and loses its original purpose. The so-called super technology defeats the traditionalism becomes a master for human beings. As a result, humanity becomes a tool in the hands of machines. "As machines get humanized, men get dehumanized. You see the outcome in psychic splits Neurosis. Breakdown of old an institution on which society has built itself over the centuries. Family life, for instance, Marriage, for instance". (DIH, p. 135)

As the disciples of Yogananda, the students of Walt Gregson analyse their culture in various aspects. Yogananda's innerself is brought out in the light of craving towards Devjani and Devjani inturns realises the strong attachment towards her guru. As Punim Jeneja points out, "The cultural confluence that takes place does not lead to any loss of national identity but to a redefining of the self in the light of new ideas and norms, as much for the Swami and Devjani as for Yogananda's American disciples".[35]

The title of the novel itself is very symbolic. 'Dream' is not the reality, but it leads to searching of self and brings out the hidden thoughts of one. In Hawaii the dream of establishment of a World Centre is not fulfilled. In otherwords the dream of Swami Yogananda ends in the beginning of his life. As Jasbir Jain rightly remarks, "*A Dream in Hawaii* is not the dream about the international cultural centre but it is Swami Yogananda's dream which brings back to him the consciousness of Neeley".[36]

Bhattacharya presents the novel with full of ironical situations. The purpose of Yogananda's visit is to bright out change in the people of Hawaii by establishing a international cultural centre through the harmonious blend of various religions. But the irony is that Yogananda himself undergoes change which makes him Neeloy again. As Harish Raizada comments, "The irony of situation is that Swami Yogananda's experience in Hawaii proves beneficial not only to the people of Hawaii but also to the Swami himself". His visit to the West is to make them cure their weakness but ironically he himself cannot come out of his own weakness for Devjani.

The aim of Bhabani Bhattacharya is not only to focus the problems of American society but the whole world. He hints at the materialistic approach of the East and the West through this novel. He expresses his view, "The problem was not American, not even Western in a wider sense; it had a world wide application". (DIH, p. 33).

REFERENCES

1. Elena J. Kalinnikova, *Some Aspects of the Contemporary Scene, Indian* English Literature A Perspective, Vimal Prakashan, Ghaziabad, 1982, p. 87.
2. K. K. Sharma, *Bhabani Bhattacharya: His Vision and Themes,* Abhinav Publications, New Delhi, 1979, p. 89.
3. K. H. Kunjo Singh, *The Fiction of Bhabani Bhattacharya*, Atlantic Publishers and Distributors, New Delhi, 2002, p. 112.
4. Bhabani Bhattacharya, *Shadow from Ladakh*, Orient Paperbacks, New Delhi, 1966, All Other References from the Novel are Indicated as SFL in Parentheses.
5. Dr. P. N. Bhatt, *The Impact of Gandhi* on Dr. Bhabani Bhattacharya's Novel's, Triveni, Triveni Publishers, Oct-Dec. 1985, p. 83.
6. K. R. Chandrasekharan, *Bhabani Bhattacharya*, Arnold-Heineman Publishers Pvt. Ltd., New Delhi, 1974, p. 117.

7. *Ibid* , p. 116.
8. H. G. S. Arulandrum, *Bhabani Bhattacharya's World View,* Common wealth *Novel in English*, Arlington, Texas, 1983, p. 45.
9. Balram S. Sorot, *The Novels of Bhabani Bhattacharya*, Prestige Books, New Delhi, 1991, p. 82.
10. Neelam Singh and Rashmi G., *Depicition of Women in the Novels of Bhabani Bhattacharya and Shobha De: A Contrastive Study,* Indian Writing in English: A Critical Study Ed. K. A. Agarwal., Atlantic Publishers and Distributors, New Delhi, 2003, p. 216.
11. *Op. Cit.*, 8, p. 87.
12. Suman Mehta, *Images of Women in Bhabani Bhattacharya's Fiction, Indian Writing in English*: Perspectives, Atlantic Publishers and Distributors, New Delhi, 2003. p. 44.
13. *Op. Cit.,* 2, p. 120.
14. *Op. Cit.,* 3, p. 111
15. G. Rai, *Bhabani Bhattacharya: A Study of his Novels*, B. R. Publishing Corporation, Delhi, 1995, p. 41.
16. Pandeya, Shiva M. and Dr. T. N. Dhar, *Bhabani Bhattacharya's Shadow from Ladakh, The Indian Novel in English*, Phoenix Publishing House Pvt. Ltd., New Delhi, 1987, p. 243.
17. Harchan Singh Boparai, *Bhabani Bhattacharya's Respons to British Colonialism in India,* Colonial Consciousness in Black American African and Indian Fiction in English – Ed. Ramesh K. Srivastava, ABS Publications, New Delhi, 1991, p. 132.
18. Shantha Krishna Swamy, The Woman in Indian Fiction in English (1950-80), Ashish Publishing House, New Delhi, 1984, p. 65.
19. Shiva M. Pandeya, *Studies in Modern Fiction*, Vikas Publishing House Pvt., Ltd., Ghaziabad, 1983, p. 237.
20. *Op.Cit.* 7, p. 185.
21. K. S. Jha, *Bhabani Bhattacharya the Humanist: A Critical Study of his Novels,* The Indian Journal of English Studies, Vol. 22, 1982-83, p. 147.
22. K. A. Agarwal, *Mind and Art of Bhabani Bhattacharya,* The Novels of Bhabani Bhattacharya Ed. Monika Gupta, Atlantic Publishers Distributors, New Delhi, 2002, p. 212.
23. Punim Juneja, *The East-West theme Indian Women Novelists* Ed., R. K. Dhawan (Prestige Books, New Delhi, 1993, p. 217.
24. H. G. S. Arulandram, *Man and Religion in A Dream in Hawaii,* The Literary Half-Yearly, Vol. 26, No. 2, July. 1985, p. 32.

25. D. Ramakrishna, *Bhabani Bhattacharaya's* A Dream in Hawaii: A Study in Post Colonial Spirituality. *Kakatiya Journal of English Studies*, Department of English Kakatiya University, Warangal, Vol., 18, 1998, p. 48.

26. Bhabani Bhattacharya, *A Dream in Hawaii,* Macmillan and Co, Bombay, 1978.

    All other References from the Novel all Indicated as DIH in Parentheses.

27. Dorothy Blair Shimer, *Bhabani Bhattacharya*, Boston, G. K. Hall and Co, 1975, p. 21.

28. B. Syamala Rao, *Bhabani Bhattacharya*, Blackie and Son Publishers Pvt., Ltd., Bombay, 1988, p. 105.

29. Harinder Sohi, *Dream and Substance Indian Book Chronicle*, Vol. 4, Oct 1979, p. 343.

30. S. Krishna Sarma and P Rangan, *What is in a Dream The Literary Endeavour*, Vol. 1, No. 3, Mysore Printing and Publishing House, 1987, p. 85

31. Bhagwat S. Goyal *Review of A Dream in Hawaii The Humanities Review*, July-Sep., 1979,. p. 17

32. Malta Grover, *Bhabani Bhattacharya as a Novelist of Social Conscience*, Shalabh Prakasan, Meerut, 1991, p. 118.

33. Balram S. Sorot, *The Novels of Bhabani Bhattacharya,* Prestige Book, New Delhi, 1984, p. 96.

34. Punim Juneja, *The East-West Theme: Some Inner Fury, The Serpent and The Rope* and *A Dream in Hawaii, Indian Woman Novelists*, Prestige Books, New Delhi, 1993, p. 233.

35. Jasbir Jain, *The Human Dimensions of Statis and Growth Perspectives on Bhabani Bhattacharya* Ed. Ramesh K. Srivastava, Vimal Prakashan, Ghaziabad, 1982. p. 64.

36. *Ibid*, p. 97.

5

A Study of Human Instincts

Before discussing in detail Bhabani Bhattacharya's contribution to short-story a brief history of the short-story is taken up. The short story is one of the oldest literary forms known to the human mind. Since the beginning of civilization, man has had the urge to convert the beginning of imagined experience into a story and hand it down to the generations. A tale thus has its roots in the oral tradition. The short-story predates and forms the nucleus of the ballad and epic. It has existed from the earliest times up to the present. It is co-equal and co-terminal with the history of man.

About the characteristics of short-story Henry Holt remarks, "From the earliest times, the short-story has served as allegory, fable and moral example. It has drawn themes from matter supernatural and natural, romantic and realistic, grotesque and mundance. It has portrayed the abnormal as well as the representative personality, mental processes as well as physical activity, and casual happening, as well as arresting incident".[1]

The stories have existed throughout history in one form or the other. The methodology of Greece, the Fables of Aesop, the Scandinavian sagas, the bestiaries of the middle ages, the legends of the celt, the parables of the New Testament in the West, the *Upanishad* and the *Panchatantra*, the *Hitopadesa*, the *Arabian Nights* in the East are rich treasuries of short stories. The Old Testament stories such as those of Jonah and Ruth date back to some three hundred years before the birth of Christ. The early Greeks and Romans imparted incidents and episodes in their classics. In the middle age, story telling as an art flourished in the form of fables and epics about beasts and also in the medieval romance.

The tales of ancient times mostly aimed at moral and religious instruction rather than mere entertainment. Later when the short story had developed into a popular literary form, it yields very varied literary pleasures. Regarding the development of short story, Edward Albert points out, "It was in the Nineteenth century that the short-story came into being as an art form, drawing upon and deriving from the periodical essay of the eighteenth century".[2]

The short-story is often seen as the little sister of the novel and because it is defined in terms of the novel, it is bound to fail in many respects when it comes up for judgement. It is considered that the short-story in comparison with the novel, lacks 'breadth' or scope and university of the fragmentary, partial, subjective etc., But in practice, it is not the case. The short story is a complete 'genre' in itself, it is different from the novel and it has characteristics that set it apart from the novel, besides giving it a definite identity.

In India we have fables in Sanskrit which later became, the model of Aesop's Fables in Greece. There are long and romantic stories of the lovers and adventures of Gods and Goddesses and kings and princes. There are also stories of merchants and courtesans, which prove the existence of highly, developed and sophisticated society. But short-story as a distinct art form developed in India in the nineteenth century. As Humayan Kabir rightly remarks, "Short story in the proper sense developed in India only, in the modern age and mainly as a result of the impact of Europe".[3]

As Edgar Allen Poe has shown, a story can be constructed to achieve unity of impression through strict unity of form. A short story deals with a single character, a single event, a single emotion or a series of emotions called forth by a single situation. A novel on the other hand, has a series of episodes that breaks and mars this unity of impression. It can be said that a short-story is a concentrated and distilled essence of literature, a drop of which contains the whole. If a novel attempts to reflect life in the totality, short-stories offer only a still life picture of reality. The short-story began to show greater interest in a situation or an aspect of character as against the novel's concern with the growth of character.

Creative writing, whether it is a novel or a short story must contain mainly four ingredients character, action, setting and a basic idea or a theme. The character must act out a situation against a setting, a background, and the way in which they act, must mean something, or convey an idea or a theme to the reader. While some stories are action-oriented some may be character-oriented. Stories in ancient and medieval India were more concerned with events and plot than with character or individuality.

Due to the new awakening of the Indian creative writers, the modern short story attained a special place in the art of literature. The emphasis is laid on the growth of character rather than on mere events. The earliest influence on Indian writers was Sir Walter Scott, who not only influenced novel, but also the short-stories. Then Freud and Marx are the two thinkers of Europe, who made a deep imprint on the mind of contemporary Indian writers. Humayum Kabir comments, "Freud was for some years worshipped almost as a demi-god. It becomes a fashion to delve into the inconspicuous and the sub-conscious to look for new subjects and themes. The Freudian influence on Indian literature was soon equalled and at times exceeded by that of Marx". [4] Later on the great masters of short-story like Tolstoy, Arton Chekhor, O. Henry, W. Somerset Maugham and Others influenced the short story writers in India.

The Indian-English short story is a successfully established art, which is in no way inferior to the short-story of any other country. Most of the Indian-English short-stories are proudly comparable with the Western short-stories. The writers write creatively in English and successfully try to capture and convey the Indian spirit, Indian values and cultural, heritage in their writings. The short-story writers try to portray the modern sensibility with all its complexities. They treat variety of themes and demonstrate different techniques very effectively. Madhusudan Prasad rightly remarks, "That the Indian-English short-stories can stand comparison with the best continental short-stories is enough evidence not only of their thematic and technical maturity but also of the confident ease with which the English language is being handled".[5]

At the turn of the 20th century, the Indian writers found the short-story as a convenient medium to express their literary consciousness and their response to the contemporary life. In the pre-Independent India, the attitudes of the Indian writers were determined by the needs of the time. They started writing short-stories, which echo the nation's cry for freedom. In the Post-Independence period there was difference in the approach of the Indian short-story writers. The troubles of a nation after freedom, its hopes and expectations, its frustrations and disillusionments have changed the form and control of the Indian English short-story.

During the first three decades of twentieth century, Tagore and Gandhi shaped India's life and literature in a novel way. The influence of these two great personalities was irresistible that many Indian writers started writing short stories. Sarala, Jag Mohan comments, "An influence as powerful as the impact of Western literature was that of Rabindranath Tagore. He influenced the Indian short story as much as he influenced Indian Poetry". [6] As in so many other fields, Tagore is the pioneer of this work of art. He is the first writer of India who gave a distinct character to the short-story. He is not only the first but also the foremost and one of the greatest masters of the short story. He described in his short-stories the life of

Bengal as seen through the window of his moving boat. He also suggests that there is no completeness or totality in the short-story as the view is only from a window.

Indo-Anglian short-story writers Mulk Raj Anand, R. K. Narayan, Khushwant Singh, Bhabani Bhattacharya, Raja Rao and Ruth Prawar Jhabvala maintained a high level of competence in this form of literature. They have shown reality with Indian characters and Indian milieu. Mulk Raj Anand is a down to earth realist, who feels for the oppressed and the suffering. His stories centre in the village and the poor villagers, combine the realism of Anand with the telling narration of Tagore. His collection of Short-Stories, *The Cow of the Barricades and Other Stories* are based on rural South India. He portrays the innate goodness and the inherent virtues of the rural folk amidst their poverty and hunger. He also deals with the national movements and independence.

Of all the Indo Anglian writers, R. K. Narayan has varied collections, nearly more than a hundred short-stories. *'Malgudi Days, Dodu and Other Stories, Cyclone and Other Stories,* Lowley Read and other various themes which touched, the heart of the readers. His collection *'Gods, Demons and Others* creates a new path in short-story writing. The puranic characters find a significant place in this volume.. The humour and pathos of a tragic situation are found in most of Narayan's stories. Khushwant Singh's short-stories show his subtle skill and irony. Stories dealt with the life in Punjab, especially the life of the sikhs. B. Syamala Rao rightly remarks, "Among Indo-Anglian writers Mulk Raj Anad, R. K. Narayan, Raja, Khushwant Singh and Bhattacharya show equal brilliance with Indian characters and Indian atmosphere".[7]

Ruth Prawer Jhabvala's stories are based on the theme of East-West, encounter. Her volume *How I Became a Holy Mother and Other Stories* contains stories which are brilliantly conceived and gracefully told. In her stories she reveals herself as a writer having wide understanding of human character and deep sympathy for the suffering humanity. K. A. Abbas is another short-story writer, who is well known for this sensitive understanding and artistic characterization. His volume *One Thousand Nights on a Bed of Stones* mostly deals with the plight of pavement dwellers in Bombay in the various stories.

Bhabani Bhattacharya has established his reputation primarily as novelist. He has produced just one, collection of short stories, *'Steel Hawk and Other Stories*. It contains a collection of fifteen short-stories all written with subtlety and skills. The book is an Orient Paper Back original, published in 1968. Some of his stories are based on small incidents while in some other stories he has taken up a character and has chosen incidents and situation. In other stories he has chosen an atmosphere and realised it through actions and persons. A clear study and a careful analysis of the stories make his approach very clear.

The first story in the collection of *Steel Hawk and Other Stories* is *Glory at Twilight*. In this short-story Bhattacharya gives a touching story of Satyajit, who was once prosperous, tries to preserve his glory at twilight. It is a neatly constructed story based on the theory that human life is a compound of queer ironies, and that man is a creature of circumstances, unpredictable and inescapable. The rise and fall that the life of the protagonist's career undergoes serves as an illustration of this. Regarding ups and downs in life, Bhattacharya comments, life lay sharpening on the grindstone of hard economy, sharpening the realities that still had the semblance of an undreamable dream. (p. 7)

Satyajit is described as a self-made man, who in a short-time acquires the position as Managing Director of a City Bank due to his early promotions. He owes his elevation to the desperate act of forgery committed by an unfortunate Maths tutor. It is ironcal that the unhappy tutor resorts to forgery in order to save his T. B., striken wife. When he is caught red-handed and punished, his wife dies of shame. That man cries for punishment in the court as "Punish me as a killer...I have put my wife to shame which kills as fast as T. B". (p. 10). That unhappy men ruin paves way for Satyajit's unexpected prosperity. Satyajit who has risen so quickly in life falls even more quickly. Bhattacharya points to the reality in life "Failure had a tempo far faster than success". (p. 11).

All the situations in the story are portrayed in an ironical way. Satyajit undertakes his journey to Santipur, his hometown, in order to escape briefly from the misery caused by his unforeseen conditions. But it is ironical that he is totally unaware of further misery that awaits him. Satyajit goes to attend the marriage of his uncle's daughter in the village. His uncle Srinath has enjoyed the timely assistance of Satyajit, and continues to be under the same impression. When Srinath gives him a royal welcome and hospitality, he feels proud without being aware of the real fact.

Bhattacharya uses the theme of hunger in a different angle in this story. It is the hunger for recognition, which needed satisfaction for Satyajit. Though he knows that he is an imposter now, the reception by the villagers awakens his hunger for glory. In the words of the writer, "Let him be happy for the day even with a false echo, let him be wrapped a while in the lingering twilights, splendour of departed glory". (p. 18) To help Srinath, he has to pawn his village house and pond as security for just rupees two thousand. That house and pond here the only, left-overs, after his bankruptcy to handover to his wife and child. He is not in a position to buy a perambulator for his newborn son. It clearly shows man's futile efforts to get out of self made prestige.

The traditional customs and procedure of marriage are fully drawn in the story. Washing of Satyajit's feet with cool water by Srinath's daughter Beena, garlanding him at the railway station, waving palm-leaf fans show the traditional way of reception. The arriving of groom's party in oxcarts and palanquins conches blowing, young women gathering and greeting at the dooryard all present the typical Indian villagers' customs during marriage. The word benediction was very ironically used in the story, which shows the artistic technique of Bhattacharya.

Bhattacharya hints at the deterioration of traditional values in modern India. There is no value for trust in the society. Nobody is willing to lend money without any security. People think that property has more weight than a millionaire's signature. In this context the attention of the words of the then Prime Minister Jawaharlal Nehru called, "All the old values destroyed, where will our India be?" (p. 23)

The second story *Public Figure*, deals with an incident which is reproduced, as an episode in the novel *Shadow from Ladakh.* This theme seems to be an inversion of the theme in *Kaumudi's Renunciation* an article in Gandhiji's *Harijan.* It describes the magnanimous surrender of all her ornaments by a girl, Kaumudi, near Calicut in response to the leader's appeal. Bhattacharya refers to this incident in his book, *Gandhi The Writer.* This story presents the postcolonial period, in which most people in the society crave for publicity. The male protagonist is a rich businessman, who is crazy for his image in the public.

The protagonist is not given any name and is mentioned as public figure throughout the story. He lives in a society where people are known by their offices. For example, the Deputy Commissioner Ram Lal Sharma is known as D. C. Sharma. Public figure is also known as P. F., in his place. A Honorary Secretary of a Welfare Fund P. F., decides to promote his name using every opportunity. He is a rich business magnate who pretends to be a great social worker, but in reality only a running man striving to win undeserved fame. When the D. C., appoints him the Honorary Secretary of the fund, he decides to use his association with the fund as a chance to elevate his own image.

The theme of hunger haunts the mind of Bhattacharya even in this second story. The public figure is a man, hungry for name and fame in the society. Bhattacharya ironically remarks that to satisfy his hunger, he gets associated with a number of societies professing public welfare. For publicity a grand function organised by him is to be presided over by a V. I. P., from the state capital. To highlight this function, he makes arrangements for the donation of gold ornaments by his daughter Nolini. But his wife and daughter do not agree to his proposal. His character is revealed through the words of his wife, "If you truly want to support the good cause, you should make yourself, a pauper and walk to streets with a begging bowl". (p. 29).

The entire story is based on situational irony. It is an ironical reversal of incident that forms its climax. P. F., dreams of the publicity for his name and his daughter's photograph in the local newspaper *Seoni Herald.* For this he tries to please Muthuswami, the sole local correspondent of the newspaper by inviting him to tea at home. His wife and daughter agree to donate some pieces of their Jewelry only when P. F., promises to replace them with new ones, in latest design. On the stage, Nolini parts with her jewels one after another as planned before. But the irony is that the costly ruby set necklace that was hidden inside her saree was noticed by V. I. P. At that supreme moment, P. F., persuades her to part with that also to save his honour in the public.

The highlight of the story is the last part in which P. F.'s expectation is utterly reversed. The irony is that all P. F.'s troubles to win name and fame end in useless report in the paper. In the report, Muthuswami neither, flatters P. F.'s eminence nor highlights his daughter's generosity. The report sarcastically mentions about the donation of a few pieces of the gold ornaments of Nolini. "It is understood that there in the audience, atleast twenty other women anxious to donate all the jewellery they owned; these still remain to be collected". (p. 32). This line makes P. F., mad with fury and reveals his real character. He scolds Muthuswami and waits, for an opportunity to revenge, to punish him in good time. This shows the hypocrisy of modern men, who pretend to be good at heart to raise his position in the society.

Bhattacharya points to the feelings of traditional women regarding the publicity of their daughters in the newspapers. Nolini's mother is filed with anger. When she hears P. F., expressing his idea of Nolini's photograph in the paper, she angrily comments, "You wish every lout in this town to get a copy of her picture? After that, who will ever marry her? Tell me". (p. 29). The same feelings of a mother are expressed even in this second novel *Music for Mohini.* It shows the mind setup of Indian women who blindly accept traditional customs. The story is full of dramatic quality from the beginning to the end.

In the story *My Brave Great Uncle,* Bhattacharya deviates from his original themes. He moves into the realm of the supernatural. The protagonist of this story is the great uncle of Rangamitti village, an old man of nearly seventy. The man with a pale and wrinkled visage has become a legendary figure in his village. He impresses the villagers with his supernatural yarns and claims that the flesh creeping tales are not the products of his imagination but his true experience. Thus he has succeeded in creating an image of a very brave man who can command ghosts and goblins. As B. Syamala Rao remarks, "Here he gives an altogether different setting, taking the readers into a supernatural world of gnomes and spirits like the Rosicrucian machinery in Pope's *Rape of the Lock*". (p. 119)

Unlike his other stories in the collection, Bhattacharya gives a detailed account of the supernatural elements in this story. The mention of so many species, all unlike each other in physical shape creates a sense of fear and anxiety in the readers. A gnome looks as different from a Brahmadaitya as a monkey from an elephant. Each kind even smell different...A goblin stinks likes a fellow who has not washed his limbs for ten years! While a spook is as clean as a temple priest of ours". (p. 41). The writer even describes the fighting of two goblins in a dramatic way. Through the attitude of the villagers, Bhattacharya brings out the Indians' belief in the supernatural elements.

The old man claims that the incorporeal spirits fear him and he has the power to drive them off by clapping his hand. But the irony is that the old man is mortally afraid of ghosts and that he indulges in clapping only to save himself from possible assault by the spirits. His mask of bravery comes off finally when the villagers insist that he should spend the night in the dead priest's room. Though he is exposed, he wants to keep the mask saying that he cannot clap his hands to ward off the ghosts as one of his hands is placed on the bier all the time. Bhattacharya reveals the real self of the old man saying, "Sick with his morbid fear, he had been living in the protective shell of his brave yarns, himself the dramtised hero. He clapped his hands out of a wish – thought; his fear intense; the way he fought fear no less intense".(p. 45).

The theme of hunger occupies the prominent place, even in this story. The old man's hunger for recognition in his village makes him a self made hero. He wants to satisfy his hunger by mere prevention instead of gaining real courage. He cannot sleep alone and needs light during the nights to overcome the fear. Bhattacharya presents the Hindu custom in the villages regarding the rites to the dead body. The Hindu custom in Bengal village prevails that at nighttime a dead body must be kept under constant vigil. Someone must sit beside it, touching the bier all the time with the hand. Though the story appears to be horror filled, the false image of the old man is narrated in a humorous way. The story ends with the laughing of the villagers, who could grasp the pseudo bravery of the old man. Bhattacharya dramatically develops the character of the story through the thrilling events in a single night.

The next story *Lattu Ram's Adventure* deals with the adventure of a boy, twelve-year-old, in a town fairs. Bhattacharya presents picturesque description of annual fair in a town with number of stalls, painted dolls, variety of sweets, hair ornaments, fighting birds as well as parrots and pigeons. At night it was illuminated with thousands of colour bulbs. The boy Lattu Ram is the central character of the story. He is alone in the fair moving from stall to stall without any interest. At that time he hears an announcement from a loudspeaker. A little five year old boy Kedar Narayan is missing in the fair. The announcement is very funny about the identification of the missing boy as thin, dark, short of one upper tooth. He has a slight squint in the left eye and it can be seen only when he laughs.

Bhattacharya very humorously presents the great confusion caused by the result of this announcement. "In the next quarter – hour, every little boy in the cheeks who seemed forlorn ran the peril of having his cheeks squeezed, so that his teeth would show. The number of chin, dark youngsters short of one front tooth was large beyond expectation". (p. 47). Still more humorous is the way by which the adults examine the squint in the left eye. To make the boy laugh, a man would jab in the ribs of the boy. Some of the signboards displayed at shops in the fair provide some kind of verbal humour; *Lady Shoes, Order Suppliers Promptly Executed, Seats of Customers Properly Caned.*

Lattu Ram goes in search of Kedar Narayan, the missing boy of five years, catches hold of some other by mistake. The irony is that Lattu Ram entertains him with a pocket of salted peanuts, a bottle of lemonade and also a movie, but as he is planning to restore this boy to his parents, he discovers his mistake. His spirit of adventure ends in a comic tone. He wants a thrill by taking that boy with him away from his parents for some time. During that time he felt the excitement of a kidnapper. He imagines that there would be a talk in the town about child snatchers and many kinds of rumours about rogues with gunny backs to imprison the little boys. These thoughts make Lattu Ram happy because he has a negative attitude towards adults, those adults folks, tyrants all, serve them right!."

In this story Bhattacharya analyses the psychology of adults and children. Usually children want to enjoy the air of freedom, which is denied by adults. Lattu Ram also feels that his teachers at school, his brother and father at home did not allow him to taste the freedom. So he wishes for the freedom of the little boy, who is also denied freedom by his parents. He expresses his thoughts, "The adult folks were all like that, Lattu Ram reflected with deep disgust. You did them a good turn, you corrected their mistake, you told them something, they ought to know, and they were mad at you right mad". (pp. 50-51). This story can be viewed as a study of psychology of adults and the youngsters.

The story *Names are not Lables* is concerned with an old man's feelings about the names and numbers. The old man's identity is kept secret by the writer in order to maintain suspense till the end of the story. The old man worries about the change of names of buses in Calcutta in to A-24. The man feels that the bus with the number does not look familiar to him and he is filled with sorrow and shame. Bhattacharya remarks, "The name could n't have given the engine more speed or made the seats more comfortable".(p. 55).

The old man argues that what would happen when a wife's name is changed. He feels that it would seem strange calling her by the new name, it is as if she has become another woman. The whole story is based on the fine expression, "Call her by a number, say, A-24, and her very breath is different, names have a spiritual value. They are not just labels". (p. 56). The man wishes if he made a lot of money he would buy all the buses in town and restore their names to them. If he could get elected to the City Corporation he would persuade his fellow consellors to order that the numbers be abolished, the names given back.

Every day at the same time, the old man was seen on that particular bus and utters the same words. He had become a feature and an intrinsic part of A-24!. This gives a dramatic touch to the story. Later it was known that he had been in prison for five years. Being a Manager of a bank, he had stolen money and gone to jail. Recently he was released from the prison. The prison life haunts him because the number A-24, releases unhappy memories in him. P. Ramchandraiah remarks, "Basing on the assumption that the old man might have borne the label 'A-24' while in prison, the story tries to probe his bruised sensibility".[10]

In the next story *Pictures in the Fire,* Bhattacharya wants to stress that racial differences are of no importance. The protagonist of his story is not an Indian and he is presented as a stranger from across the seas. As the basic human nature every where is the same, there are racial similarities regarding the principles that govern man's behaviour. The atmosphere of the story also helps the total scene to achieve its appropriate tone. The narrator of the story is Bhattacharya, who deliberately introduces himself as a writer of short-stories and novels.

The protagonist, Henry Brown and the narrator meet in a trench and they expect bombardment at any moment. In the meanwhile Henry Browns tells his story and expresses his feelings to lighten his heavy heart. He introduces himself as Josephine Brown, a creative writer. As the narrator has already seen the picture of Josephine Brown in the books, he considers the stranger as a mad person. The narrator is afraid to be close with the madman, because bombs had far less horror than the breath of a mad man. But that man reveals that driven by the urge for creative expression, he writes stories, but gets them published in the name of his wife, Josephine Brown. He expressed his urge "The need for a self expression could be as strong, as the other needs for food, for sleep, for a woman". (p. 61).

The reason for hiding his own name for his creative writing is the year of rejection. He uses his wife's name not out of his affection or respect towards her but out of diffidence. He would not mind if the returned envelope were addressed to his wife. He wants to use her name as a shield against his hurt. K. K. Sharma comments about this, "The brittle male ego, apprehensive of rejection, seeks protection behind his wife's name".[11] To his surprise his story is accepted.

Initially his wife pleads against using her name and implores him to use his own name. But he continues to write in her name. He is happy because he feels that he has created her as any character in his stories. As a result, Josephine shoots up into eminence and becomes a highly respected public figure whereas Henry, the rural author remains unknown to the readers.

It is only when Josephine becomes famous as a creative writer and even starts enjoying this new image of hers as a separate famous identity that he begins to feel angry with her.

This new-won fame, instead of bringing the couple close to each other, succeeds only in spoiling their relationship. That success had given her this pride. Their spirits had slid apart as never before while they should have had a complete union. There was no union, only the pangs of a new unaccountable separation". (p. 65). Instead of blaming himself he blames his wife for all that had happened.

The vulnerable ego of man could not tolerate the fame of his wife. When a woman, may be his wife asserts her own individuality, it shocks his ego. Unable to blame her fame, Henry Brown blames the whole female race, "only a woman could misappropriate. So coldly, without shame". (p. 66) Bhattacharya presents the contrast between male and female psychology. A woman feels happy to be the wife of a famous man, whereas a man's ego is shattered when he feels that he is a husband to his famous wife.

The theme of hunger can be felt even in this story also. Henry Brown could not recognise his hunger for fame, which was dormant in him. Not only Henry, every creative writer wants to be known to the readers. The author reveals the feelings of Henry, which are deep down in him and comes to the surface at last. He felt a great need of fame for himself. After recognising this, Henry sends his new story under his own name, but it returns rejected. He decides to stop writing but his urge for self-expression is too strong to be suppressed. The irony is when his new story goes under Josephine's name gets published. The title of the strange is symbolic, which presents the strong patterns in life as pictures in the fire reveal strange shapes in the darkness. R. K. Srivastava remarks, *Pictures in the Fire* is ingeniously contrived and grippingly narrated, and is certainly deserves better attention then it has received at the hands of Bhattacharya critics."[12]

Mere Monkeys is the next story in the collection of *Steel Hawk and Other Stories.* This is based on the fact that as for as the basic instincts of hunger, fear, anger and sexual desire are concerned, there is no difference between a monkey and a man. Bhattacharya attributes human instincts to animals through his keen observation and study of psychology. The story is the vivid portrayal of the behaviour of monkeys near his house. The narrator used to watch the monkeys every day on the branches of a tall tamarind tree.

Bhattacharya presents the affection of mother monkey towards its youngling and its utmost care of nursing it. The other monkeys in the group also fondle the youngling with pleasure. While the monkeys carefully handles the youngling "the mother would sit proud and content, and she would soon claim the baby back and start to give suck again". (p. 69). The author very naturally portrays the motherly affection and pride in the eyes of the monkey. The happy and peaceful atmosphere of the place is changed suddenly due to the arrival of a huge monkey. It is an overgrown male of the species, which was loitering about the tamarind tree.

While describing about the male monkey, and its approach towards the mother monkey, Bhattacharya indicates natural masculine arrogance, in the human society, "The male dashed up the tree and crouched before the mother glaring at her, masterful, the thin-lipped slit of mouth cruel with an unmistakable leer". (p. 70). Due to fear, the mother shielded her youngling with her body. But all of a sudden the beast snatched the body away and threw it playfully up in the air. Within seconds the baby dropped to the ground and died. The male monkey deliberately throws down on the ground and kills the baby monkey that is being fondly nursed by the mother. As a typical representative of male species, the monkey is innately and instinctively aggressive.

The death of the youngling creates the tragic atmosphere in the group of monkeys. Bhattacharya presents the pathetic situation by importing human feelings and mourning at the time of death. The particular Indian way of wailing is picturised, "Like the professional mourners who in this part of India rend the air with their ritual of full throated wailing when someone is dead, the monkeys raised shrill voices and swayed their haunches and beat their breasts". (p. 72) The vivid portrayal of this scene shows the author's keen observation of human behaviour during different situations.

The next day after the death of the young monkey, the mother monkey was responding to the overtures of the brute monkey, which had killed that youngling. The narrator immediately feels the inferiority of animals and their behaviour. The word 'Animals is used sarcastically and with a feeling of superiority over animals regarding the behaviour of the mother monkey. But in the very next moment, this superiority degrades when he understands that the mother-monkey has her own sense of moral right and wrong. The mother monkey pulls down the brute monkey, along with herself, to a watery grave to avenge the death of the baby monkey. She takes revenge which is obviously present in the human beings. As K. R. Chandrasekharan observes, "*Mere Monkeys* is an unusual story which makes a powerful impact as it represents the operation of almost human feelings in a monkey's mind".[13]

With trivial details about what monkeys do the author builds the conflict between the mother-monkey and the brute monkey in a dramatic way. He enacts a deeply human drama with the background of the animals. It appears to be a beast fable with the effectiveness of the moral sense of Panchatantra tales. It makes the readers realise that sometimes animals could be less animalistic, and more value-conscious, than human beings.

Bhattacharya's next story *A Moment of Eternity* begins and ends with a tragic note. Flashback technique is used to narrate the story. The story begins in a dramatic way with the court scene. The description of the Judge is very funny. "He has to pick up the black cap and place it on his head so he may look like Yama, the death-god and mere utterance of ten words or twelve". (p. 74) The element of mercy, which the world and the heaven bless, is stressed here in connection with the justice. The same type of story appears as an episode in the novel. *So Many Hungers*!.

The pathetic condition of a lower middle class Indian woman, who is entirely dependent on her husband, is depicted. The condition of her husband, who works to earn for his wife and two children, results in his contracting tuberculosis. Due to his ill health he has lost his job and searches for a new job to save his family from poverty. While hunting for work day and night, his thoughts of the family haunts him.

The traditional Indian woman's attitude towards her husband and family is portrayed through the characters of the mother of Sona and Mona. She prays day and nights for the welfare of her husband and prepares to save him by giving her life. She utters. "Oh, I could die a hundred deaths so he could be happy for a day. And I was helper, for I had no art needed to make a living. I has I was helpless, for I had no art needed to make a living. I had nothing to give him save my soul". (p. 77) Bhattacharya gives appropriate references from mythology to show the fighting spirit of Hindu women to save her husband. He narrates the story of Satyavan and Savitri to produce more effect. According to this story when Savitri's husband Satyavan dies, Savitri follows the death-God Yama. Because of her sincere worship, Yama offered her any boon except the life of her husband. She refused the riches offered by the God. At last she asked him to bless her with seven children and the death God granted her the wish. So with intelligence, Savitri got back her husband from the clutches of death God.

The spirit of Savitri is seen in Indian woman who forced the mother to save her husband. But as she could not tolerate the death of her husband, she wanted to follow him. In the utter misery she loses her senses and takes a tragic decision. She gave opium to both of her daughters Sona and Mona and later she herself consumed it. She feels, "In you we three live in your dying we three die'. Savitri will not be denied. Savitri, who is ever in every woman". (p. 82).

The tragedy is further heightened when the children face cruel death but mother is saved and arrested for the case of murder and suicide. The mother wants to die as fast as possible but the Judge gives her four years imprisonment. She feels that she has to wait for death for four more years. She longs for death punishment for her crime, which is denied. There is nothing left for her but a prayer for madness. Because the thoughts of her children's death haunt her like a shadow and madness is the only way to escape from the memories. It is the pathetic tale of a woman, who is driven to disbar poverty, worry and disease. As R. K. Srivastava observes, "The cycle of destitution-starvation death which is the characteristic core of Bhattacharya's novels is also the theme of "*A Moment in Eternity*".[14]

The next story *Just Coincidence* stands for unity of time, place and action. The setting of the story is the two-berth compartment of an express train. The whole action is confined to a small span of time, just about an hour. The whole atmosphere is that of a detective fiction. The story has an arresting beginning "This is a true happening, but the strangeness of it gives it perhaps the semblance of imaginative fiction". (p. 85) The characters involved in the action are only three – The narrator, his wife and another fellow – Passenger.

The first-person narrator, travelling by a Delhi bound train with his wife, is reading about the exploits of Machine-gun-Kelly. He picks up a magazine of detective fiction to pass his time. The fiction was full of bullets and blood. Just at the point, where Kelly fires a shot in the story, the narrator hears a bullet sound and finds the window-pane of the compartment blown to pieces. The sudden incident and wonders at the coincidence of actions shock the narrator. At this moment the fellow passenger also shows the symptoms of shock.

Bhattacharya has given an instance of human psychology and man's premonition in just coincidence. He presents a link between the gun shot and the premonitions of the narrator's, co-passenger. The co-passenger expresses that he felt that evil were about to happen before his journey. For the first time he rang up to his friend and requested him to look after his family during his absence. He further explained that his office clerk, wrote down his name and address on the luggage as never done before. He exclaims that it may be because of his premonition or nothing but coincidence. After hearing of Kelly's firing and the gun shot just at the moment, the narrator questions himself whether it is just coincidence or something else? The writer uses the techniques of steam of consciousness through out the story. The story begins and ends in a dramatic way, which reveals that the writer artistically portrays each and every incident in life.

The life style of acrobats and their love and respect for their skill is emotionally portrayed in the next story *Acrobats.* The skill of acrobats is passed on from generations to generations as a profession from parents to children. But in modern times the younger generation is not interested in this art which was loved and practiced by older generations, Bhattacharya presents this conflict between father and son in this story. The father compels his son to adopt the centuries old inheritance, which the boy hates and revolts. The father deep-rooted in traditional feelings questions "And put to shame the fourteen generations of our forefathers in Heaven land". (p. 94) The father beats his son in anger but after-words requests his son to forgive him for his madness.

The author very realistically presents the father-son relationship. Recognising his son's reluctance towards his art, the father allows the boy to select his way of living but one day, he saw his son processing the feats in the backyard with full concentration. The father watches his son with delight and excitement. The affection towards his fathers makes the boy accept the traditional art. He wants to satisfy his father and asks. "The fore-father in Heaven land–are they pleased?" (p. 96)

Bhattacharya's power of close observation of the skill of the acrobats has made the story very lively. He describes skill of the father acrobat. He stood erect and rigid, his firm feet planted apart holding a lost a ten froot pole at the end of which a boy lay spread eagled, precariously balanced on his belly". (p. 90). The skill of the father and the son is compared to show who is the better acrobat. While observing the feelings on the faces of the folks, it is felt that the alarm could not be on Father's account. Because nothing would happen to the father if his muscles failed but the boy could break his legs or his skull if he was little careless. There is a danger for boy's life if he would drop down on the stone pavement. With father it is sheer strength, but with boy it is a great skill.

The father and the boy live and perform their acrobatic feats together on the streets. The father has undivided love for his motherless son and the boy has constant devotion to his father. Inspite of the difference in their age they live like true companions, and there deep understands between them. The performance is given again and again in front of a particular house. The boy looking down into his father's face notices that he is looking with longing eyes on a servant maid standing on a balcony. Though he is unable to understand it, he feels his father's attraction for a maidservant coming between him and his father. He instinctively resents this outsider because it represents a threat to his love. "There was something new between himself and his father, something that he had to understand". (p. 93).

When his father's eyes are fixed on the balcony with a new and curious expression, the son is hurt inside. He observed the maid at the balcony who is watching the face of his father deeply. Those two are watching each other in an odd way without caring for the outer world. The boy expressed his feelings in a different way to his father by commenting that the maid is watching a free show without giving single paise. But the father hurts his son's feelings by asking him to stop his silly chatter and walks in silence. Balancing on his back the boy watches the looks of the woman but could not make out the rapt look. The boy feels "that he had no existence for them, he was a segment of the tall pole on his father's mouth". (p. 97) Bhattacharya dramatically presents the inner feelings and expressions of the father and his son in a natural way.

The perfect balance of affections between the father and the son is suddenly upset by the intrusion of a servant maid. The father does not care for the injured feelings of the adolescent lad. The boy wants to run away from this miserable situation but 'Unbreakable bonds' of his love for his father hold him helpless. At last he decides to express his anger against this maid in a harsh way. In order to show his unhappiness, the boy deliberately loses his balance on the pole and falls on the stone pavement. He is taken to hospital in an unconscious state, and luckily escapes death but his right leg is broken. When he gains consciousness in the hospital, he finds his father caressing his legs. The father realises the core of his son's inward storm. There is a violent struggle in his mind and at last, he decides to forsake the woman. The father learns his lesson and the acrobats are no more to be seen in the street, "with his strength of a lion, father fought his battle". (p. 99).

The union of the father and the boy signifies the synthesis and the harmonious living of older and younger generation, the ancient and the modern. The loss of balance and the affection is restored. As K. R. Chandrasekharan observes, "The deep attachment between father and son, the sadness and jealousy felt by the boy and their common respect for the memory of the dead mother are brought out with breath-taking force". The love of father and son dominates the story, while the attraction of the intruder woman is discarded.

The short-story *The Quack* is a sketch of the business techniques of a quack and the attitude of village folks. Bhattacharaya's observation of the familiar scene of Quacks, vociferously advertising their medicines on Indian Pavement. The story reveals the author's knowledge of the psychology of the quack as well as that of gullible masses who blindly believe the eloquent advertising. He realistically presents the scene in the village market, "That hand held a pair of tongs at the end of which was live evil-visaged scorpion with a curved tail. Thrusting it forward as it writhed, he whirled about along the crowd's edge and all the while his talk came unceasingly". (p. 100).

The words of the Quack are very attractive, which makes audience fall a prey to the speech. He describes the magical power of the coal black powder, which is very cheap but powerful. The pinch of the black powder' works like a magic and deadens the venom. The pain of the poisonous creature's bite is vanished by applying the power. He compares it to the treatment of modern Allopathy, which is very costly. Very intelligently he strikes at the attitude of the village folks, who don't spend much on the medicines. Attributing some spiritual powers to the powder awakens the religious beliefs of the People. The Quack narrates that a great yogi gave the secret of its preparation to him and advised him to work for the welfare of the people. He reflects, "Pass on the drugs to needy ones and take in return nothing more than its bare cost". (p. 101).

Bhattacharya focuses attention on the theme of hungers in this short story also. In order to earn his daily bread the Quack has to fight a battle. His struggle is not for himself alone but for his dear ones, his wife and children. When the initial eloquence of the quack falls flat on the audience the lines of dismay grow graven on his face. He has to feed his family with his skill of quakery. The author comments, "Their fate lay on what his tongue could achieve. Failure would mean hunger for them, Starvation". (p. 102). In that particular day not even one packet was sold which shows his failure. But the Quack would not allow the failure to come his way. So, he tactfully changes his advertising. He mentions that the black powder can do only four things cure stings, bites, kill belly ache, ease headache and last of all it can make loose teeth strong and stand pillar like.

The psychology of the village folk who buys such medicines is clearly analysed. Somebody or other falls a victim to the tact of the Quack, whose statement makes everything appear like truth. The old man in the story, who meets the author in the audience, buys the black powder packets. He shows his decaying teeth and says that the dentist has already told that nothing can be done for his teeth. Yet he hopes that the black powder may help him because there is no other way. He expresses, "Why not hope a bit against all hope? why not give every stupid thing an honest trial? Quackery? Yes. I am no trustful ask. "But.... what if it just happens to be otherwise this time?." (p. 104). His faith in the miracles makes him fall a prey to the quack and buys four packets of that powder. This story conveys the idea that human mind is prone to have faith in the miraculous things despite a deep awareness of the modern and real facts of life. Bhattacharya presents the synthesis of ideal and real elements in human nature very artistically.

The short story *the Faltering Pendulum* is mainly the characterization of an old widow who is the central character of the story. The childlessness and resultant loneliness have given her a harsh temperament and a sharp tongue. She has no kin to stay with her and no consolation in her life. She collects rags from door to door and lives with the cast off clothes of man and woman. This shows the poverty of the old woman, which lives, in her imaginary world. Bhattacharya attributes a speciality to the clothes of different types of people in society. He describes, "A smell of life clung on to the cast-off clothes of man and woman. Each had its own individual smell of life. The rag woman lived with the smells. They kindled a zest in her and fed her fancies". (p. 106) According to him, each cloth of men and women has a meaning and a story of its own, which signified the way of their life.

The writer has not given any name to the woman. She draws some consolation from the company of the rags, which raise in her mind curious pictures of the men and women to whom these clothes once belonged. As a childless woman, she curses her barrenness and longs for company to satisfy her inner urge. She tries to cover her sense of loneliness and longing with her intolerant talk. Her desire for motherhood forces her to buy a month old goat youngling and the three ripe pumpkinseeds after selling the rags. She wants to fill the emptiness by growing the seed and making them fertile. Since her own barren condition is beyond her control, she tries to identify herself with the vines seeking some fulfillment. This barren woman's interest in the vines is a case of transferred goal, "The individual may resort to indirect means of obtaining gratification choosing an alternate goal towards which to direct his energies".[16]

The pumpkin vines provide an outlet for the woman's expressions and can afford some satisfaction. Her actions show the repressed thought and impulses, which she cannot control. She could feel the rhythm of the growth and the movement of vine from the deep earth. She is thrilled at the bloom of flowers and eagerly waits for the fruits. But after some days she observes that the vines are barren like other traditional women, she thinks that whatever she touches will become barren. This shows her psychological attachment with the vines. The writer comments, "She was strongly close to the life of the vines, that lone despised woman of a remote Bengal village, for her they had a being". (p. 109).

As a mother she fondles the goat youngling and like her child, she clasps it to her breast. She feels that the goat can understand her talk and knows everything. She starts her new kinship with the goat youngling and all day long she reveals her suppressed heart to it. Bhattacharya's theme of hunger can be felt in this story also. The hunger for motherhood, which is foremost in the women, prevails from the beginning to the end of the story. As K. K. Sharma rightly remarks "The eternal woman with her all encompassing hunger for motherland emerges from the pages of *Faltering Pendulum*".[17]

With a great thrill of a mother, the rag woman watches and waits for the full cycle seeds, flowers-fruits, seeds'. When the blooms die without producing fruit, it appears to her that her own sterile being has affected them also. One day she observes that the goat youngling starts nibbling the vine inspite of her repeated warning. In a mood of frustration, she is over powered with such fury that she strangles her little pet. Infact, she is angry at her own sterile fate. The killing of the goat symbolizes the removal of hindrance for her expected goal. As a result of disappointment she loses her reason and acts in a mad way. Later in the evening, young girl points out the two little pumpkins, which have been lying unnoticed.

At the end of the story, Bhattacharya brings out the philosophy of life that light comes after darkness and life springs up the side of death. After many expectations and disappointments, a balance is maintained in life. Bhattacharya symbolically presents his view as "But the pumpkin vines had springs to fruitful life, after their long barren dead-aliveness, a balance was achieved. The faltering pendulum had regained its swing". (p. 112) The whole story is a case study of a faltering pendulum regaining its normal swing.

The story *Pilgrims in Uniform* is quite different from the stories in the collection due to philosophical and spiritual aspects. The hunger for spiritual awakening and the satisfaction of soul determines the action of the characters in the story. The settings of story are the customary annual tour of pilgrims to the historic temple of Jagannath, which is organised by the novitiate Bharagava. The peasants strongly believe that they can be relieved from the bonds of the earth by undertaking the pilgrimage. Bhargava stirred the emotional feelings of the devotees through his discourses, on his way to the holy place. He asserts the Hindu belief regarding the cycles of birth and death, "O brothers rebirth has no reality for those who have glimpsed the Lord on the Car in the month of Asadh!" (p. 113)

Bhattacharya turns to the traditional beliefs of peasant folks about there past lives and the theory of Karma. During their journey they are ready with open mind to wash away their sins of previous birth. They lead their lives with a strong belief in their religion, which holds that everything is written on the brow of human beings based on their Karmas. Fate is inscrutable and man cannot modify the will of Destiny. Indeed there is a divinity that shapes our ends. Bhattacharya expounds Hindu philosophy with effective sentences.

Bhattacharya presents the difference between materialism and spiritualism through the characters of the pilgrims and a co-passenger. The co-passenger criticizes the blind belief of the peasant folk that they have overmuch religion in their bones. He questions them "Tell me, why should gay living villains sit above you and let money flow like water, while all the time you honest folk have not enough to stop your hunger? call this God's Justice?" (p. 115). He comments on the injustice attitude of all-merciful God towards innocent children and the good people of the soil. The answer of the peasants reflects the ancient Hindu concept that this life on earth is the result of the past deeds. They express their philosophy of life as "All deeds are recorded by unseen hands and each bears the fruit sweet or sour I as we sow in one birth so we reap in another". (p. 116). The story gives an idea of wavering and doubt among the city bred and there methods of reasoned arguments.

The co-passenger considers belief of peasant as the Philosophy of opium. He feels that their faith has only negative values. The traditional values make them too much long-sighted so that they do not see the present. They only thinks about the past and the future, and live in the state of drug addiction. Bhargava could not accept this memory of fatalism and expresses, "It is not the kind of opium that hurt. It only makes us happy". (p. 117) The peasant faith is not altered with the argument of the co-passenger, who mocks them all as a sort of opium addicts. Like him, many materialists believe that faith in God and religion is no better than opium which immunes men to misery.

Bhattacharya symbolically presents the inner beauty of soul through the dark visage of the Lord Jagannath. There is a description of saint Sri Chaitanya and his devotion, which makes him, intoxicated with the divine lordliness. Though the idol of Lord Jagannath has no beauty of shape or face, Sri Chaitanya is beholden by the beauty of the Lord. The prime preaching of Hindu philosophy and the vedas is the inner purification and beauty rather than the external attraction. The image of Lord Jagannath is the symbol for this vedic concept. "The exterior, the shell, does not count. The within alone has value". (p. 117) The man who has the pollution of evil in him cannot see the image of the lord except the black stone throne, the lamps of oil, the gold ornaments. The polluted one sees ugliness and emptiness which shows his evil thought.

There is an important episode of Ram Lal, a lad of sixteen, which is vital for the effect of the story. Ramlal, a young professional thief, travels one day in the guise of a pilgrim along with a band of peasant pilgrims and their leader,

Bhargava. He has no desire to make the pilgrimage, but only the evil motive to rob the pilgrims of their money when they are asleep. But, before he carries out his task, he listens to the discourse of Bhargava about Lord Jagannath and comes under the magic spell of the Lord. He understands the intense faith of those pilgrims who are prepared for any hardship in order to partake of the divine loveliness of the Lord.

Ram Lal is miraculously transformed into a real pilgrim after hearing of God's mercy and love from the discourse of Bhargava. Bhargava preaches that all men are equal in the Lord's strain. There is no difference of caste like Brahmin and the Untouchable. They can sit together and eat from the same bowl at the abode of God. The writer expresses his views through Bhargava, "The Lord is there not for the Brahmin aloof in the dignity of learning, not for the devotee, pure-minded, God – Conscious, truth knowing. He is there for the ignorant and the ignoble, for the lowly in spirit, the bruised in body and soul, the polluted, the thief". (p. 119) Ram Lal is anxious to wash off pollution by joining the pilgrims to attend the car festival and have the darshan of the lord. But due to his evil background, he doubts whether he can have a darshan of the deity or just an empty throne and only the gold ornaments. He feels that his innersoul is strongly purified by his divine thoughts. He is satisfied with the clarification of Bhargava, "My son, a thief may repent and wash off pollution". (p. 121). The conversion of a thief at the end of the story exhibits Bhattacharya's belief in the basic goodness in each individual.

She Born of Light is a story where realism in life and art is wonderfully depicted by Bhattacharya. The whole story centres around an artist called Dhruba and a peasant girl, Suta. The whole scene is laid in the Ajanta caves and the plot is carefully developed leading to the growth of an artist's mind. Suta is a simple peasant girl tall and well-shaped nearing twenty and she has pretty eyes and a pretty voice. Dhruba, a young master sculptor from a far off city starts painting a picture of her on the wall of Ajanta. The artist's eye captures an unusual quality of light in Suta's personality and so he calls her Aloka Suta or a girl born of light.

Bhattacharya briefly mentions the history of picture making at Ajanta caves. It is believed that generations before, many wandering shilpis came to the caves and made pictures so that the art would be safe from irreverent eyes. The walls of the caves are filled with the work of artists of many faiths like Buddhism, Jainism and the Paintings of Vishnu, Krishna and Shiva. These artists left there the impress of their thoughts, feelings and vision. In addition to that there are beautiful paintings of women in the caves. Bhattacharya describes the artists as "They were casteless in a way, for, Brahmin or Kshatriya, Vaisya or Shudra, they did not follow the caste profession to which they were born, to which they were committed by dharma, the supreme Law". (p. 123).

The first meeting of Dhruba and Suta is portrayed in a romantic way. Suta longs for the arrival of an artist to the cave. The appearance of Dhruba fills her heart with a strange feeling. She feels that though a stranger the artist touches her heart with romantic feelings. It appears that her dream of many years comes to reality through her words, at last, "from where have you come? Ages, you made me wait, needless one". (p. 126). Dhruba also keeps his glance on her with great pleasure, and discloses his love for her.

As an artist Dhruba has a dream to realise, before his union with Aloka-Suta. He is presented as a rebel in advance of his times. He wanted to change the traditional conventions, which neglected reality in art. He wants to give a new realism to art and bring it closer to life. He dreams of making the art inseparable from life. Regarding conventional artists, Bhattacharya comments, "Artists painted not from life, only from memory. The memory pictures gave art a mannerism that had no tree regard for anatomy". (p. 129).

Dhruba who makes a picture of Suta is more interested in giving a new realism to art. Though he is very well aware that Suta loves him, 'he was denying himself life while he created it in his picture'. She feels tonguing for him but the shilpi in him dominates and he calmly goes on with his painting. Even when she agrees to denude herself so that he can give realism to his art, it is the artist in him that prevails. All immersed in his art, he ignores the woman in her and feels happy in painting the trapped soul of a woman. He awakens her to her woman-hood and then disappoints her by his artistic coolness. Dhruba hopes and believes that he will have Aloka-Suta once his painting is accomplished. But he does not realise that she is now mere Suta and no longer Aloka–Suta. After completion of her painting, she quietly goes back to her once discarded lover, the simple peasant Nakul.

The story reveals the deep psychological feelings of an artist and a peasant girl. Dhruba could not read girls thoughts and the crisis of her feelings. Something is happening deep in the spirit of Suta, who is ready to surrender to the artist, Aloka-Suta having given her as dead, whom she loves. The writer comments "She had moved out of the flesh-image that had been hers and merged herself into her other image on the cave wall. Suta remained". (p. 133).

The story shows the influence of Tagore's philosophy, that true fulfillment comes only the claims of body and soul is satisfied. Tagore pleads for fullness of life and reconciliation between the claims of earth and heaven in his writings. As P. Ramachandraiah remarks, *She Born of Light,* another important story in the collection is rich with Tagorean echoes, in both theme and treatment".[18] For Dhurba, the artist in him is satisfied and recognition is ensured, his physical desires can wait. But for a peasant girl, Suta, love is upper most. She could not digest the artist's negligence of her desire. Bhattacharya delicately presents the spirit of a girl with this deep psychological insight.

The story *Steel Hawk* that the book is named after, is the last in the collection but not the least in construction. Bhattacharya very aptly coins the word 'Steel Hawk' for the aeroplane. The story brings out the wonder and fascination in the minds of rural folk in India by the arrival of the aeroplane. Simple-minded men and women go on foot in a remote village of Sonamitti and some villagers go by bullock-cart to have a look at the marvel the modern innovation as the wonder of wonders that has descended to their land. Bhattacharya portrays the realistic scene of country side through the riding of an ox-cart and the excitement of the people of village on the cart.

The characterization of Grandma and her grandson, Bishan makes the story remarkable and highlights the effect of the story. Grandma is described as an old woman with countless years of age, and she is mad about the modern tricky machines. Grandma is not directly introduced as a character, but comes to life through Bishan's reference to her. She cannot think of any conflict between her old world interests and the products of new technology. She is as ready to welcome the Steel Hawk as she was when the rail-road first came to the village. With great wonder, she watched the hundred wheels and the coaches made of metal and wood. Through her eyes, Bishan portrays the enthusiasm of villagers at the movement of engine, which reminds them of the iron horse. Infact, she had even saluted to the image of wonder as one did to God and expressed her feelings as, "Truly, such a thing exists to this I must have earned merit by a hundred and one good deeds". (p. 139).

In this story, Bhattacharya highlights the blending of the old and the new, the ideal and the real elements in Indian life today. Through perfect symbols he presents the synthesis of the ancient and the modern. The 'cart' signifies the old and the people of the village considered it as ideal, whereas the 'Steel Hawk' stands for the modern that is very much real today. Grandma is the virtual symbol of synthesis of old and new. She represents the old, traditional out look of the past, but she is not altogether rigid in her attitude toward the modern technology. In her early youth, she had felt immensely happy at the sight of a railway engine. Even in her old age she is the admirer of the new inventions of modern science. She is very anxious to know about the 'flying wonder' which catches her spirit. The author comments about the changes in the attitude of people like her, "She who was of yesterday was possessed by Today, then how could one who was of today be otherwise?" (p. 142)

The character of Bishan in the story presents the synthesis of the traditional and the modern elements. As a village cartman, he represents the old way of life but he does not adhere rigidly to the ancient ideals and attitudes. He broods over the implications of the new culture and tries to answer for himself the question, "Why must speed greedily eat up farmers?" (p. 142) The question focuses on the issues, which are real to people like him in the village. They may feel that these machines and their speed are going to kill the thrilling of the village life. The journey in the skypath makes the people miss many things on the road like talking to the folks, plucking blooms from fields and watching greenery on earth.

But the modern age has influenced his mind and he imagines that he is enjoying the ride with his grandma in the sky. His fancy reveals the acceptance of modernism by the older and younger generations of India. Commenting on his reveries, the author remarks, "for the cartman of Sonamitti village had yielded to the impulse of the age and was riding the Steel Hawk with his Grandma, Zooming away mightily". (p. 143).

Bhattacharya refers to the customs and ideas of the old people in one village. After hearing the wonder of modern aeroplanes, grandma thinks about the existence of flying things even in the Ramayana the epic of the olden times. Grandma sums up the philosophy of life as "Life is a great wheel. It spins slowly in the stream of time a finger width in a hundred years. Things on top get lost to the view with the wheel's turning but, as time flows on, they rise again". (p. 140) Through his characters, the author not only presents the human nature but also the nature of animals and birds. The innocent child Babla questions her mother "What happens if birds attack the flying wonder?" The mother replies, "Birds have no malice darling. They have clean thoughts". (p. 141). This shows Bhattcharya's perception of earthly creatures including human and animal. He touches upon all aspects of life right from the Ox-riding to the heights of Hindu Philosophy.

Bhattacharya's short-stories have an independent concern of their own. His volume of *Steel Hawk and Others Stories* covers a wide range of theme and tone and they show the author's keen sense of perception. The stories are named for their varied topics ranging from the natural instincts of a monkey rope-dancing to the depths of philosophy. He continued his dictum that Art must have a social purpose even in the short stories. With the background of realities of life, his stories attempt a genuine reform of the society. This is a special and salient feature of Bhattacharya, which keeps him far above the other Indo-Anglian writers.

Bhattacharya's main view is to bring, an awareness and awakening in the minds of men and women and set things right. We can notice that some of the characters in the short stories have their extension in his novels, and some other characters in his novels find their miniature in his short-stories. Dr. Chandrasekharan rightly remarks. Bhattacharya's short stories on the whole, show his seriousness of purpose as a writer even as the novels do. They give us a glimpse of his personality, his awareness of the human predicament, his interest in what goes on the inner chamber of the human mind and his philosophy of moderation and compromise".[19] (pp. 137-138). As Monika Gupta rightly comments, "With the help of Indian myths Bhattacharaya makes the story of the novel and short stories realistic and expressive".[20]

REFERENCES

1. Henry Holt, *Short-Stories for Study an Anthology*, Henry Holt and Company INC New Delhi, C 1956, pp 1-11.
2. Edward Albert, *History of English Literature*, OUP, London, 1923, pp. 217-218.
3. Humayun Kabir, *Contemporary Indian Short Stories,* Series – I, Sahilya Akademy, New Delhi, 1976, p. ix.
4. *Ibid.* p. xii.
5. Madhusudan Prasad *'Contemporary Indian-English Stories,* Sterling Publishers Private Limited, New Delhi, 1988, p. ix.

6. Sarala Jag Mohan, *Modern Indian Short Stories,* Indian Council for Cultural Relations, New Delhi, 1976, p. 2.
7. B. Syamala Rao, *Bhabani Bhattacharya*, Blackie and Son Publishers, Pvt. Ltd., New Delhi, 1988, p. 114.
8. G. S. Balarama Gupta, *Steel Hawk and Other Stories: An Evaluation* Perspectives on Bhabani Bhattacharya Ed. Ramesh Srivastava, Vimal Prakashan, Ghaziabad, 1982, p. 169.
9. *Op. Cit*, 7, p. 119.
10. Dr. P. Ramachandraiah, *The Short Stories of Bhabani Bhattacharya* The Literary Endeavour, Vol. VI, No 1 to 4, 1984, p. 72.
11. K.K. Sharma, *Points of View* Vol. 1, No. 2, K. K. Publications, Ghaziabad, 1994, p. 86.
12. *Op Cit.*, 8., p. 172.
13. K. R. Chandrasekharan, *Bhabani Bhattacharya*, Arnold-Heinemen Publishers, Pvt. Ltd., New Delhi, 1974, p. 135.
14. *Op. Cit.,* 8, p. 173.
15. K. R. Chandrasekharan, p. 136.
16. Floyd L. Runch, *Psychology and Life*, Foresman Company, U. S. A Scott, 1958, p. 181.
17. *Op. Cit.*, 11, p. 87.
18. *Op. Cit*, 10, p. 77.
19. K. R. Chandrasekharan, pp. 137-138.
20. Monika Gupta, *The Novels of Bhabani Bhattacharya*, Atlantic Publishers and Distributors, New Delhi, 2002, p. 215.

6

Towards Truth and Non-violence

Bhabani Bhattacharya attempts to assess the literary aspect of the greatest man of India, Mahatma Gandhi, focusing mainly on his writings and the influence of his personality on the millions of people not only in India but all over the world. He probes the diverse impressions which contribute to the mental make up of the Mahatma. Being a historian, Bhattacharya is impressed to see a simple man aspiring to undertake a Herculean task of achieving political independence for his country. Gandhi's personality, which exhibits the connection between words and deeds deeply, impresses him and the result is this biography of the greatest man of India. As Dorothy Blair Shimer rightly observes, "Bhattacharya the writer is interested in Gandhi as the writer and in revealing this one particular facet of multi-faceted career".[1]

Regarding the aspects of a writer, Bhattacharya expresses his view that he who wields words effectively for a creative purpose is a writer. He draws a dividing line between the writer and non-writer based on the nature and dimension of their purpose. In the first chapter, *Preview*, Bhattacharya presents Gandhiji as a perfect writer with social purpose. He does not agree with the opinion of a Gandhian scholar, who views Gandhi as a man of action than a writer. According to Bhattacharya, no one has ever used the stuff of words on a massive scale as purposive as Gandhi. He comments on Gandhi's qualitative writing as, "No one has used words with such intense longing to be down to earth on the one hand and paradoxically, to reach for the stars on the other".[2] (*Gandhi The Writer*, p. 2).

As a writer, Gandhi gives an outlet to this thoughts, dreams and dedication through language. He produced his works in clear-cut lucid prose in his mother tongue Gujarati, Hindi and in English. Mahadev Desai, his faithful secretary and companion translated the works of Gandhi from his mother tongue to English. Gandhi's own English writing alone exceeds two million words. He filled the pages of *Young India*, the weekly Journal, which was founded in 1919, mainly with the product of his own pen. Gandhi himself acknowledges, "I write to propagate my ideas".[3]

The writings of Gandhi extend to the periodicals like *Navajivan*, a Gujarati weekly and *Harijan*, weekly issued in English and several languages. The contents of these periodicals are the principal source material for Gandhian study. In addition to this, his works include *An Autobiography*, *Sathyagraha in South Africa, Hind Swaraj*, *Key to Health* and numerous letters written to people of all kinds and even children. These collections are meant for the great and the humble, old and young and even children, which hold a mirror to the writer's personality. The graph of the great political philosopher is not evolved in a day or a decade. Gandhi himself is quite aware of his steady growth and points out, "I have never made a fetish of consistency...As my vision gets clearer, my views must grow clearer....A careful eye would notice a gradual and imperceptible evolution".[4]

Hind Swaraj or *Indian Home Rule*, the work of Gandhiji attracted the highest acclaim even after thirty years of its publication. Reviewing a reprint of the book, John Middleton Murry stated, "The greatest Christian in the modern world is

Gandhi and *Hind Swaraj* is (I believe) the greatest book that has been written in modern times".[5] During his stay in South Africa, Gandhi began writing in his early youth, with an extraordinary measure of humanistic approach. The period of his South African days are a severe self-preparation for his growth as a writer, that helped later in his homeland.

Key to Health, which has been listed among Gandhi's basic books, had surprisingly large circulation in the East as well as the West. Bhattacharya views that History and life-Force became two significant elements that turned into one which made Gandhi to continue his contribution deep down in his heart and led him from untruth to truth, darkness to light, death to immortality.

Though Bhattacharya wants to confine himself to the literary aspect of Gandhi, he could not control his enthusiasm for the various aspects of the great man. Since his fortieth year Gandhi was thoroughly immersed in a kind of Nirvana, passionlessness, which reminds one of Gautam Buddha. Even in the highly sophisticated era, he could attain absolute control over his innerself, which equals him with Buddha. Regarding Mahatma's greatness, he quotes Nehru, "It may be that if many attempts to write his life, they may succeed in throwing light on some aspects of this unique career".[6]

In the *Second chapter, Early Reading and Writing*, Bhattacharya deals with various literary influences on Mahatma Gandhi during his early age. Though his house was filled exclusively with religious works, Gandhi had no interest on them at school going age. Even at school, his intellect was not of a higher range and he rarely won any prizes. His study confined to his school text-books and his lessons were no pleasure for him. But he was not a dunce at school and never received an unfavourable progress report. To his amazement, Mohandas sometimes won prizes and scholarships and he truly reveals about this as, "an achievement for which I have to thank good luck more than my merit".[7]

The first strong influence on Mohandas is the Gujarati play, *Harishchandra*, which laid the foundation of truth in his mind. Though born in a staunch Vaishnava house, he showed no interest in religious beliefs. Bhattacharya brings out the curious circumstances that led to Gandhi's reading of the ancient epic, *The Ramayana*. Recitation of religious verses from *The Ramayana* is to escape from the fear of ghosts, thieves and serpents during his school age. For him, God, Rama and Truth became synonymous which remained in his heart till the end. Even at the time of death, the last words he uttered are 'Hey Ram'.

Though Gandhi's religious belief started only after his college days, it had a great influence throughout his life and widened his knowledge. The Rama of his prayers is not the historical personage of the great epic. In the opinion of Gandhi, Rama is the symbol of the Eternal, who is omnipotent. Bhattacharya quotes Gandhi, "He belongs equally to all. Is their one god for the Mussalmans and another for the Hindus, Parsis or Christians? No, there is only one omnipotent and omnipresent god. He is named variously".[8] Bhattacharya expresses this universality in almost all his works.

The influence of ' Manusmriti', the law of Manu, the giver of ancient times is presented to bring out the cause for the deep roots of morality in the mind of the Mahatma. This shapes the vision of Gandhi and confirms his belief that morality is the basis of all things and truth is the substance of all morality. Truth becomes his sole objective, growing in magnitude day by day. The influence of Shamal Bhatt, a seventeenth century Gujarati poet is a major one, which is reflected by the principles of Gandhiji. He refers to the wonderful lines of the verse in his *Autobiography*:

> *"For a bowl of water give a goodly meal;*
> *For a kindly greeting bow thou down with zeal;*
> *For a simple penny pay thou back with gold;*
> *And return with gladness good for evil done".*[9]

Bhattacharya mentions Gandhi's reading of English Philosophical works and their influence on him. Inspite of his friends compulsion, Bentham's *Theory of Utility* has no impression on the mind of young Gandhi. Henry Salt's *Plea for Vegetarianism*, a book from a vegetarian restaurant strengthened his views and vows to this mother. As the book is reason-oriented, it provoked him to read other books on the subject of vegetarianism. Gandhi is convinced by Howard William's *Ethics of Diet* that all Prophets and Philosophers from Pythagoras and Jesus down to those of today have been vegetarians. Due to his contact with Sir Edwin Arnold, eminent among the vegetarians, Gandhi arrives at the truth that, "the real seat of taste was not the tongue, but the mind".

The vegetarianism that Gandhi discovers in England is rooted in the current humanitarian and socialist ideals. It has close links with the Transcendentalism of Emerson, Thoreau and Walt Whitman. Regarding the influence of Thoreau's works, Pyarelal writes, "Thoreau's thoughts percolated down to him indirectly through the English vegetarians. The well from which he imbibed was thus the one in which the buckets of both the East and the West had often dipped and grated together".[10]

Gandhi's ethical and moral outlook is strengthened by Sir Edwin Arnold's *Translation of Gita* and *The Light of Asia*, the story of Gautama Buddha's life and teachings. Madame Blavastsky's *The Key to Theosophy* shaped Gandhi's doctrine of Universal brotherhood and religious tolerance. The reading of New Testament makes on immediate impression on him and the *Sermon on the Mount* moves him intensely. His principle of Passive resistance is the outcome of the impact of the *Sermon on the Mount*. He unified the teachings of *The Gita*, Buddhism and Christianity to have a broader outlook. The total ethical and moral outlook affirmed in the works of Bhattacharya is drawn from the Gandhian vision of life.

Bhattacharya discusses the, early writing of Gandhi during his stay in London. Gandhi started writing a book called *London Diary*, which constitutes the chronicle of events during the author's stay in London from 1888 to 1891. The writing was frank and rich in detailed information. About his literary effort Bhattacharya remarks "*The London Diary* holds vivid glimpses of an immature but eager youth embarking on his great voyage of destiny". (GTW, p. 25) Gandhi's literary endeavour continued with his contribution to a magazine called *The Vegetarian.* The articles are almost informative especially on aspects of India's dietary ways. As Gandhi is already preoccupied with ethics, his religious reading in London enabled him to achieve a fusion and harmony throughout his life. Bhattacharya rightly observes, "Ethics and religion ceased to have separate identities. Completely integrated, one succouring the other, they became one indivisible piece". (GTW, p. 28).

In the *Third chapter, The Next Phase* Bhattacharya deals with Gandhi's self-searching in a sincere way among various pressures in his life. His life turns at a crucial stage with the offer of a wealthy Muslim merchant of Porbander who has a big business in South Africa. Despite the earnest efforts of his friends, he could not accept Christianity 's claim to be the only truth. The vital aspect of 'Sin' in Christian theology could not satisfy Gandhi and Bhattacharya comments on this, "he sought redemption not from the consequence of sins committed but from the very thought of sin itself". (GTW, p. 31).

Bhattacharya focuses on Gandhi's religious tolerance and his principle of unity in diversity by stating his belief that the *Sermon on the Mount* was not a treasure of the Christians alone but for the whole universe. He quotes from Gandhi's article titled 'Truth is God'; "I have not been able to see any difference between the *Sermon on the Mount* and the *Bhagavad Gita.* Today, supposing I was deprived of *The Gita* and forgot all its contents, but had a copy of the sermon, I should derive the same joy from it as I do from *The Gita*". On the other hand, Gandhi has no delusion about Hinduism. For him the untouchability, an intrinsic element of Hinduism appears senseless.

The influence of Edward Maitland and Anna Kingsford shaped his personality and moulded his mind. According to new interpretation of Bible, "the aspirant to Christ-like perfection must accept self-denial for a spiritual purpose, as also vegetarianism and close communion with nature he should take the vows of abstinence, prayer, watchfulness, meditation, self-restraint, fearlessness and voluntary poverty".[12] The system of universality captured the mind of Gandhi and he started to follow it throughout his life. In his articles, Gandhi stressed the utter inadequacy of materialism and the invention of the terrible weapons of destruction in the world of civilization.

Gandhi's passion of self-discovery is seemed to be realised thorough his close association with a Gujarati sage, Raychandbhai, Gandhi considered him as a great religious leader, who made great impression on his moral views. In addition to this, Patanjali's Yoga Sutra awakened his interest in yogic discipline and paved way for his mental control. Later, the Russian writer, Tolstoy emerged as a mighty force in his life and made him realise more about the infinite possibilities of universal love.

In Bhattacharya's opinion, Gandhi is intellectually more mature and ready to start writing of his own due to his early reading of literature on Christian, Hindu and other religions and biographies of Indian national leaders. It is evident from his two pamphlets, *An Appeal to Every Briton in South Africa* and *The Indian Franchise*. In both of them, he logically condemns every objection of the Natal whites to Indians exercising the right of franchise. He argued "To separate the two communities is easy enough, to unite them by the 'silken cord' of love is difficult".

Due to his contact with the Theosophists who were under strong Hindu influence, Gandhi's religious consciousness sharpened and there was a change in this intellectual status. The Theosophists expect guidance form the young Indian intellect and he is expected to give rather than to receive. He began to study Swami Vivekananda's *Raja Yoga*, Patanjali's *Yoga Sutras* and many other books to help his friends.

Bhattacharya rightly remarks, "This was also the time when Gandhi drew close to *The Gita* which now became his infallible guide to conduct. It is his 'dictionary of daily reference, offering his a ready solution for all his trials and troubles", (GTW, p. 37). The cardinal rules of *The Gita*, 'Non-Possession' and 'non-attachment' became his life principles.

The impact of John Ruskin's work *Unto This Last* on Mahatma Gandhi is dealt with in the *fourth chapter*, *The Magic Spell of Book*. Through his friend Henry Polak, Gandhi happened to read the book throughout his journey of twenty-four hours. When he reached the last page, he had come to a firm decision that he would change his life in accordance with the ideals set forth by John Ruskin. About the great influence of the work, Bhattacharya comments, "Gandhi found in this book, expressed in clear terms, the innermost echo of some of his own growing convictions". (GTW, p. 39)

This book of Ruskin, held Gandhi with so much power and led him towards an entirely new order of life. Ruskin's call to mankind for equality and brotherhood touched something that had been dormant in Gandhi himself. Gandhi acknowledged that the book affected him more than any other in his life. Gandhi himself remarked, "Great Britain gave me Ruskin, whose *Unto This Last* transformed me overnight from a lawyer and city-dweller into a rustic, living away from Durban on a farm three miles from the nearest railway station",[4] Gandhi strongly believed and followed the principles suggested by Ruskin throughout his life.

After Gandhi's arrival at Durban, he resolved to change his life in accordance with the ideals of the book and at once decided to establish a farm settlement in Phoenix, fourteen miles from Durban. Gandhi's associates settled here and lived in the simplest manner. They were involved in agricultural work and spent their spare time to bring the journal *Indian Opinion*. According to Bhattacharya, the Phoenix settlement marked the first decisive step in Gandhi's progress towards his doctrine of aparigraha or voluntary poverty.

Bhattacharya analysed Ruskin's writings in totality and brings out the essence of his philosophy. It may be summed up as a synthesis of thought and conduct, of targets and deeds, of the harmony attained between word, belief and work. It is the discrepancy between word and deed that leads civilization to its doom. Ruskin's economic principles appealed to Gandhi because they supported his own concept of an ashram organisation. Both Ruskin and Gandhi sought the conversion of the upper classes by a change of heart. John Bondurant makes a subtle distinction between Gandhi and Ruskin, "Gandhi recognised the power of common man and placed before him the means whereby he could assure himself the 'Justice' about which Ruskin could only speculate".[15]

According to Bhattacharya Gandhi tried to achieve harmony and eliminate discrepancy between thought and action. By turning word, creed and deed into one, man could become an integrated personality. Gandhi expressed his feelings in 1940 after four decades of his reading Ruskin's work and the vital experiences he had been subjected "If mankind was to progress and to realise the ideal of equality and brotherhood, it must adopt and act on the principle of *Unto This Last* a, book written with blood and tears".[16]

An interesting point was made by Louis Fischer regarding the influence of Ruskin's works on Gandhi. According to him nothing that Gandhi read in Ruskin's works need have suggested the drastic course of action. The fact was that Gandhi himself was ready for a back to nature move and Ruskin pushed him gently towards the great decision. Gandhi himself acknowledged that his habit was to forget what he did not like and to carryout in practice what he liked. Louis Fischer comments, "He frequently read into texts what he wanted them to say. A creative reader, he co-authored the impression the book played on him. He put things into it and took them back with interest".[17]

In *Fifth Chapter, Indian Opinion: The Rugged Pathway*, Bhattacharya discusses Gandhi's contribution to the weekly which formed a basis for his future freedom struggle in India.

Indian Opinion, a weekly journal was launched at Durban in 1903 by two of Gandhi's associates. Gandhi who was the force behind it, finally took it over in 1904. Since 'Indian Opinion' did not accept advertisements, the major part of the expenses had to be borne by Gandhi alone out of the income from his legal practice. *The Indian Opinion* was a mirror of Part of Gandhi's life. Gandhi mentioned about it in his *Autobiography*, "Week after week, I poured out my soul in its columns, and expounded the principles and practices of Satyagraha as I understood it".[18]

The best compliment paid by Gandhi was that Satyagraha would probably have been impossible without *Indian Opinion.* It was the means for the study of human nature in all its casts and shades. There was always the closet communion between the editor and he readers, who sent a wide variety of outpourings to the paper every week. The paper belonged to the publisher and the reader in equal measure. For the welfare of hundred thousand of Indian Coolies in South Africa, Gandhi, who was known to the white people as a 'Coolie barrister', had to stay there, though he was anxious to go back to his homeland.

It was in the alien land of South Africa, Gandhi devised and brought into use his historic instrument, under the compulsion of circumstances. He started a battle against violence in a strange new manner that had no technique except an abstraction called passive resistance and a weapon named Satyagraha (Truth force). To give an Indian name to the instrument, Gandhi introduced a new term to our vocabulary. With vivid brilliance, as a great writer, he contributed certain words to our Indian language. Satyagraha was one such word more meaningful as Satya (Truth) implies love and firmness, Agraha that indicates the force, which is born of Truth, love and Non-violence.

The Journal carried a vivid portrayal of the sufferings of the Indian community in South Africa. The objects of the paper, as stated by Gandhi were threefold: *First*, to make Indian grievances known to the Governments in South Africa, in Britain and to the people of India. *Second*, to make the Indians in

South Africa aware of their own shortcomings and try to overcome them. *Third*, to eliminate the prevailing distinctions between Hindus and Muslims, among Gujarati and Tamilians and others. Gandhi expressed, "The British rulers in India...Follow a different policy. They do not desire that we should come together and become united. Here in South Africa these groups are small in number. We are all confronted with the same disabilities...we can easily essay an experiment in achieving unity".[19]

Gandhi's life during the period 1906-14 in South Africa was not only the history of the Satyagraha movement their, but what Gandhi has called his experiment with truth. He narrated the incidents in the book *Satyagraha in South Africa*. He agreed that it was on the South African battle-filed that he had discovered himself. It was the same instrument of non-violent resistance, which was a weapon to the Indian people, led to the ultimate goal of complete independence. Regarding the development of Gandhi in South Africa, Bhattacharya remarks "It was there, in the heat of the strife, that his personality had attained a moulding that was to last a life-time. He had evolved and tried out in action a new political philosophy and attained a spiritual maturity of the rarest kind". (GTW, p. 53).

Bhattacharya analyses the circumstances that led to Gandhi's work *Hind Swaraj* or *Indian Home Rule*. When Gandhi was in London in 1908, the vision of Indian freedom took more precise outlook in his mind. During his return voyage to South Africa he set forth his thoughts on this subject. In London he had come in contact with several Indian patriots including terrorists. Though the courage and self-sacrifice of terrorists moved him, he was convinced that these acts of violence were no remedy for Indian's ills. The booklet is a severe condemnation of modern civilization and teaches love in place of hate. He presented his intention to replace violence with self-sacrifice.

Bhattacharya presents the philosophy of Gandhi on modern civilization in this chapter. According to Gandhi, civilization in Europe meant nothing but the emblems of material welfare like physical comforts and new luxuries. Such civilization was sure to be self-destroyed. People think that passive resistance is a weapon of the weak, but it is mightier than a sword. The soul force is superior to armed force, which does not shed even a drop of blood. Gandhi stated about this in Hind Swaraj as, "Passive resistance is a method of securing rights by personal suffering. It involves sacrifice of self...Sacrifice of self is infinitely superior to sacrifice of others"..[20] Gandhi specified four disciplines that passive resisters need and they are: *(i)* complete chastity, *(ii)* voluntary poverty, *(iii)* truth and *(iv)* above all fearlessness.

Bhattacharya presents the philosophy of Thoreau and the similarly between Gandhi and the American poet in the *Sixth Chapter, Thoreau and Gandhi*: *Two Ends of a Bridge.* A great man in America, Henry David Thoreau was a writer, philosopher, poet and above all a practical man. His writings are pondered by millions of people and some of them put his ideas into practice. He was considered a great man because Thoreau himself was a man who practiced what he preached. A sense of duty forced him to write much against his own country. He considered it a great sin that the Americans held many persons in the bonds of slavery.

Thoreau was imprisoned when he stopped paying the taxes due to him. During his imprisonment, he put down in papers whatever thoughts occurred to him and were published in book form. Campaigning for the abolition of Negro slavery, Thoreau wrote his famous essay *On the Duty of Civil Disobedience*. In Volkshorst prison, Gandhi read Thoreau's essay on civil disobedience and it went deep into his heart and strengthened his conviction. Gandhi stated "Thoreau furnished me through his essay on 'Civil Disobedience', scientific confirmation of what I was doing in South Africa".[21]

Bhattacharya tries to analyse the thought process of both Gandhi and Thoreau, which appears in a similar mode. The prison house is the creative place for happiness by undergoing sufferings for the sake of their people. Both of them gave importance to soul-force than the sufferings of the body. Their thoughts flowed without any hindrance even inside the confined walls of prison. Gandhi expressed his feelings regarding his prison life as, "The real road to happiness lies in going to Jail and undergoing sufferings and privations there in the interest of one's country and dharma".[22]

Gandhi recollected the words Thoreau had written in 1849 that he did not feel for a moment confined, and the walls seemed a great waste of stone and mortar. He laughed at the locked doors, which could not reach him, they had resolved to punish his body. References to Thoreau continued in *Indian Opinion* even after civil disobedience movement. In 1911 Gandhi published a paper under the title *Thoughts from Thoreau.* George Hendrick remarks, "The Walden philosopher was a practical man willing to practice his beliefs... The Mahatma was especially indebted to Thoreau who defined society and government to follow his consicence".[23]

Though Gandhi and Thoreau adopted the techniques of resistance against a tyrannical state, there was a vast divergence between the problems each faced and the circumstances in which these problems were set. According to the situations, their approach had to be quite dissimilar. Thoreau's sole concern was the individual. The individual in conflict with the state would offer civil disobedience for his inner satisfaction. In this aspect, Gandhi too had the greatest faith in the individual. He asserted that no society could prosper on denial of individual freedom.

It may be noted that there was a wide gap between their respective positions and fields of action. Bhattacharya points out that Thoreau's revolt was a one-man affair. It was directed against a state that was powerful and the civil war for the abolition of Negro slavery was not within Thoreau's sight. On the other hand, Gandhi was wholly concerned with the arousal of mass revolt. His task was to organise the resistance of the oppressed millions against an alien state. The similarity between the two men was the idea of defeating the weakness in one's own self. A second thing was an innate belief in the adversary's change of heart. Both of them keep away from the path that led to violence.

According to Bhattacharya, Thoreau was thinker with nothing in him of the man on a battlefield. But Gandhi was both, in equal measure. Thoreaus's dream of Negro emancipation became a reality only after his death, whereas Gandhi translated an idea into a technique and developed it step by step over a span of forty years. With his soul-force he won the hearts of millions of people and achieved victory. As Bhattacharya rightly observes, "It may be said that where Thoreau's bridge-building stopped, Gandhi's began. And the Mahatma, walking the bridge to its end, stepped off onto solid earth and still walked on – he walked on and on towards the remote horizon". (GTW, p. 63).

Chapter Seven, Communion with Tolstoy, deals with the impact of Tolstoy and his writings on Mahatma Gandhi. Bhattacharya remarks, while Ruskin gave the doctrine of manual labour, Tolstoy led Gandhi to the avowal of complete non-violence. Gandhi expressed his views that Europe mistook the bold and brave resistance of Jesus for Passive resistance, which is the instrument of weak. But Gandhi detected no passivity, no weakness about Jesus as depicted in the four gospels. Tolstoy's *Harmony of Gospels* shaped the views of Gandhi and the meaning of Gospels became clearer to him. Gandhi felt overwhelmed by Tolstoy's *The Kingdom of God is within you* which propagates the strong denunciation of war and violence. The Great Russian writer, Tolstoy's other works that had powerful effect, on Gandhi's mind include *Gospels in Brief, What to Do. The First Step*, *Reason and Religion* and *How Shall We Escape.*

Gandhi was tormented by the same spiritual problems faced by the Great Russian. Apart from the creative artist of the world, Tolstoy was vested with a second personality.

Bhattacharya remarks, "That other Tolstoy, the seeker of spiritual truths and one of the greatest thinkers of all time, drew Gandhi's intense interest and homage". (GTW, p. 65)

Tolstoy's writings, but the example he set by the reorientation of life that he adopted did not only influence Gandhi. He believed that in the Western world, there is no man so talented as Tolstoy. In a letter addressed to Henry Polak in 1909 Gandhi wrote, "I should like all in Phoenix to read Tolstoy's *Life and My Confessions* both are soul-stirring books. Tolstoy is incomparable in chastity of thought. His definition of the purpose of life is unanswerable". (GTW, p. 68).

Gandhi had a great urge to communicate with the great writer and in 1909, he wrote letter to him about the Satyagraha movement in Transvaal seeking his advice on the problems. Tolstoy answered the letter promptly and praised the passive resistance of Gandhi. Tolstoy considered the struggle as the fight between gentleness and brutality, humility and love on one side and conceit and violence on the other side. Gandhi considered Tolstoy as one of his guides and remained a humble follower of that great leader. Tolstoy warmly remarked about Gandhi as, 'a person very close to us, to me' in a letter to his friend.

Bhattacharya briefly mentions about Tolstoy Farm in South Africa. Gandhi's rich and idealist friend, a great admirer of Tolstoy, Herman Kallenbanch, gave eleven hundred acres of land to the passive resisters for their use, free of rent. Gandhi accepted this gift and named this farm after Tolstoy. With his family and co-workers Gandhi came to live here in extreme simplicity verging on poverty. Men and women of several religions and a variety of languages were the inmates of Tolstoy Farm. Gandhi informed Tolstoy about this new experiment in community living.

Tolstoy expressed his pleasure in the progress of Gandhi's passive resistance movement in his last letter to Gandhi in 1910. Tolstoy wrote that human beings should realise the value of love and avoid violence even in small issues in their life. If violence is permitted even in a single case the law of love becomes in effectual. He further stated "What one calls non-resistance is in reality nothing else but the discipline of live. Love is the supreme law of life. That law has been promulgated by all the philosophies – Indian, Chinese, Hebrew, Greek and Roman. It has been most clearly expressed by Christ". (GTW, p. 70) Tolstoy considered Gandhi's work in Transvaal is the most important of all the works in the world.

Tolstoy's call for absolute chastity for both the married and the unmarried, gave strong colouring to Gandhi's thoughts. His life and message, which are purely based on love, are never-failing sources of inspiration for Gandhi. Gandhi believed that, as mankind for the peaceful living will practise time pass on Tolstoy's teaching. When Tolstoy died on November 20, 1910, *Indian Opinion* remarked "Tolstoy is not dead he lives through the lives of his innumerable followers throughout the world".[24] The teachings of Tolstoy were a matter of great encouragement and satisfaction to Indian passive resisters. But his critics commented that his life was a failure because he never found his ideal. Gandhi did not agree with critics and considered the great writer's failure as only human. He regarded Tolstoy's inconsistencies as constant development of his dogmas.

Joan Bondurant pointed out the influence of Western thinkers, Tolstoy, Ruskin and Thoreau on Gandhi. She brings out the difference between Gandhi and Tolstoy by stating that like Thoreau, Tolstoy remained primarily a theorist and has no technique for mass action. Joan Bondurant further observes, "The contribution of Gandhi lies in his transformation of just such principles as these into the dynamic techniques of action, Satyagraha".[25] Gandhi himself admitted that while he had benefited greatly from Tolstoy's ideas, he had developed his own methods and made his own form. According to Bhattacharya, Gandhi acted as a capable pupil who had built upon the foundation lay by his teacher.

Bhattacharya analyses the growing image of Gandhi in *Eighth Chapter*, *The Image Rechiselled*, Gandhi's image was not constant from South Africa to India. His life was marked throughout by slow evolution. He underwent a gradual intellectual development as the years rolled on. Bhattacharya comments, "It was a compulsion of his inner nature that he would perpetually, ceaselessly reassess his ideals and values. No wonder that at different stages of his life, he seemed to contradict himself". (GTW, p. 75) Gandhi followed the path of truth in every aspect of life. Whatever was lost not an iota of truth could be sacrificed. For him truth mattered more than anything in the world. Bhattacharya views that truth was more than the lives of thousands of men and women and even the country's freedom from foreign rule. Hence, Gandhi could adhere to the principal, 'Truth was God' throughout his life.

Gandhi himself grew up along with millions of combatants in Satyagraha struggle and he was vested with more self-awareness than others. Unlike other people, he possessed mirrors to findout his inner being and moulds himself in accordance with the times. Bhattacharya remarks, "It was history that chiselled continuously the incomplete, uncertain Gandhian image". (GTW, p. 75) He had major share on giving shape to his time. The period between 1915-47 is considered as the Gandhian era in India. On the Indian scene, he appeared equally great as a thinker and a man of action.

Bhattacharya quotes Gandhi's writings in *Young India* and tries to bring out the changes in the image as it grew. Though Gandhi's ideals 'selfless services' and 'action without attachment' continued from his *Indian Opinion* to *Young India*, there appeared some change in his attitude. Gandhi expressed, "I long for freedom from the English Yoke. I would pay any price for it. I would accept chaos in exchange for it. For the English, peace is the peace of the grave. Anything would be better than this living death, of a whole people".[26] After the Great war and terrible massacre of Jallianwalla Bagh, it was out of the travial of repression that the new Gandhi emerged.

Bhattacharya briefly mentions Gandhi's contributions to the two great Journals, *Young India* and *Navajivan*. Through his writings in the Journals, Gandhi aroused feelings of the nation for non-co-operation. He called the people of India for the great Satyagraha movement without violence in any form through his articles. After the death of Lokmanya Tilak, Gandhi made his remark in *Young India*, "Let us erect for the only Lokmanya of India an imperishable movement by weaving into our lives his bravery, his simplicity, his wonderful industry and his love for his country".[27] The Great Trail in 1922 at Ahmedabad was mentioned to indicate the non-violence principle of Gandhi and its success even after the arrest of the great leader. When Gandhi was sentenced to six years imprisonment, the people of India showed no violent reaction. Gandhi expressed, "A Government that is evil has no room for good men and women except in its prison".[28]

Chapter Nine deals with Gandhi's writing in Gujarati and his contribution to literature with new directions. Gandhi's articles in *Navajivan* attained popularity and the influence was immense on the public. As Editor of *Navajivan*, he started remolding the language in accordance with his own concept and ideals. He brought about a remarkable change, "In simple, easy Gujarati he addressed the people, directly, argued with them, coaxed and rebuked them…In the process, he freed the languages from the artificiality of an exclusive tradition of writing and ushered in a new era in Gujarati literature."[29]

Gandhi's *Atmakatha*, Gujarati version of his Autobiography acquired place among the best works in Gujarati prose. K. M. Munshi comments about the work, "It is not the expression of an exuberant temperament and has a hard metallic quality. One of the most precious human documents".[30] Bhattacharya deals in detail with Gandhi's *Autobiography* in a separate chapter.

Bhattacharya mentions valuable letters of Gandhi, which are filled with high thoughts. These letters served as practical guidance to their recipients, with intense humanity. Regarding the effect of letters K. M. Munshi states, "These letters have provided him with his greatest instrument of controlling the conscience and conduct of his friends and adherents".[31] His style is clear, lucid, precise, full of practical things and there is no place for imagination. Because of the qualities of simplicity and brevity, Gandhi was ranked as one of the topmost writers of Gujarati. His aim was to have simple and unpedantic language, which could reach the masses directly.

The *Tenth Chapter* is the detailed study of the technique of truth force, which was designed by Gandhi. The entire Gandhian thought may be conveyed through the word Satyagraha. This is the outcome of the evolution and maturity of Gandhian mind. He described Satyagraha as a science still in the process of evolution. S. A. Bari rightly remarks, "Gandhi made Satyagraha a Science. It is a Science in the making there could be no finality or perfection about this Science... It is dynamic, not static".[32]

Gandhi asserted that Satyagraha has two essential qualities of self-suffering and fearlessness. It involves complete non-violence not in deed alone but also in thought and word. According to him, truth is what the voice within oneself speaks and it comes out from disciplined conscience. It is then a weapon of those who are strong in spirit and dare enough to face the opponent. As Dr. M. A. K. Sukumar rightly remarks, "Gandhiji's concept of non-violence is not a fad. It is the only sensible way of life which could make the world a better place to live in".[33]

Bhattacharya upholds Gandhian philosophy of basic goodness in mankind. It was Gandhi's firm belief that all men had the inner capacity to mould themselves, to be strong-willed, to be fearless and true satyagrahis. Gandhi identified himself with the common people and touched the minds and hearts of millions of people and influenced them. Bhattacharya believes, "This faith in the latent power of the common man drew him to the vast masses of the people, and in his mode of life he made himself one with them, indistinguishable". (GTW, p. 93).

Gandhi insisted on the interdependence of means and ends throughout his life. He considered both as the facts of non-violence and they do not have priority over one another. He proved that right ends could not be achieved by wrong means. As he pointed out, it is evident that an end-result attained with violence, as its instrument would have to be perpetually maintained by more and more violence. U. Thant Secretary – General of the United Nations pointed out, "To him the means merged in the end, and the end sanctified rather than justified the means. Here again is a proud thought which all of us at the United Nations should keep in mind when pursuing the goals of the Charter".[34] Gandhi's philosophy of Satyagraha has a significance far beyond the confines of India and has an universal appeal.

In *Eleventh Chapter*, Bhattacharya meticulously brings-out the similarities and dissimilarities between the two great persons of India, Mahatama Gandhi and Rabindranath Tagore. He quotes the words of Jawaharala Nehru, "No two persons could be so different from each other in their make-up or temperaments...Both were at the same time wholly Indian. They seemed to represent different but harmonious aspects of India and to complement one another".[35]

When Tagore was awarded Knighthood in the list of the British King's birthday, he at once renounced the honour to protest against the British atrocities in the Punjab. Gandhi was given the Kaiser-I-Hind gold medal and he too renounced the honour to make his protest. He expressed his thoughts to the Viceroy that the medal was not the symbol of respect that it only shows government's immorality. Tagore too felt the same and wrote to the Viceroy of India, "The time has come when badges of honour make our shame glaring in their incongruous context to humiliation, and I, for my part, wish to stand, shorn of all special distinctions, by the side of those of my countrymen who, for their so-called insignificance, are likely to suffer a degradation not fit for human beings".[36]

Tagore shared his views with Gandhi and expressed his beliefs in the ways of restraint but not retaliation. His faith in

Gandhi shines out in his letters to the great leader. He compared Gandhi with Lord Buddha of the present time by conquering anger by the power of non-anger and evil by the power of good. At the same time Tagore expressed his disagreement for Satyagraha movement. He felt this as a hindrance for the establishment of Viswa-Bharat, the World University, because it could be misinterpreted in the West as isolationism. It would further erect barriers between India and the West on the path of intellectual co-operation. Tagore expressed his feelings, "It hurts me deeply when the cry of rejection against the West rings loud in my country with the clamour that Western Education can only injure us. That cannot be true".[37]

Gandhi answered Tagore that such fears about non-co-operation were baseless. Further Gandhi viewed that it would bring about honourable and voluntary co-operation based on mutual respect and trust. About the English Education Gandhi was worried that if the system of government was evil, it was sinful to let children be associated with the schools it maintained. He wrote, "It was as necessary to reject untruth as it is to accept truth...If India is ever to attain the swaraj of the poet's dream, she will do so only by non-violence and non-cooperation".[38]

Later Tagore recognised the greatness of the Satyagraha movement, appreciated Mahatma Gandhi's urge for patriotic self-sacrifice. Gandhi himself agreed with Tagore's concept of universal humanity and had given the title the 'Great Sentinel' to the poet. Though there are many disagreements between them, their friendship became stronger. They complemented each other's work in several regions and even in the field of writing.

Bhattacharya analysed the circumstances in the *Twelfth Chapter*, which moulded Gandhi as a writer though the was not a born writer. His pen achieved literary power through relentless effort, which involved lot of patience and perseverance. As an editor of the magazine *Indian Opinion* his initial prose style was simple, straightforward, precise, lucid and persuasive. But as an editor of the magazine *Young India*, there was significant development in his writing and technique. Bhattacharya points out the maturity of Gandhi's writing, "His economy in words was a reflection of his fast-growing inner restraint...he now wrote impassioned passages that could set the reader's blood afire". (GTW, p. 106).

The time when Indian writing in those days was marked by pomposity, Gandhi's writing was a sharp departure from the current literary ingredients. He simply expressed what he felt deep down in his heart. His American admirers viewed that the most important quality of his literary art was clarity and Gandhi mastered his medium. His style was perfect for his purpose of communication.

According to Bhattacharya, Gandhi's term of imprisonment at Yeravda Prison gave him the leisure which he needed for his extensive reading. His solitary confinement gave him an opportunity to the outside world. During this two years of isolation he read about 150 books, through the prison library. He read the books on Hindu Philosophy, Buddhism, Islam, The Bible, Social Sciences and Western literary works. The result of literary assimilation could be felt in his way of self expression. His mastery of simple and lucid English and the high standard of his productivity strongly influenced the writing of his time. Indeed many Journalists tried to emulate his style. As K. R. Srinivasa Iyengar rightly remarks, "Gandhi had neither the time nor the inclination to cultivate the so-called art of writing. No straining after emphasis, no colour, no irradiating brilliance. Yet they are Gandhi's words, and their very bareness constitutes their strength".[39]

In the *Thirteenth Chapter, The 'Gita': Impact and Re-Interpretation*, Bhattacharya analyses Gandhi's views and discourses on the *Bhagavad Gita*. This sacred epic has indelible effect on the father of our nation. He preached and practised according to the verses in the song celestial. His wide reading of translations and commentaries widened and strengthened his knowledge. About the influence of the epic, Gandhi wrote, "When doubts haunt me, when disappoints stare me in the face, and when I see not one ray of light and find a verse to comfort me: and I immediately begin to smile in the midst of overwhelming sorrow".[40]

The impact of *The Gita* can be found on Gandhi, through his own, talented way of interpretation. He strongly believed that *The Gita* is an allegory describing the inward conflict in which mankind is forever involved. He regarded it as the fight between the baser impulses and the higher impulses in each one of us. It is the external war not only between cousins but between the two natures in us, good and evil. He considered it from the moral aspect of people. Gandhi accepted the book as a solution to all the problems of people. He wrote, "Some basic problems which are hard to solve, but it is free from any kind of dogma and it gives us in a short compass, a complete reasoned moral code, which satisfies the intellect as well as the heart. It's appeal is Universal".[41]

According to Gandhi, the central teaching of *The Gita* is not violence but non-violence, which forms a deeper kind of interpretation. His logic was that violence is impossible without anger, attachment and hatred, which are the basic principles in *The Gita*. The futility of war was proved as the victories, amid the debris of destruction have produced nothing but misery. The message of desirelessness and self-realisation obsessed the mind of the *Mahatma*. He argued if there is no desire for fruit, there can be no ground of violence. But many scholars challenged the Gandhian interpretation of The Gita. They criticised that he has distorted the meaning of *The Gita*, superimposing on it his own concept of non-violence.

Gandhi has made Karma Yoga, the great principle in *The Gita*, the keynote of his life. Karma Yoga, the path of action without attachment captivated his mind and motivated him to do his duty. He strongly believed that the success of an act lies in performing it, and not in its result. Gandhi in his work, *Discourses on the Gita* expounded the message of selfless action and the means of practicing it. He insisted that one must be unaffected by pleasure or pain, success or failure. He said, "*The Gita* is not an aphoristic work, it is a great religious poem. The deeper you dive into it, the richer the meanings you get...with every age, the important words will carry new and expanding meanings. But its central teaching will never vary".[42]

The writings of Mahatma Gandhi during his solitude in Yeravda Jail for the second time are discussed in the *Fourteenth Chapter*, *Words from a Prison Cell.* During this time, Gandhi wrote a series of letters to the Satyagraha Ashram, dwelling on the Ashram's principles. These letters are known for remarkable exposition of Gandhi's ideas and concept. This collection was issued as a booklet titled *From Yeravda Mandir*. He felt the jail as a temple and Bhattacharya comments that Gandhi's presence had turned the prison into a temple in the truest sense.

In the series of letters, Gandhi stressed the importance of vows that the Ashram inmates are made to observe. Bhattacharya discusses the vows one by one in detail. Gandhi's wider sense of truth includes truth in thought, speech and action. He quotes, "Truth resides in every human heart and one has to search for it there, and to be guided by truth as one sees it".[43]

As a writer, Gandhi poured out more about ahimsa than about any other subject in his letters. He strongly stated that non-violence was the law of the human race and violence was the law of the brute. He has drawn a clear cut line between non-violence and cowardice. He made it clear that non-violence did not mean running away from danger. Non-violence should not be considered a cover for cowardice, but it is the supreme strength of the brave. Gandhi wrote, "The path of true non-violence requires much more courage than violence".[44]

Gandhi expressed his views about the observance of brahmacharya, which is one of the vows of his Ashram. He insisted on the control of the palate and advised the inmates of the Ashram, to eat to sustain the body. In his other letters he dealt with the vows of non-possession, fearlessness,

Swadeshi and untouchability. The themes of 'Bread Labour', 'Equality of Religions', 'Humility' and 'Sacrifice' also dealt with in his letters to Ashram devotees. He wrote about bread labour, "God created man to work for his food, and said that those who ate without work were thieves".[45]

Bhattacharya briefly discusses the autobiography of Gandhi, *The Story of My Experiments with Truth* in the *Fifteenth Chapter*. Initially it appeared as a serial every week over a span of almost-three years. As it was written in Gujarat, Mahadev Desai translated it into English for *Young India*. Finally it appeared in book form in 1927 and it consisted of 170 chapters. Regarding his work Gandhi commented, "I have gone through deep self-introspection, searched myself, through and through...Yet I am far from claiming any finality or infallibility about my conclusions".[46]

In his *Autobiography*, Gandhi records ordinary happenings, which are historical, political, social and even personal. According to Bhattacharya, Gandhi enables the reader to make use of his own imagination by reading between the lines. Without the intention of self-dramatising, Gandhi casually deals with his every day life. Bhattacharya remarks, "As a document of uninhibited revelation of his inner being, these memoirs must be, considered as unique". (GTW, p. 131)

The 170 chapters of *Autobiography* fall under five divisions or parts, arranged in accord with the phases of the author's life, the first part deals with author's childhood days, his education and early friendship, his marriage and finally his sojourn in England. Gandhi revealed his shyness and incapacity for making speeches in public. But later he had completely overcome his early diffidence and addressed vast audience.

The second part is the narration of the way Gandhi began life in India. It consists of his bitter experience in South Africa. It is the record of many fields of his experiences in the new country. The next part shows Gandhi in the midst of the storm that burst upon him during this second voyage to South Africa.

The fourth part of his *Autobiography* reaches a turning point. It deals with *Indian Opinion*, the birth of Satyagraha and training of the spirit. He dwells on his experiments with the boys and girls at Tolstoy Farm and in Phoenix. The last part is the longest in the book and it is set entirely in India. It is about Satyagraha Ashram. The book ends after a discussion of the Nagpur Session of Congress in 1925.

The *Autobiography* is full of experiments of a Truth seeker, who imposed self-suffering for the moral fall of his Ashram inmates. His penance made the guilty ones realise their fall. Gandhi commented about his work, "If every page of these chapters does not proclaim to the reader that the only means for the realisation of truth is Ahimsa, I shall deem all my labour in writing these chapters to have been in vain".[47]

Gandhi's *Autobiography* was known to the West through John Haynes Holmes. Then C. F. Andrews brought out an edited version in 1930-31. In the frankness, the work recalls Rousseau's *Confessions*. It stands for the noblest and bravest character of all times. Reginald Reynold remarks, "The *Autobiography* reveals a very ordinary man who became a saint by setting himself impossible standards and the spiritual power to live up to them".[48]

The *Sixteenth Chapter* is about Gandhi's visit to Europe in 1931. It resulted in cultural contacts with France. Gandhi was introduced to the French people through Romain Rolland's work *Biography* (1924). The establishment of International Study Group in Paris followed his visit. As a result several studies of Gandhi were produced in French. Pere Regamey stated that it was Gandhi who shook the Christians out of their lethargy and recalled to them the Gospel of the master of non-violence.

C. F. Andrews, Henry Polak, John Haynes Holmes and many others at London, warmly welcomed Gandhi. In a welcome address at the meeting, the distinguished author Laurence Houseman said, "We welcome you as bringing something which is not generally understood, the unification of politics and religion...You are a strange man. You are strange to many, even in your own country".[49] In London, Gandhi stayed at Kingsley Hall in preference to sumptuous quarters because it was situated in an area where the poor lived and was dedicated to their service. Muriel Lester, who stayed at Sabarmati Ashram during 1926-27, ran the centre of social workers, Kingsley Hall.

Bhattacharya states that Gandhi's visit to Europe was to interpret India to the people of Britain and to meet the best minds of the country. The writers and other intellectuals who established contact with him included George Bernard Shaw, Charlie Chaplin, Harold Laski, Lloyd George, and Francis Yeats – Brown, Randolph Churchill and many others. Gandhi's contact with the Oxford intellectuals served the purpose of a true cultural exchange.

During his visit, Gandhi was impressed by Maria Montessori's Training College and expressed his warm appreciation. In a great reception given to him by the Vegetarian society, Gandhi emphasised on the physical and moral consequences of vegetarianism. Regarding Gandhi's personal contacts with British intellectuals, C. F. Andrews points out, "His unique personality gripped the best English minds and his originality of thought set those whom he met thinking as they had never done before. They were not always in agreements with him; but they all immensely respected the greatness of soul which they found in him".[50]

Bhattacharya devoted a whole chapter to discuss Romain Rolland's biography of Gandhi, *Mahatma Gandhi*, subtitled, *The Man Who Became One with the Universal Being*. This work was translated to several European languages and had a wide circulation. Through this book, Gandhi was being presented to Western readers for the first time. For his work on Gandhi Rolland greatly benefited from conversations with Tagore, C. F. Andrews, Madeliene Slade (Mirabehn) and others. Bhattacharya considers Romain Rolland as great a man as Gandhi. He was well known for his humanism during the First Word War. He quotes Rolland's words, "For one year, I have been rich in enemies. Let me say this to them: They can hate me, but they will not teach me to hate".[51]

Romain Rolland's internationalism forced him into exile from his homeland, France to Switzerland. He viewed Gandhi as a unique personality who had transformed a vision into reality. He wrote biographies of the two great saints of India, Sri Ramakrishna Paramahamsa and Swami Vivekananda. His biography of Gandhi interprets the message of non-violence and the spirit of soul. He stated, "Gandhi is more than a word; he is an example. He incarnates the spirit of his people...If the spirit of India now surges forth from temples and forests, it is because it holds the message for which the world is sighing..."[52]

Bhattacharya mentions a significant outcome of Romain Rolland's book on Gandhi. The work has tremendous effect on Miss. Madeleine Slade, the daughter of a British admiral. It brought a spiritual awakening in her and changed her life. She stated that the book made her soul follow the path of Truth. Later she came to Sabarmati Ashram and dedicated herself completely for the service of India. She was called Mirabehn by Gandhi. In a letter to Roland, Gandhi wrote, "What a treasure you have sent me! I shall try to be worthy of the great trust. I shall...assist her to become a bridge between East and West".[53]

When Rolland questioned Gandhi about his opinion on God, Gandhi answered that though in his early youth he considered God is Truth, later he changed his opinion. He observed that 'Truth is God' rather than 'God is Truth'. As he considered God as an eternal principle, he viewed that Truth is the basic principle in the nature. Bhattacharya comments that Romain Rolland found his ideas in Gandhism and expressed his strong faith throughout his life.

In *Eighteenth Chapter*, Bhattacharya quotes some hymns and songs, which were recited at the Sabarmati Ashram during prayer time. The hymns include passages from *The Gita* and *The Upanishads*. They stressed the triumph of Truth and the emptiness of material possessions. Gandhi issued a small book titled *Ashram Bhajanavali* which showed his universalism. It includes songs of Tulsidas, Surdas, Kabir, Nanak, Mira, Narasimha Mehta and some other writers. These songs exhibit universal brotherhood, self-purification and renunciation. In addition to these, Gandhi was interested in the poems of Rabinadranath Tagore and he translated some of them into English, Gujarati and Marati. He was deeply moved by some Christian hymns and Shelley's *The Mask of Anarchy*. Gandhi loved reciting the lines as they touched his heart and satisfied his soul.

The emergence and the success of the new weekly *Harijan* is discussed in the *Nineteenth Chapter*. During Civil Disobedience Movement, Gandhi established Harijan Sevak Sangh (Servants of the Untouchables Society) and launched the weekly *Harijan*. It was devoted mainly for the welfare of the untouchables. Bhattacharya states that initially Gandhi used the word asprishya but later an untouchable correspondent suggested the name Harijan. The weekly was devoted for the cause of rural reconstruction, problems of nutrition and politics was excluded.

Bhattacharya points out, "Once in a while, *Harijan* was enriched by Gandhi's depiction of the human scene out of his experiences". (GTW, p. 188) Gandhi wrote an article, *Kaumudi's Renunciation*, which was his experience during his tour in South India for collecting Harijan welfare fund. It was about a girl's donation of all her gold ornaments at Calicut. During the Second World War, Gandhi appealed to the British, through his article titled *To Every Briton*. He appealed to adopt the method of non-violence instead of war, "I do not want Britain to be defeated, nor do I want her to be victorious in a trial of brute strength...I want you to fight Nazism without arms or with non-violent arms".[54]

In 1942, when 'Do or Die' movement started, the Government confiscated the old files of *Harijan* and destroyed them. Later the weekly was revived in 1946 and was devoted to the major issues of feeding and clothing and the problem of communal frenzy. When some ideological differences aroused between Gandhi and his colleagues, he expressed the idea of closing down *Harijan* rather than compromise.

Though Gandhi revolted against imperialist rule of the British, he realised the importance of English language. When there was a complaint that English edition of *Harijan* was getting more importance than the Indian language editions, Gandhi did not agree to stop the English edition. Regarding the value of English language, Gandhi observed, "As Hindustani is the national language of the country, so is English the language of the world. Its international position cannot be disputed. Imperialist rule of the Englishman will go, because it was and is, an evil. But the superior role of the English language cannot go".[55] the periodical *Harijan* had a number of article which convey the essence of Gandhian principles.

In *Twentieth Chapter*, Bhattacharya discusses Gandhi's important Book, Hind Swaraj published in 1908. The new editions of the work were came out in 1921 and 1938 in *The Aryan Path*. Bhattacharya briefly mentions the responses of Western scholars like G. D. H. Cole, John Middleton Murry, Gerald Heard, J. D. Beresford, Claude Hougton and Irene Rathbone to the new edition after 30 years.

Mr. Cole in his article agrees with Gandhi's view regarding rejection of Western civilization not only for India but also for all humanity. Gerald Heard accepts Gandhian idea that non-violence is the weapon not of the weak but of the strong. Claude Houghton highlights the themes of *Hind Swaraj*, the misfortune of influence of Western civilization on India and the supreme power of love.

John Middleton Murry calls *Hind Swaraj* a great book with clarity and beauty. Bhattacharya views that Murry sees no essential difference between Gandhi's vision of real Swaraj and the Christian vision of the Kingdom of Heaven. John Middleton Murry states, "The greatest Christian teacher in the modern world is Gandhi; and Hind Swaraj (I believe) the greatest book that has been written in modern times".[56] The novelist, Irene Rathbone, impressed by Gandhi's doctrine of passive resistance based on fearlessness and she treats Gandhi and his words equal to Christ's, the son of God. In this chapter, Bhattacharya presents a different viewpoint of Western writers about Gandhi's work *Hind Swaraj*.

Literary Pilgrimage is the *Twenty First Chapter* in which Bhattacharya presents Gandhi's visits to Santiniketan after his return from South Africa along with the Phoenix students. In 1915 Gandhi planned to set up an Ashram which would be a projection of Phoenix in India. Till then they had temporary abode at Tagore's Santiniketan. According to Bhabani Bhattacharya, "Two of India's greatest men met at last. It was a memorable moment in India's cultural history". (GTW, p. 204) Inspite of ideological differences, their bonds of affection and regard for each other remained forever.

Gandhi's second visit to Santiniketan in 1925 showed his interest towards the system of education founded by Tagore. At the same time Tagore was attracted towards Gandhian principles of Truth and non-violence. He paid a visit to Sabarmati Ashram in 1930. To the inmates of the Ashram, he gave a message, "The sacrifice needed for serving our country must not be mere emotional enthusiasm, which is a sort of luxury, it must be a severe discipline of truth".[57]

On the issue of the Communal Award, Gandhi began his fast unto death and wrote to Gurudev, asking his blessing for the noble cause. Their personal relationship deepened and in the year 1932, Tagore undertook the long journey to Poona to be at Gandhi's bedside and extend his support. When Tagore was in a crucial stage regarding financial support for Viswa Bharati, Gandhi came there to assist him. Gandhi gave an impression of his visit, "The visit to Santiniketan was a pilgrimage to me...Old age has made no difference to the elasticity of (Gurudev's) mind...In my reply to his touching appeal, I have promised all the assistance".[58] Bhattacharya comments that the last visit of Gandhi to Santiniketan in 1940 is the symbol of their unity.

The *Writer in His Mud Hut* is the *Twenty Second Chapter.* Bhattacharya presents the simple life of Gandhi at a remote village, Segaon near Wardha. It was Mirabehn, devotee of Gandhi, who first thought to settle in a country side and spend her life in solitude. Later Gandhi himself decided to settle at Segaon all alone. Mirabehn built a one-room cottage with open verandas in the village Segaon. It was so simple that split bamboo made the roof of the meeting and the walls were plastered over with mud.

In 1936, at Nagpur Conference, Gandhi announced his intention to live in the village, "My heart is in the villages...I have been asking (my) co-workers to go and settle in villages and to serve the villagers. I feel that I cannot do so effectively, until I go and settle in a village myself".[59] Gandhi persuaded the villagers to support the removal of untouchability. After Gandhi's settlement, his mud hut became the pilgrimage centre for many writers, intellectuals, social workers not only from India but from all over the world.

Segaon is replaced by the name Sevagram in 1940. The inmates were dedicated to the service of the poor. Irrespective of cultural differences the inmates included Hindus, Muslims and Christians, men and women the rich and the poor and foreigners. The daily routine begins at four O'clock in the morning with communal prayers and spinning. On the whole Sevagram was beyond all limitations and narrow mindedness. Stanley Jones rightly remarks, "Sevagram represents the body of Mahatma Gandhi – it is the outer expression of his inner life".[60] As a result, Sevagram became a place of pilgrimage for the intellectuals all over the country.

Bhattacharya analyses Gandhi's *Impact on Indian Literature* in *Twenty Third Chapters.* The simple personality of Gandhi attracted many poets, novelists and dramatists. The principles of Gandhi inspired the creativity of artists and this brought a change in Indian Literature. Regarding the influence of Gandhi, Bhattacharya writes, "He has been what one may call a writers writer. While he produced no creative work of his own, he inspired creativity on a scale surpassed by none. Some part of the best writing everywhere in India bears his counter – Signature". (GTW, p. 224)

Gandhi's simplicity, love for common man, villages and the poor brought a change in the emphasis of writings from the rich to the poor, sophisticated to simple and the educated to the illiterates. His revolutionary thought and practice made the writers to focus on social reform in their works. Hindi literature came under the full impact of Gandhian ideas of patriotism and national independence. The poets Mahavir Prasad Dwivedi, Makhan Lal Chaturvedi, Subhadra Kumar Chauhan, Maithili Sharan Gupta and many others had strong impact.

In Gujarati literature the impact of Gandhi was stronger than any other Indian literature. He gave a new direction to the writers and their prose style became less ornamental, simple, direct and natural. The writers imbibed Gandhian philosophy and adopted it for their writings. Kaka Kalelkar, Ram Narayan Pathak, Mahadev Dasai, K. M. Munshi are prominent among them. Regarding the influence of Gandhi, Padamsingh Sharma Kamalesh rightly remarks, "The writers of their age may be said to have belonged to two groups. There were those who imbibed Gandhian philosophy and made it the main content of their literature and those who were influenced by Gandhi but adopted an independent".[61]

Gandhi's devotee, Kaka Kalelkar successfully handled creative literature in Gujarati, though his mother tongue is Marathi. The Private Secretary of Gandhi for nearly twenty five years Mahadev Desai, probed into his master's personality in his Diaries. In Kannada literature the influence of Gandhi is felt through many writers like V. K. Gokak, Basavaraj Kattimani Inamdar, T. R. Subba Rao etc. In Assamese literature, several writers in prose interpreted Gandhi's life and thought. In the literature of Bengal, Rabindranath Tagore dominated the scene. In Tamil literature, Subramanya Bharati, Kalki, V. M. Kodainayaki Ammal, C. Rajagopalachari, V. Kalyanasundaranar wrote under Gandhian influence. Marathi and Malayalam literature also had strong impact of Gandhiji.

Bhattacharya presents Gandhian influence on Indian Writing in English. The novelists, Raja Rao, R. K. Narayan, Mulk Raj Anand and K. A. Abbas have dealt profoundly with the Gandhian impact. Bhabani Bhattacharya himself was greatly influenced by Mahatma Gandhi. His whole works are ample evidence for the impact of Gandhian principles. Among the biographers, Pyarelal, B. R. Nanda, D. G. Tendulkar achieved great success. As a whole, Gandhian literature in English is vast and varied. Bhattacharya comments, 'The Gandhian revolution in Politics' coincided with a literary revolution". (GTW, p. 24).

The *Twenty Fourth Chapter*, Many Bridges – West to East, deals with the contact of Western writers with Gandhi and their appreciation of the great leader of India, Mahatma Gandhi. Thesis writers built a bridge between West and East. The earliest among them was Romain Rolland, the great French writer. His biographical study of Gandhi as early as 1922 was a pioneering work.

C. F. Andrews, a British scholar was attracted towards Tagore and stayed at Santiniketan. He met Gandhi in South Africa during Satyagraha movement and became his disciple. His book Mahatma Gandhi's ideas dealt with Ahimsa, Passive Resistance, Tolstoy Farm, Satyagraha in India which are still new to the West. Gandhi spoke of him as, 'We are as blood brothers' and called him Deenabandhu.

J. H. Holmes was greatly influenced by the great leader and considered him as a man with the supreme soul. He considered Gandhi equal to Jesus and confirmed to West that M. K. Gandhi is the greatest man in the world. He remarks, "He was everything I believed but hardly dared to hope. He was a dream come true".[62] He wrote on Gandhi in the American magazine and stressed that Gandhi is a saint worshiped when dead.

Louis Fisher was another bridge between the West and the East. He wrote of Gandhi as "One of the saviours of mankind", during his homage that followed the assassination. Gandhi so impressed Reginald Reynolds that Reynolds contributed number of articles about the leader's viewpoints to the British periodicals. His remarkable book, *A Quest for Gandhi* is a record of his earlier and later visits to India.

Bhattacharya mentions about Frederick Fisher of America, who was an outstanding interpreter of Gandhian thought. Influenced by Gandhi, he had lived in India for twenty-eight years. Frederick Fisher said in his Foreword, "I use Gandhi as a telescope through which to view this balancing of forces because he is without controversy, the outstanding personality of the new East. Without him, India, infact the whole modern Orient, is like France without Napoleon, like America without Lincoln".[63] Fisher tried to explain the way, how a naked little man held the fate of the British Empire in his bony palm.

Sarojini Naidu was the most prominent among the Indian disciples of Gandhi, who went to West to spread the gospel of non-violence. She had won fame as the great interpreter of India to the Western world. With her wonderful oratory, Sarojini Naidu has won the hearts of millions of people abroad. The impact of Gandhi can be recognised through the articles of more than fifty famous Western thinkers' contribution to the work, *Mahatma Gandhi: Essays and Reflections on His Life and Work* edited by Dr. S. Radhakrishan in 1939.

In the *Twenty Fifth Chapters*, Bhattacharya throws light on Gandhi's concept of freedom. Gandhi urged for India's regeneration through various means of self-purification. The constructive work for the welfare, of the people was to touch every aspect of nation's life and the village should be the focal point. Gandhi said, "If the village perishes, India also will perish. The revival of the village will be possible when it is no more exploited".[64] The plan of Gandhi was "to wipe every tear from every eye".

Regarding means and ends, Gandhi viewed no wall of separation between them. He could not compromise with his philosophy of life for the freedom of his country. This is evident from his words, "I will not sacrifice Truth and non-violence even for the deliverance of my country".[65] Gandhi insisted that freedom should not be confined to mere change of rulers from white to brown. He was against the doctrine of Asia for Asians. For him, Nationalism is not possible without internationalism. His mission was the universal brotherhood of man without any hostility towards other countries.

As a great observer of events, Gandhi could draw a vivid picture of the realities in the Congress and the divergence between himself and his colleagues. As a result, he resigned from the Congress in 1934 and issued a statement, "Take non-violence. After fourteen years trial, it still remains a policy with the majority of Congressmen, whereas it is a fundamental creed with me...it has not yet become an integral part of the lives of Congressmen".[66]

The *Twenty Sixth Chapter* is titled *Epilogue*: *An American Dream*. Bhattacharya asserts the warmest sanction of Gandhi's ideals outside India. In this regard he presents the success of Gandhian technique of non-violent resistance for the use of the American Negro-Community against the race bar. Dr. Martin Luther King followed the footprints of Gandhi and attained his goal. He came into contact with the life and teachings of Mahatma Gandhi by reading books on his life and works. Dr. King observes, "As I delved deeper into the philosophy of Gandhi, my skepticism concerning the power of love gradually diminished, and came to see that the Christian doctrine of love operating through the Gandhian method of non-violence, is one of the most potent weapons available to an oppressed people in their struggle for freedom".[67]

Dr. King was greatly moved by the idea of Satyagraha and the Gandhian doctrine of "Return good for evil". His struggle for civil Rights of the American Negro was strictly disciplined, attuned to non-violence principle of Gandhi.

Bhattacharya comments, "Dr. King's belief in the basic goodness of man and the ultimate triumph of non-violence was on the same plane as that of Gandhi". (GTW, p. 273) Dr. King became the first person in the United States to apply Gandhian non-violent technique to a social movement.

When Martin Luther King received Nobel Peace Prize, he acknowledged the source of inspiration. He asserted that the approach to the problem of racial injustice has a successful precedent, Mahatma Gandhi, who challenged the British Empire and freed his people from exploitation. Dr. King considered Gandhi as his master and Jesus Christ as his Lord; while his inspiration comes from his Lord, the method comes from his master, Mahatma Gandhi.

In the *Last Chapter*, *The Full - Splendoured Image*, Bhattacharya presents the image of Gandhi through the eyes of world-renowned men and women. He quotes brief extracts from Albert Einstein, Rabindranath Tagore, Romain Rolland, S. Radhakrishnan, Jawaharlal Nehru, C. H. Keyserling, Indira Gandhi, Gilbert Murray, Edward Thompson, J. H. Holmes, Arnold Toynbee, Salvador de Madariage, C. E. M. Joad and Earl Mountbatten of Burma.

Albert Einstein considered Mahatma as a man of wisdom and humility who has confronted the brutality of Europe, with the dignity of simple human being. Rabindranath Tagore remarked him as a great politician, organiser, moral reformer and above all a man for humanity. Romain Rolland wrote about Mahatma, "He has inscribed his named among the sages and saints of humanity; and the radiance of his figure has penetrated into all regions of earth".[68]

S. Radhakrishnan considered Mahatma as a symbol whose purpose was to develop a world – civilization, a world – culture and a world – community. Jawaharlal Nehru regarded Gandhi as a spirit of India, who has changed and moulded the minds and spirits of millions of people. Mrs. Indira Gandhi portrayed Gandhi as a living man who has rejected the politics of the elite and found the key to mass action. According to her, his life is noble and his thoughts stand for timelessness. His words and deeds are the solution for eternal problems and the inner guidance of individuals. In the words of Mrs. Indira Gandhi, "He fashioned his ideas as tools in the course of his experiments in the laboratory of his own life".[69]

Regarding the influence of Gandhi, Bhabani Bhattacharya himself was greatly overwhelmed by the noble principles and their relevance to modern times. Gandhian imprint can be observed in each and every aspect of his literary career. Particularly this biography of Mahatma Gandhi stands for Bhattacharya's everlasting interest in the father of our nation and the greatest personality of the world.

REFERENCES

1. Dorothy Blair Shimer, *Bhabani Bhattacharya-Gandhi Biographer* The Journal of Indian Writing in English Ed. G. S. Balarama Gupta, Gulbarga, July 1974, p. 14.
2. Bhabani Bhattacharya, *Gandhi The Writer. The Image As It Grew*, National Book Trust, New Delhi, 1969, p. 2.

   All other References from the text are Indicated as GTW in Parentheses.
3. *Harijan*, A Journal of Applied Gandhism, 1933-55, Navajivan Publishing House, Ahmedabad June 18, 1946, p. 210.
4. *Harijan*, Sep 28, 1934, p. 260.
5. *The Aryan Path*, Hind Swaraj Number, Sep. 1938, Theosophy Company, Bombay, 1948 p. 82.
6. D. G. Tendulkar, *Mahatma*, Vol. I, Forward by Jawaharlal Nehru, Publications Division, New Delhi, 1962, p. xi.
7. M. K. Gandhi, *An Autobiography*, Navajivan Publishing House, Ahmedabad, 1983, p. 10.
8. *Harijan*, Apr 28, 1946, p. 111.
9. *Op. Cit.*, 7, p. 25.
10. Pyarelal, *Mahatma Gandhi: The Early Phase*, Part-1, Navajivan Publishing House, Ahmedabad, 1965, p. 240.
11. *Young India*, Navajivan Publishing House, Ahmedabad, Dec. 22, 1927.

12. Anna Kingsford and Edward Maitland, *The Perfect way or the Finding of Christ* Preface, pp. viii-ix, John H. Watkins, London, 1923.
13. *The Times*, London, Jan 27, 1896.
14. *Op.Cit*, 6. Vol. VI, p. 177.
15. Joan V. Bondurant, *Conquest of Violence: The Gandhian Philosophy of Conflict*, Oxford University Press, Bombay, 1958, p. 156.
16. *Harijan*, Aug. 25, 1946, p. 281.
17. Louis Fischer, *Gandhi-His Life and Message for the World*, Tauchinty, Stuttgart, 1953, p. 30.
18. *Op. Cit.*, 7, p. 214.
19. *Indian Opinion*, Phoenix, South Africa, Apr. 23, 1906, p. 12.
20. M. K. Gandhi, *Hind Swaraj*, Navajivan Publishing House, Ahmedabad, 1982, p. 79.
21. *Op. Cit*, 6, p. 177.
22. M. K. Gandhi, *From Yeravda Mandir*, Navajivan Publishing House, Ahmedabad, 1932, p. 23.
23. *Indian Opinion*, June 10, 1911.
24. *Op.Cit*, 10, p. 645.
25. *Op.Cit*, 15, p. 179.
26. Young India, Jan 12, 1928.
27. *Young India*, July 28, 1920.
28. Young India, Sep. 22, 1921.
29. *Collected Works of Mahatma Gandhi*, Vol. XVI, The Publications Division, New Delhi, 1959), p. ix.
30. K. M. Munshi, *Gujarat and Its Literature*, Longmans Gree and Co, Bombay, 1935, p. V.
31. *Ibid*, p. 316.
32. S. A. Bari, *Gandhi's Doctrine of Civil Resistance*, Kalamkar Prakashan Pvt Ltd., New Delhi, 1971, p. 63.
33. Dr. M. A. K. Sukumar, *Gandhi and the Bible Relevance of Gandhi to Modern Times* Ed. N. H. Sitarama Sarma, B. Sudhakara, V. Chandra-mouliswar Rao, S. V. University, Tirupati, 1994, p. 91.
34. U. Thant, *Mahatma Gandhi: 100 Years* Ed. S. Radhakrishnan, Gandhi Peace Foundation, New Delhi, 1968, p. 372.

35. Jawaharlal Nerhu, *The Discovery of India,* The Signet Press, Calcutta, 1946, p. 405.
36. Edward Thompson, *Rabindranath Tagore, Poet and Dramatist,* Oxford University Press, London, 1926, pp. 273-274.
37. *The Modern Review,* The Modern Review Officer, Calcutta, 1935, p. 12.
38. *Young India*, June 1921.
39. K. R. Srinivasa Iyengar, *Indian Writing in English*, Asia Publishing House, Bombay, 1962, p. 216.
40. *Young India*, Aug. 6, 1925.
41. *Young India*, Aug 8, 1927.
42. Young India, Aug 6, 1951.
43. *Harijan*, Nov 11, 1933.
44. *Harijan*, Aug 4, 1946.
45. *Young India*, Oct 13, 1921.
46. *Op. Cit*,7 p. X.
47. *Ibid*, p. 382.
48. Reginald Reynolds, *A Quest for Gandhi*, Doubleday, New York, 1952, p. 131.
49. Muriel Lester, *Entertaining Gandhi*, Ivor Nicholson and Watson, London, 1932, p. 56.
50. C. F. Andrews, *Mahatma Gandhi's Ideas*, Allen and Unwin, London, 1930, p. 84.
51. Romain Rolland, *Above the Battle,* The Open Court Publishing Company, Chicago, 1916, p. 18.
52. Romain Rolland – Mahatma Gandhi: *The Man Who Became One with The Universal Being*, Shiva Lal Aggarwala and Co. Ltd., Agra, 1922.
53. *Gandhi Marg*, Gandhi Smarak Nidhi, New Delhi, 1966, p. 43.
54. M. K. Gandhi, *Non-Violence in Peace and War*, Navajivan Publishing House, Ahmedabad, 1949, pp. 318-21.
55. D. G. Tendulkar, Mahatma, Vol. VIII, The Publications Division, New Delhi, 1962, p. 243.
56. *The Aryan Path*, pp. 437-41.
57. *Op.Cit*, 55, p. 4.
58. *Harijan*, Mar 2, 1940.
59. D. G. Tendulkar, *Mahatma*, Vol. IV, p. 85.

60. E. Stanely Jones, *Mahatma Gandhi, An Interpretation*, Hodder and Stoughton, London, 1948, p. 159.
61. Padam Singh Sharma Kamalesh, *Gujarati Aur Uska Sahitya,* Rajkamal Prakashan, New Delhi, 1960, p. 34.
62. John Haynes Holmes, *My Gandhi*, Harper and Co, New York, 1953, p. 27.
63. Frederick B. Fisher, *That Strange Little Brown man Gandhi*, Ray Long and Richard R. Smith, New York, 1932, p. viii.
64. *Harijan*, Aug 29, 1936.
65. *Young India*, Jan 20, 1927.
66. D. G. Tendulkar, *Mahatma*, Vol. III, p. 297.
67. Martin Luther King, *Strength to Love*, Pocket Books, New York, 1963, p. 138.
68. S. Radhakrishnan. Ed. Mahatma Gandhi: *Essays and Reflections*, Kitabistan, Allahabad, 1944 pp. 193-9.
69. S. Radhakrishnan, *Mahatma Gandhi: 100 Years*, Gandhi Peace Foundation, New Delhi, 1968, p. 90.

7 Conclusion

A Novelist Insearch of Peace and Social Values

In almost all his works, Bhabani Bhattacharya deals with various aspects of Indian life. He deals with the social, religious, economic, political and even psychological aspects of India life. As India is a land of unity in diversity, the diversified elements of the country are portrayed and concluded in unity. As B. Syamala Rao remarks, "Bhattacharya presents the different aspects of Indian life-clash between the past and the present, caste and reform, man and machine, tradition and modernity, mysticism and materialism, science and superstition, myth and reality and individual and society".[1]

Bhabani Bhattacharya has made his mark as a translator, a creative historian, a biographer, a storyteller and finally a novelist. His works carried out the nineteenth century progressive ideals. Like other great Indian novelists, his works present him as a revolutionary social writer. Commenting on the attitude of Indian novelists, T. D. Brunton says, "Indian novelist has instead an extra ordinary cultural multiplicity to contemplate, embracing differences of age, caste, religion, wealth and politics.......The novelist is complimentary to the modern sociologist, psychologist even economist (one thinks of *Robinson Crusoe*)".[2]

As a sociologist, Bhabani Bhattacharya identifies and analyses the issues and problems of the society. As a committed artist he identifies himself with the society, and has an inner urge to express the contemporary issues to create awareness in the people. As a psychologist he deals with a variety of characters in his novels, and analyses their behaviour in day to day situation. He peeps into the minds of character and portrays them in a realistic manner. As an economist he insists on the principles of Gandhiji and Jawaharlal Nehru. He firmly believes that the country's economy is based on the countryside, which is the chief source of production.

About Bhabani Battacharya's art H. G. S. Arulandram rightly points out "a novelist then for Bhattacharya is a man among men, gifted with an extra measure of sensitivity and keen powers of observation. What he sees around him creates an inner urge, a compelling need to express himself then and only then a novel is born".[3]

Bhattacharya's first novel *So Many Hungers*! is born out of the Bengal famine and the sufferings of the millions of people. His second novel *Music for Mohini*, is born out of the conflict of modernity and tradition which the Indian society faced after the independence. His third novel *He Who Rides a Tiger*, is born out of the exploitation of the pseudo sadhus. His fifth novel *The Goddess Named Gold*, is born out of the eagerness of the money mongers. His fifth novel *Shadow from Ladakh* is born out of the Chinese aggression in 1962. His last novel *A Dream in Hawaii*, is born out of the East-West encounter from the spiritual aspect.

The characters in Bhattacharya's novels are very much realistic and their behaviour in almost all situations in life is realistic. The conversation between husband and wife, father and son, brother and sister is lively. This shows his keen observation of day to day incidents. He asserts that, "I have not missed a single opportunity of observing incidents, happenings where I can gain something for the writer in me. Most of my characters have shaped themselves from real earth".[4]

It's true that Bhattacharya's character like Rahoul and Manju, Kajoli and Kishore, Kalo and Chandra Lekha, Mohini and Jayadev, Meera and her grandmother, Suruchi and Sumitha, Neeloy and Devjani behave as any other person would behave in a particular situation. He makes his character all flesh and blood and portrays them in their moments of strength and weakness. In this aspect he never turns aside from reality. M. K. Bhatnagar aptly remarks, "Bhattacharya's characters mark the triumph of the artist in their creator. They are not bundles of ideological platitudes, grinding their maker's axe, but mortals who have psychological compulsion to adopt a particular course of action".[5]

There are both positive and negative characters in the novels of Bhabani Bhattacharya. This is due to the objectivity of the novelist in his creation of character. Rahoul, Jayadev, Satyajit, Bhaskar, Meera, Suruchi, Mohini are on the positive side. Samarendra Basu, Seth Shamsundar, Kalo, Walt Greson are examples of the negative side, While creating the different type of persons, the main aspect is the touch of human instinct, which is the basic for life. As Bhabani Bhattacharya writes , "The most heroic character must have his feet on common earth; and the dastardly villain, even more difficult to create, needs to be redeemed by the 'human touch'. Otherwise, credibility is lost".[6]

While handling the male and female characters in his fiction Bhabani Bhattacharya focuses special individuals as symbols. Kajoli is the symbol of Mother India, Mohini is the symbol of Modern India, Meera is the symbol of newly won freedom, Suruchi is the symbol of unity in diversity and Sumita is the symbol of an ideal woman. All these women characters are dynamic and brave enough to take active steps.

In the fiction of Bhabani Bhattacharya men derive motivation and inspiration from women. The role of women in Indian society and in a family is complex and multidimensional. She is the heart of family life and renders her duties as wife, daughter, mother, daughter-in-law and mother in law and finally grandmother. In the fiction of Bhattacharya woman plays a vital role for the maintenance of values in the family. As Marlene fisher points out, "In one after the other, from *So Many Hungers*! to *Shadow from Ladakh*,-women are either the central character themselves, are of atleast equal importance with the male characters, or provide the inspiration and meaning from which a man derive his strength".[7]

The women share many qualities in common with men such as maturity, compassion, love, suffering, courage, support, sacrifice, independence of will, charm and a sense of responsibility, they crave for fulfillment as women and as responsible human beings in a community. His characterization of women in this fiction shows his bios. He openly admits, "I think the women of India have more depth more richness, than the men. The transition from the old to the new, the crisis of value adaptation, strikes deeper into the lives of our women than of our menfolk".[8]

Bhattacharya presents man-woman relationship very realistically in his fiction. As a creative writer, he has the perception the analytic mind of a sociologist and provides an exact picture of the relationship. He deals with family relationships with high seriousness because the traditional heritage of India gives great importance of the family. He artistically handles the natural tension between man and woman due to the traits of asceticism and aestheticism. This tension plays a major role in man-woman relationship in his novels. It may be observed in Rahoul-Manju, Jayadev-Mohini, Biten-Lekha, Sohanlal-Meera, Satyajit-Surchi, Bhaskar-Sumita and Yogananda-Devjani relationships. As Harcharn Singh Boparai remarks. "In projecting this type of tensions in man-woman relationship Bhattacharya has objectified the psychic conflict between man's idealistic, centrifugal pursuits, and woman's home-making, centripetal instincts".[9]

While Rahoul, Jayadev, Satyajit, Lekha Meera and Sumita exhibit the ascetic strain; Manju, Mohini, Biten, Sohanlal, Suruchi and Bhashkar reflect the aesthetic strain in them. This tension is epitomized, in Yogananda-Devjani relationship in

A Dream in Hawaii. Professor Neeloy struggles under the haunting influence of his student Devjani. Bhabani Bhattacharya successfully portrays the basic instincts of men and women, their different pursuits and psychologic approach.

A careful study of Bhabani Bhattacharya's fiction presents a technique of handling two different types of character. By using the technique of contrast between the characters, he highlights the qualities of good and evil. Devata and Samarendra Basu in *So Many Hungers*!, Mohini and Sudha in *Music for Mohini*, Kalo and Biten in *He Who Rides a Tiger*, the minstrel and Seth Samsunder in *A Goddess Named Gold*, Satyajit and Bhaskar in *Shadow From Ladakh* and Yogananda and Vincent Swift in *A Dream in Hawaii* are compared and portrayed to idealize good and condemn evil. As G. Rai remarks, "Bhattacharya has used Parallelism and contrast to set off his characters. It is a favourite device with him. Two characters are usually set in contrast or comparison with each other and there by explained in a fuller way".[10]

Bhattacharya's novels are symbolic in their settings, their characters, and their actions, as well as in their diction. He transforms the reality into artistic pictures in his novels. He creates the events or settings in his fiction for the sake of symbolic significance. The characters in the novels are symbols of contemporary real life personalities. In *So Many Hungers*! Kajoli and family are the symbol of poverty and hunger. Devesh Basu is the symbol of a true patriot, who sacrifices his life for the village of Baurni and participants in freedom struggle. Samarendra Babu is the symbol of Black-marketers. In *Music for Mohini*, Jayadev is the symbol of modern youth who opposes supersititions and orthodox. In *He Who Rides a Tiger*, Kalo is the symbol of evils of caste system and Chandra Lekha is the symbol of victims who suffers at the hands of brothels.

In *Goddess Named Gold*, Seth Samsunder is the symbol of corrupt political leaders; Meera is the symbol of a selfless girl who suffers for the sake of poor villagers. In *Shadow from*

Ladakh, Satyajit is the symbol of followers of Gandhian principles and Suruchi is an ideal wife who supports and assists the noble cause of her husband. As Harish Raizada points out. "Bhabani Bhattacharya is the most prominent of the contemporary Indian English novelists to make a consistent use of symbols in his novels to convey the intense reality of Indian life and present his own vision of a new and progressive social order in the country".[11]

Symbolism is a device used by Bhattacharya to convey a hidden meaning. He depicts the Indian situation after independence through his heroines. The innocent girls Kajoli, Mohini, Lekha, Meera and Sumita all symbolize mother India. They face the same conflicts, tensions and traps and as India. The Pseudo priests who exploit the people in the name of religion is presented through Kalo. The priests exploit the ignorant masses; so that they remain satisfied with their wretched lot under the fear of religion and God. The Yagna ceremony symbolizes the attempt of priests to keep India under the bondage of religion.

The exploitation of capitalists and profiteers in free India is symbolically presented in his novels. The Seth's deeds and thoughts symbolize the blind principle of capitalism which is the root of all exploitations On the other hand, me aims of Meera symbolize the ideals of a welfare state. Narsingh Srivastava rightly remarks, "As an allegory is built on the texture of interlinked symbols, the action in the novel centres around the symbolic names of things and persons which the novelist has aptly chosen to signify the two opposing truths of good and evil or service and exploitation".[12]

Bhattacharya ironically portrays the contemporary issues indicating the seriousness of the problems with a comic touch. In almost all his novels, the appeal is universal. Though the characters are Indians, they are the symbols of universe. As human nature is same everywhere, people have same human instincts, the joys and sorrows, Kajoli wants to lead a happy life with her husband Kishore, Chandra Lekha thirsts for family life and for that she becomes ready to throw away the mask of divinity. Satyajit dedicates his life for non-violence and peace in the country.

In *A Goddess Named Gold* the touchstone is used as a powerful symbol to utilise the freedom for the development of the downtrodden. Minstrel is portrayed as a guide to show the path for the attainment of ideals of a welfare state. Bhattacharya comically presents the acts of kindness and the blind belief of villagers regarding the miracle of touchstone. He humorously depicts the typical Indian rural life and the attitude of the ignorant masses. All the incidents, actions and situations in his fiction have an universal appeal. As Balaram S. Sorot Points out, "The use of symbolism and irony, unfailing sense of humour and sincerity of purpose further enhance the appeal of his fiction which though dealing with the contemporary Indian life, has a wider and universal significance".[13]

In *A Dream in Hawaii*, Yogananda is the symbol of spiritual craving in Indian society, Walt Gregson is the symbol of practicality of American society. Stella is the symbol of search for spiritual nourishment in modern American society. These characters symbolize the good and evil in different cultures. *In Shadow from Ladakh*, the two different places Gandhigram and Steeltown symbolize the necessity of synthesis of cultures and mutual understanding and co-existence. As R. S. Singh observes, "In Bhabani Bhattacharya's *So Many Hungers*!, Kajoli's tricolour sari symbolized her identification with the case of dependent India.......Satyajit and Bhashkar, Sevagram and Steeltown, charkha and turbine, idealism and pragmatic renunciation and involvement – these are juxtaposed and compared to vivify the changes that the history of India has undergone during the past fifty years".[14]

Bhabani Bhattacharya is a novelist of social vision. In his novels and short stories, there are number of incidents which everyone faces, observes and reacts in day-to-day life. The nature of human beings is presented through his first hand observation. From the pathetic condition of Indian peasant to the spiritual discourses of Indian Yogi, there is an element of naturality. As K. R. Chandrasekharan says, "Bhattacharya is a realist and at the same time a visionary. He depicts the eye in the country as he has seen it with his observant eyes".[15]

Social realism is a tool in the hands of Bhabani Bhattacharya to expose the social evils. As a realistic artist, he identified the evils of contemporary society and suggested solution to overcome those problems. He exposed corruption and profiteering in the society through his characters Samarendra Basu, Motichand, Sri Abalabandhu, Seth Samsunder, Jogesh Misra and Vincent Swift. According to him, corruption is the main cause for the inhumanity. The Indian society is filled with this social evil from neck to heel. From his first novel to last novel, he hints at the evils of corruption in social, economical and political fields.

Bhattacharya predicts the modern corruption and criminalisation of politics immediately after Independence. He hints at hoarding and black marketing at the cost of millions of lives in his first novel. Corruption during Bengal famine results in making the rich richer, the poor poorer. The immoral election methods, the cheap tricks of politics, profiteering, the corrupt practice of bribery in his novel *A Goddess Named Gold* bring the modern political scenario before the eyes. Though the political freedom gives an opportunity to work for development of the country, the exploiting attitude of the politicians leads to social misery. As Ramesh Kumar Gupta rightly remarks, "Bhattacharya expresses the belief that only political liberation is not the remedy for all social and economic evils".[16]

The economic inequalities in the corrupted Indian society give rise to so many social evils. In *He Who Rides a Tiger*, the novelist hints at the flesh trade in the city to meet the demands of body. The poverty in countryside forces many innocent girls to accept the wages paid by the brokers. The evil is intensified due to the greediness of politicians to gain money and power. C. D. Narasimhaiah aptly states, "Bhabani Bhattacharya and Khushwanth Singh in very different ways, give us valuable insights into the pathos of economic improvement, maldistribution of wealth and human degradation caused by political upheavals".[17]

The caste system is the worst evil that is prevalent in the Indian society for ages. In *Music for Mohini* there is an undertone of casteless society. Bhattacharya advocates inter-caste marriages through his characters Harindra and Sudha. The central character of the novel Jagadev also encourages inter-caste marriages in his village. Through the younger generation of modern India, the novelist putsporth the view that the casteless society is the foundation to build strong India.

The sufferings of the poor people in the Indian villages due to the caste hierarchy is the main theme of his novel *He Who Rides a Tiger*. The central character Kalo is illtreated due to his kamar caste. The exploitation of high caste people makes Kalo take revenge on the society by wearing the mask of the Brahmin. By wearing the sacred thread he becomes Mangal Adhikari to hit back the caste-ridden society. As K. R. Chandrasekharan observes, "*He Who Rides a Tiger* is a novel of protest....not only against a political and economic system which degrades the human being but also against an established social order which labels men as superior and inferior by virtue of the accident of their birth".[18]

To overcome the barriers of caste system, Bhattacharya, advocates inter-caste marriages not only at the national level but also at the global level through inter-continental marriages. In his novels, a kamar girl marries a brahmin and the brahmin girl marries a low caste man. Through the character Bhattacharya suggests inter-caste marriages for the welfare of the society. Bhattacharya writes to Arulandram on his opinion of inter-caste marriages, "I have no patience for artificial barriers in human relationships. In don't understand casteism and things of that kind. Nor do I understand narrow chauvinism of any calibre".[19]

Indian society is deeply rooted in blind beliefs and superstitions. Bhabani Bhattacharya has written his novels with the purpose of bringing out a transformation in the attitudes of ignorant people. In *Music for Mohini*, Jayadev's mother is the symbol of typical Indian woman who has orthodox beliefs. She believes in astrology and fears about her son's life, longevity. In order to get a grandson to save her son's life, she compels her daughter in-law, Mohini to offer blood from her bosom to the Goddess. But Jayadev rescues his wife at the right time. The life of Sudha is ruined due to the belief in astrology. Sudha is named as Saturn eye and no one comes forward to marry her. The blind belief of magical powers to talisman and the miracles due to that is portrayed ironically. The public easily believes the trick of Kalo as the grace of Lord Shiva.

Religion plays a dominant role in Bhabani Bhattacharya's novels. Religion is used as a weapon for exploitation in the Indian society. The novel *He Who Rides a Tiger* is mainly based on this kind of exploitation. The wickedness of the exploiters in the name of religion is the chief theme of this novel. Harish Raizada points out, "In *He Who Rides a Tiger*, Bhabani Bhattacharya exposes the wicked practices of the hollow religion exploited by the vested interests to exploit the blind faith of simple and credulous people. It is turned into a spiritual merit in exchange for merchandise".[20]

Bhattacharya respects all religions and never considers one religion superior to the other. He is mainly concerned with man-centred religion rather than God-centered religion. His primary concern is to establish perfect interpersonal relationships through the preachings of religion. In addition to this, religion should be helpful to achieve self-fulfillment. He values the ethical aspect of religion. In a letter written to Malta Grover, he remarks, "Religion is a purely personal matter. It is usually an-opiate, a tranquilizer, but we do need that kind of medication in our moments of tension........far more important are the moral values".[21]

Through his characters, Bhattacharya not only reflects but also revolts against the social evils in the society. In *So Many Hungers*! Kajoli protests against seduction, Rahoul protests against the exploiters. Devesh Dasu protests against the British rule. In *Music for Mohini*, Jayadev protests against the superstitions, blind beliefs and customs. In *He Who Rides a Tiger* Kalo protests against the caste-ridden society. Chandra Lekha protests against the exploiters who seduce young country girls. In *Goddess Named Gold* Meera protests against the political and economic exploitation. In *Shadow from Ladakh*, Satyajit protests against the industrialization and modernity.

Regarding the element of protest in literature, Pritish Nandy rightly remarks, "Protest has always been essential feature of literature. It has reflected the writer's concern, work, social reality and the human predicament and almost all writers have at sometime or other in their protest against the established order of things, to express their disapproval of prevalent literary tradition or social norms".[22] Bhattacharya's fiction is true to this aspect of protest.

One can observe the complex nature of human life and its eternal struggle between good and evil in the novels of Bhabani Bhattacharya. His characters struggle for existence in the society. In this process they face so many problems, suffer a lot and then strive hard to stand firm. Kajoli struggles hard to save her family from the clutches of hunger. In this struggle she loses the members of her family, but she is courageous enough to withstand the problems. At last she decides to lead her life with honest earnings by selling newspapers in the city rather than losing her chastity. The freedom fighter, Devesh Basu suffers till his end but hopes for the best in the prison. Rahoul struggle hard to help the poor destitute from hungry deaths.

Jayadev in *Music for Mohini* struggles hard to enlighten the people of the village and free themselves from blind belief and superstitions. Mohini struggles to adjust with the new life after marriage and to co-operate with her husband in the field of social awareness. Kalo in *He Who Rides a Tiger* faces a struggle due to the caste barriers in his village. In the city of Calcutta he struggles due to injustice and corruption. His struggle for existence makes him revolt against the society.

Satyajit in *Shadow from Ladakh* struggles hard against the evils of industrialization through non-violence. During Chinese aggression, he strives hard for negotiations following the principles of peace and Sathyagraha. As K. K. Sharma points out, "The struggle in the novels of Bhattacharya takes various forms. It is against hunger, superstition, ignorance, unjust forces, tradition, base desires of man, matter with its various manifestations corruption, sin etc. But in the totality of the situation it emerges as a conflict between good and evil".[23] The struggle in *A Dream in Hawaii* is internal, while in other novels it is external. The central character Yogananda struggles to eliminate his love towards Devjani. But after years of practice, he could not come out from his inner weakness and the struggle continues.

Regarding the nature of human beings, Bhattacharya disagrees with the idea of perfectibility of humans. He has hegelian belief in this aspect. Hence the characters in his novels are a mixture of good and evil, virtue and vice. The heroes have some qualities of the villain and the villains have some qualities of the hero. There is a blend of both contrary things. For example in *He Who Rides a Tiger*, Mangal Adhikari who is a kamar by birth, feels polluted with the touch of a low caste born Vishwanath.

The daughter of Kalo, Chandra Lekha is a girl of virtue. But due to hunger in those days of famine, she yields to Steal a pumpkin from the garden of an old woman. Kalo also steals bananas in the train to save his life. When he could not find a noble job, he works as a pimp in the harlot house. Satyajit in *Shadow from Ladakh* is a Gandhian and selflessly works for the welfare of his village. Though he leads a simple life and follows the principles of Gandhiji, he could not come out of his ego and pride.

In *A Dream in Hawaii* Yogananda gives discourse on Bhagavad Gita and preaches others to control the sense. But he himself could not control his urge for this beloved Devjani. He fails to practice what he preaches, though he is a Swamiji.

In an interview with Janet P. Gemmill, Bhattacharya putsforth his view when he says, "Most of us are made up of some good, some evil, some virtue, some vice. The proportions vary of course. But we are never made in the proportions of Rama and Ravana, all hero and villain".[24]

The presence of two different aspects of Indian society – past and present, tradition and modernity, science and superstition, ritual and reason is clearly portrayed in Bhattacharya's novels. His stand is that of compromise or synthesis of both the aspects. He never blindly approves or disapproves. He views the issue in a broader sense and analyses it in totality. There is a compromise between ancient and modern in the novel *Music for Mohini*, charka and steel in the novel *Shadow from Ladakh.* As K. K. Sharma rightly remarks, "In the beginning, the two contrasting values are shown in sharp conflict with each other, but by and by the clash becomes less severe, and ultimately reaches the ideal stage of reconciliation and synthesis".[25]

According to Bhattacharya the bright future of India rests on the compromise but not on the conflict between the two aspects. He highlights the synthesis of asceticism and aestheticism in his fiction. The marriage between Jayadev and Mohini, Bhashkar and Sumita, Satyajit and Suruchi symbolizes the union of asceticism and aestheticism. Jayadev, Sathyajit and Sumitha stand for ascetic qualities while Mohini, Suruchi and Bhashkar represent emotional side of human life.

The synthesis of thought and action predominates in the novel *Music for Mohini.* The very rare union of two contraries is presented through the character of Jayadev. The philosopher has to come down from these thoughts to carryout the work to end social inequalities. Bhattacharya putsforth his views in the novel as, "One cannot live effectively in two altogether separate worlds, Jayadev had said one day to his wife, yet his need for twofold living was inherent in his work. Thought had to be related to action. Abstraction had to be resolved in human terms".[26]

Bhattacharya views modern science as a boon to mankind. Science and technology can change the life of man in a constructive side. But at the same time it has some adverse affects also. He insists that machines should not be the masters of man, but man should be the master of machine. Other wise it will lead to destruction. This particular view is applicable to all times of past, present and future. Bhaskar in *Shadow from Ladakh* insists on the effective use of modern technology while Sathyajit protests it. Later Sathyajit realises the positive side of technology, Steeltown full of machines stands for protection but not destruction.

The influence of Indian thinkers and phiolosophers like Raja Ram Mohan Roy, Swami Vivekananda, Gurudev Tagore, Mahatma Gandhi and Pandit Jawaharlal Nehru's ideals have great impact on Bhattacharya. Tagore's Santiniketan and his ideals of aestheticism occupy vital role in the novel *Shadow from Ladakh*. Satyajit reflects Tagore's world religion, the religion of man while Suruchi reflects the fullness of life. This can be observed from the words, "Integration – that was the poet's life long quest, integration of the simple and the sophisticated, the ancient and the modern; city and village; East and West".[27]

Tagore's principle of harmony of two different cultures is the basic theme of the novel *Music for Mohini*. His views of cross-cultural issues and synthesis form the central idea. This theme of harmony is not only limited to different parts of a country but extends of different nations of the world. In his last novel, *A Dream in Hawaii*, the theme of integration between native and alien cultures becomes the central idea. It crosses the national boundaries and includes international diversities. Through the character of Swami Yogananda, the diverse values of cultures are highlighted. He makes an attempt for the healthy blending of East and West. As R. S. Pathak rightly remarks, "Bhattacharya has treated the theme of integration of values more fully in his latest novel, *A Dream in Hawaii*. The locale of the novel presents a blending of the old and new values of the East and the West respectively".[28]

The broad world view of Bhabani Bhattacharya shaped his views of interculturation during his stay at the East-West centre in Honolulu. He asserts that the greatest need of the hour, the world peace can be achieved only through mutual tolerance and understanding between diverse cultures. As an optimist he tells that most of the problems would be solved through this feeling. Rabindrantah Tagore often insisted on the oneness of different and various cultures. He strongly believes in the ideal of unity in diversity. Bhattacharya reminds the ideals of Tagore in this aspect "I have no doubt about there being just one world. The West and the East share common human values basically. Tagore often stressed the point that unity does not mean uniformity. A thread of unity runs through the obvious diversities".[29]

The influence of Mahatma Gandhi and his moral and ethical values are found in almost all the novels of Bhabani Bhattacharya. Gandhiji's principle of non-violence dominates the freedom struggle of the central characters in *So Many Hungers*!. Devata, the freedom fighter was modelled on the ideals of Mahathma Gandhiji's presence is felt through the preachings of Devata and the words and deeds of his followers. In *Music for Mohini*, Jayadev's village reconstruction and awareness programmes for rural people shows the clear influence of Gandhiji. The village Gandhigram is the symbol of Gandhiji's rural self-dependence and self-employment through small scale industries in *Shadow from Ladakh*.

Sathyajit is modelled on Mahatma Gandhiji's principles of Sathya, Dharma, Shanti, Prema and Ahinmsa. His Sathyagraha, Peace March, Self-sacrifice, Khadhi and Charka movement are typical examples. He describes, the peace mission to Ladakh, during the time of Chinese aggression "The demand for peace will be our only weapon and the faith in the spirit of man, our only shield".[30] During the time of crisis in the country, many people began to rethink the validity of principles of Mahatma Gandhi after Independence. As the enemies have no reasoning ability, the value of Ahimsa is questioned.

While Gandhiji's influence on the struggle for independence is dealt in *So Many Hungers*! the pragmatic view of the evolving Indian society from independence to the Chinese aggression is dealt in *Shadow from Ladakh*. As T. Asoka Rani points out, "If *So Many Hungers*! upholds the Gandhian ideals of non-violence and passive resistance, *Shadow from Ladakh* questions the validity of the very ideals of Gandhji in the changed context of post-Independence Scenario".[31]

The abolition of caste system in India is life long ambition of Gandhiji. Bhattacharya's novel *He Who Rides a Tiger* is mainly based on this idea. The evils of casteism in rural areas makes the central character a rebel against the society. This evil leads to many other special evils in the society. The novelist insists on the elimination of caste hierarchy in the country. The novel *A Goddess Named Gold* is centered on political corruption about which Gandhiji warned the political leaders to cut the roots off. Bhabani Bhattacharya asserts that real fruits of Independence can be achieved by only following the Gandhian way of life. Regarding this K. K. Sharma rightly remarks, "*A Goddess Named Gold* embodies Bhabani Bhattacharya's view that people should strenuously work to secure economic freedom through the Gandhian way of peaceful Satyagraha and procession".[32]

The life and principles of father of the Nation have also influenced the last novel of Bhattacharya, *A Dream in Hawaii*. The basic values of life Sathya and Dharma are incorporated in the character of Yogananda. The journey from Professor Neeloy to Swami Yogananda is treated with the touch of Gandhian values. When Yogananda could not control his love towards Devjani, he reveals his true self to her regarding his honesty of establishment of world centre of religion, even the selfish Vincent Swift could not demoralize his aim. As R. Jha points out, "The ultimate disenchantment of its hero, Swami Yogananda, with the commercialization of ancient Indian religion and Philosophy in the United States of America and his return to India are enacted under the beacon light of Gandhian truth".[33]

As Gandhiji was a nationalist, patriot humanist and a man of religion he not only brought revolution in politics but also in Indian Writing in English. The Gandhian influence has brought vital themes and elegant portrayal of character in the novels of Indo-Anglian writers. The actual Indian with simplicity and nobility is brought out with sincerity. R. K. Narayan and MulkRaj Anand make Gandhi himself a character in some of their novels. But Bhabani Bhattacharya without introducing Gandhi as a character, makes his presence felt throughout the novel. Gandhiji's ideals are the basic for his fiction from beginning to end. As Harcharns Singh Boparai observes, "Bhattacharya has critically examined the continuing impact of various aspects of Gandhism in post-independence India. Thus Bhattacharya's response to the Gandhian phenomenon is more comprehensive than that of his contemporaries".[34]

As a historian, Bhattacharya carefully observes and analyses the current events with the experience of the past. History includes only the past story of humanity and a series of events which are sometimes remote and sometimes immediate. Through his fiction, Bhattacharya presents the cause and effects of historical happenings and warns the humanity to be cautious about the present events. The historical interpretation is prominent for the treatment of contemporary events. The evils of second world were in his novels caution people about the dangers of famine, hunger and exploitation. As Mallikarjun Patil remarks "like Dickens, Tolstoy and Anand, Bhabani Bhattacharya portrays a historical cataclysm in a way that does not look historical but present always. It is a fascinating tale told for the present mankind not to imitate the evil motifs of the last generations".[35]

According to Bhattacharya, the modern India novelists have not been able to write books on the theme of the two world wars, the crisis on the borders, the freedom movements and the partition. But these issues are focused in the literature of the West. In this regard, the Western writers present a contrast to the Indian writers. Bhattacharya points out, "It would be somewhat odd to say that the writers have been too dazed by recent history to make it their material. In contrast, the two World Wars are adequately reflected in the best literature of the West. The writers have lived through history undazed".[36] In his opinion, this is due to the Indian writer's conception that historical events are not suitable subjects for a work of art.

Bhattacharya does not agree with the critics like C. Paul Verghese who think that contemporary reality can produce only journalistic literature. Bhattacharya has wide scope of the modern novel which can artistically treat recent or remote events. He holds that contemporary events can form a fitting theme for fiction. He distinguishes journalism from work of art in his theory of fiction. He views that journalistic literature does not emanate from inner urges and has no spontaneity. On the other hand, a genuine work of art, should have both these elements. He takes Steinbeck's the *Grapes of Wrath* for example and comments, "That good book depicting an immediate and acute problem of the time of its writing, could easily have become brilliant journalism instead, it became a true piece of fiction".[37]

The fiction of Bhattacharya recreates the political atmosphere of the country before and after independence. The focus is mainly on a specific political context with broad approach of the protagonists. It also reflects the political consciousness of the people at that time. The famous speech of Indian Prime Minister Jawaharlal Nehru and the emotional response of the villagers, in *Goddess Named Gold* perfectly presents the political scenario. The very spirits of India during early sixties with the problems of Chinese borders, the attack of Chinese emperors on Tibet are intelligently woven in *Shadow from Ladakh*. As M. K. Bhatnagar remarks, "for Bhattacharya the ethic of 'political art is: a compulsive experience a living image, a dominant emotion and a meaningful expression. Anything contemporary is not denied artistic value purely for the reason of its being contemporary".[38]

Bhattacharya presents the political happenings during the period of Bengal famine, freedom movement and Chinese aggression in a wider human framework. The endeavors of the protagonists are interwined with the chronicle of the nation. As a creative writer, Bhattacharya presents truthful account of the bare facts of history including the names and dates with artistic touch. His treatment of the events and persons of the thirties and the later period projects him as a perfect chronicler, who has succeeded in rendering artistic approach to historical forces.

Being a writer of objective outlook, Bhattacharya discussed the vital aspects of Indian life in totality. Along with the social, cultural and economic aspects, the historical and political forces influence the presentation of his fiction and short-stories. His aim is to transform the society, which is deep rooted in evils. This can be observed in his literary output. As Shalieswhar Sati Prasad points out. "The socio-economic and political forces shaped both the realistic content of the novel and the novelist's desire for social transformation".[39]

Bhattacharya pleads for positive change in the society and in the lives of people. The change must be in the beneficial way, which does not destroy the basic quality of the people. The fundamental values of the Hindu tradition should not be eliminated in the name of modern development. The blind beliefs of the people due to illiteracy should be rooted out. But at the same time the age old traditional aspects should be reconsidered keeping in view the moral and ethical values of humanity. As R. Shanti observes, "the need for a change of social outlook and re-orientation of social values is Bhattacharya's major concern. He pictures the society of today and invites attention to many beliefs and practices which have become deeply embedded in the lives of human beings".[40]

The Indo-Anglian writers for the purpose of their novels use the ascetic as a symbol. But very rarely this character is portrayed as an individual character in fiction. This can be observed in R. K. Narayan's Raju in *The Guide* and Bhabani Bhattacharya's Kalo in *He Who Rides a Tiger*. As the saffron robe generates respect in public, people derive benefits from him. Sometimes it can be turned into a symbol of evil. The ascetic can play upon the faith of man by exploiting his influence. It depends on how the novelist uses this symbol for the development of his novel.

The role of ascetics in Indo-Anglian fiction varies from simple to complex. The ascetics influence the other characters in fiction by their words and deeds. As Meenakshi Mukherjee remarks, "They often solve problems raised by worldly men or bring peace to a troubled situation. This is the simplest pattern, seen in novels as different as Bhabani Bhattacharya's *A Goddess Named Gold*, Sudhindranath Ghose's *The Flame of the Forest* and Kamala Markandaya's *Possession*".[41] The wandering minstrel gives an amulet to his grand daughter Meera and leaves the place. When the situation gets beyond solution, he appears again and resolves the crisis. The influence of minstrel is felt even in his absence.

Bhattacharya writes with a purpose keeping in view the changing needs of the country. His novels covering the period of nearly five decades face a particular problem, his fiction reflects that aspect. The concern for social well being is uppermost in his mind. Keeping in view of the situation he suggests measures for improvement. His understanding and approach of the issues is centred on the progress of humanity. As K. Venkata Reddy observes, "His art being purposive, the novel in his hands becomes an instrument of social change. He has, however, succeeded in his attempt to bring about a harmonious fusion of his social concerns and artistic values".[42]

Bhabani Bhattacharya believes that people everywhere are linked together by certain common bonds. National boundaries cannot separate the common humanity. He insists that the process of interculturation take places, most effectively in Hawaii, which is the theme for his last novel *A Dream in Hawaii*. As a visiting Professor of Honolulu Bhattacharya has a wider knowledge of many cultures. As Cromwell Cramford remarks, "Unlike the monocultural individual who knows only his own native culture, and the bio-cultural individual who has native culture, and the bio-cultures, Bhabani Bhattacharya is a working knowledge of two cultures, Bhabani Bhattacharya is a multi-cultural person who is uniquely equipped to mediate between several groups in a culturally diverse world".[43]

Regarding the language of his fiction Bhattacharya often renders the native proverbs in English. The dialogues in his fiction reflect the rural lifestyle and the mentality of the various categories of people. As a story-teller, he uses many techniques to catch the attention of the readers. He makes use of traditional method of narration and at the same time the modern techniques. As Ramesh, K. Srivastava points out, some of Bhattacharya's dialogues are so natural and so typical of rural life that to read them is to hear them in the vernacular with appropriate gestures and tones while one is transported mentally to the scene of action".[44]

The stream of consciousness is used in the last novel, *A Dream in Hawaii.* The protagonist, Yogananda's monologues illustrate to the readers the thoughts in his mind. He makes use of Indian myths in his novels and short stories to make them more interesting. In all his novels from *So Many Hungers*! to *A Dream in Hawaii* Bhattacharya uses allegorical mode to convey certain spiritual values which are essential for the reconstruction of modern India.

Along with the serious treatment of theme Bhattacharya creates comic situations in his fiction. Even the serious characters like Seth Samsunder and Motichand behave in a humorous way. The literal translation of English names in their mother tongue (Bengali) creates a delicate humour. The quarrel of Mohini and her brother ends in a funny way. The acts of kindness proposed by Seth lead to comedy. As K. Agarwal comments, "He is like R. K. Narayan a master of creating humour through his characters like Seth Samsunder, Motichand and comic situations".[45]

The vision of Bhattacharya extends from individual to humanity, national to universal at large. As a historian, he is well aware of historical events in Indian and other countries.

He strongly believes that the peace and prosperity of the nation depends on its healthy relationship with other countries. As man is a part of nation, he is a part of the universe at large. So, welfare, of the individual depends on the welfare of the world.

The concept of universal brotherhood is foremost in the mind of the author. To achieve this, one should develop love towards the people of other countries. Hatred towards any other country should be avoided. Regarding his world view H. G. S. Arulandrum remarks, "Bhattacharya is a universal man, whose interest in man extends from individual to humanity at large, And so if he corners forward to outline the future of mankind it is because of his interest in man and his well-being and also because of his firm belief that in this complex world, the welfare of the individual rests rot only on the welfare of this society or nation, but also on the welfare of the world".[46]

Bhattacharya is lover of world peace. In the novel *Shadow from Ladakh* which was written during the period of Chinese aggression, he pleads for eschewing war and expresses his desire for world peace. Due to different ideologies, there is scope for disputes over many things. But Bhattacharya advocates that all disputes must be settled at the table and not at the field of battle as that would endanger world peace. War destroys human values apart from other aspects. Condemning and denouncing war, Bhattacharya observes, "war destroys not only human lives but something no less important human values. Modern war with its terror-weapons is as activistic as Tamurliane path of conquest marked by mounds of several human heads".[47]

Bhattacharya presents the evils of war in his novels. War gives opportunities for people like selfish Samarendra in *So Many Hungers*! to find out means of exploiting war conditions. The result was hunger and poverty. There fore to Bhattacharya, war is a mass murder, a murder of peace, happiness, security and above all human values.

Bhattacharya has so much faith in man, so he believes that it is possible to establish permanent world peace. He quotes Gandhiji in *Shadow from Ladakh*, "Not to believe in the possibility of permanent peace is to disbelieve in the godliness of human nature". (p. 82) Inspired by the ideals of Gandhji and Nehru, Bhattacharya pleads for meeting of minds to settle all disputes. In *Shadow from Ladakh*, Suruchi, the Indian delegate to the World Peace Conference explains India's faith and hope in establishing satisfactory peace even at the times of crisis. Endorsing her view a Chinese delegate quotes Nehru's letter again. India and China look toward each other and past memories crawl in their minds, again pilgrims of new kind cross or fly over the mountains that separate them bringing messages of good will and creating fresh bonds of friendship". (p. 10).

Through the characters in these novels, Bhattacharya pleads for peaceful co existence in both the countries. Sometimes negotiations may fail. On such occasions Bhattacharya pleads for the adherence to and practice of the principle of non-violence. War is the last resort for gaining political freedom for a nation and for safeguarding the freedom and liberty of a nation as in the case of Vietnam war and Indo-China war. But it should be avoided by all means. For the welfare of the world, Bhattacharya pleads of eschewing war and expresses his desire for establishing world peace.

With the aim of world peace in his heart and mind, Bhattacharya gives importance to moral values in his fiction. The society, which adheres to morals, can spread the same to the whole world. As K. A. Agarwal observes, "He becomes a moral artist. In his novels he zealously exposes and attacks the social evils of the contemporary society. He concerns with a provocative moral vision of a meaningful life for his common folk".[48]

While presenting the theme of spiritualism, Bhattacharya extends his\outlook from a single unit of society to whole universe. Hence in his last novel, *A Dream in Hawaii*, the setting shifts from one country to another. The thoughts, response and approach of the West are portrayed with a broader outlook. The spiritual craving of the West gives an universal appeal. As Anita Myles rightly remarks, "In shifting the scene from India to America, Bhabani Bhattacharya has shown that the search for tranquillity in religion and spiritualism is not only found in India but the world over. It's a basic human need; one could even explain it as the anchor of existence; hence, the desire is universal".[49]

The theme of permissiveness and occultism in the contemporary, American society is well presented in the last novel *A Dream in Hawaii*. The action of the story is based on Bhattacharya's first-hand knowledge of the Hawaii island where he stayed nearly for three years from 1969-72. After his return from the island, he started to write the novel having gone through experience in the United States. Bhattacharya gained "that knowledge which gave the urge to transcreate realities in contemporary American society: the metallic grip of supercivilization, the behavioural contradictions; the agony of futilities; the search for direction, for self-identity".[50]

Bhattacharya satirically comments on the growth of Science and technology in the West and its impact on human life. The great society with all its splendour in shaken to its very foundation due to violence, which is the outcome of scientific advancement. The young men of America experience the danger far more than their elders. This is presented through the inclination of American youth towards the spiritual movements of the East. The Bhakti Movement of Mahaprabhu Chaitanya is popular as the Hare Krishna Movement in America.

The Transcendental Meditation of Mahesh Yogi is a fast – growing cult in the West which attracts the youth of sophisticated society. The people of West began to realise that the materialistic achievements have made human proved distortions to humanity. The super technological society is outwardly, glamorous but is actually stinking. Bhattacharya symbolically presents the contemporary situation with the animal imagery.

The animal imagery used in his novels, is suggestive of the evils in society. The imagery of a tiger in *He Who Rides a Tiger*. The spider trying to trap ant and in *A Goddess Named Gold*, the hawk; jackal, in *So Many Hungers*! are some examples. In *A Dream in Hawaii* the image of a 'dead rat is crucial to the theme of the novel. It points to the disease of the American society. The image of bee represents the youth that are looking for thrill and excitement in life.

Bhattacharya realistically conveys that the discovery of Indian gurus is first made in the West. The spiritual influence of four great Indian personalities, Gautama Buddha, Swami Vivekananda, Gurudev Tagore and Mahatma Gandhi is felt in the West more than in India, which is the is birth place. K. H. Kunjo Singh comments, "Bhattacharya reveals the Indians' callous attitude towards Gandhi who is much respected and worshipped as a living presence in foreign countries".[51]

Apart from six novels, Bhattacharya has produced a collection of fifteen short stories named *Steel Hawk and Other Stories*. These stories provide insight into the psychological aspects of human beings. He satirizes the hypocrisy in the society through these short stories. His theme varies from comedy to tragedy and presents the realistic picture of mankind. He stresses the philosophy of Tagore even in his stories and aims at fullness of life. He deeply analyses even the simple incident in life and brings out the attitude of men and women.

Gandhi The writer: The Image As It Grew is a work of Bhattacharya published in October 1969 to commemorate the centenary of Mahathma Gandhi's birth. In this work, he studies Gandhiji mainly as a writer. In addition to Gandhiji's writings, Bhattacharya deals with other aspects like the evolution of political issues. Gandhiji's contacts with other great personalities and his influence in the West. He also evaluates Gandhiji's life style and his philosophical ideas.

Bhattacharya achieves a variety of effects by carefully handling it in his fiction. Time is an integral part of Bhattacharya's narrative technique, which projects him as a talented artist. In a work of fiction, time has a direct relation with its structure and every narrative essentially involves some kinds of time scheme. As E. M. Forster observes "the basis of a novel, is a story, and a story is narrative of events arranged in time sequences".[52]

The introductory chapters in Bhattacharya's novels are very significant from the narrative point of view. The novelist places the reader before a particular scene, an occasion, which he is to follow in the course of the novel. In *So Many Hungers*! The opening scene presents the evil consequences of Second World War and the determination of Rahoul to work for the welfare of nation. The opening scene in *Music for Mohini* presents the central character Mohini as a young girl interested in romantic novels and this gives rise to the subsequent events in the story. *He Who Rides a Tiger* opens with an introduction to the background of a blacksmith, Kalo. The opening scene in *A Goddess Named Gold* presents the planning of the six women of the cow house five to launch a movement against the Seth. The narrative in *Shadow from Ladakh* begins with a short scene, which shows Suruchi and the airhostess in conversation which reminds the threat of Chinese aggression. The introductory chapter in *A Dream in Hawaii* opens with the musings of Swami Yogananda which leads to the central theme of the novel.

Bhattacharya employs the various devices of story telling to make his narrative strongly to hold the reader's mind. It involves several stimulating moments that provoke readers. It invites the participation of the reader in the execution of the story. As Lowry Nelson remarks, "Involvement of the reader or spectator as accomplices or collaborators in essential is the curious situation of artistic communication".[53]

Bhattacharya has so extensively used role-playing as a technique for the development of character in his fiction. He successfully handless this in *He Who Rides a Tiger*, in which Kalo plays the role of a brahmin. The growth to awareness during this role-playing comes through many experiences such as his contact with a destitute kamar and an orphan boy, the procession of destitute demanding food which reminds him of his previous state. Above all, the revelation of the fact that Biten is Bikesh Mukherjee who has cast off his brahminism leads to Kalo's courageous exit from the role. As Harcharn Singh Boparai rightly remarks, "The growth of character in Bhattacharya's novels usually takes place through role-playing".[54] In *Shadow from Ladakh*-, Satyajit assumes the role of a little Gandhi in Gandhigram. He tries to impose his Gandhin asceticism upon his wife and daughter as also upon his people of Gandhigram. But in the end he comes to realise that man cannot play a role bigger than his own social stature. Compared to Bhattacharya, Narayan has made a very limited use of this technique in *The Guide*.

From a thorough study of Bhabani Bhattacharya's works, it is observed that he has a prophetic vision. His novels hold a mirror to the current issues and crises. The present conflict and compromise of various cultures is a clear example, which was advocated by him some decades ago. The cultural synthesis propagated by him can be observed in all walks of life. As R. S. Pathak rightly comments, "The message conveyed by the novelist, the message of synthesis, accommodation, compromise and understanding is even more relevant today than it was when his novels were published".[55]

REFERENCES

1. B. Syamala Rao, *Bhabani Bhattacharaya*, Blackie and son Publishers Pvt. Ltd., Bombay, 1988, p. 129.
2. T. D. Brunton, *Critical Essays on Indian Writing in English* Ed. M. K. Naik, S. K. Desai, G. S. Amur, Macmillan, Madras, 1977, p. 214.
3. H. G. S. Arulandram, *Bhabani Bhattacharya's Novels, Triveni* Journal of Indian Renaissance, Vol. 46, Oct-Dec., 1977, No. 3, p. 69.
4. Sudhkar Joshi, *An Evening with Bhabani The Sunday Standard*, April 27, 1969, p. 43.

5. M. K. Bhatnagar, *The Message and the Medium, The Novels of Bhabni Bhattacharya* ed. Monika Gupta, Atlantic Publishers and Distributors, New Delhi, 2002, p. 165.
6. Bhabani Bhattacharya, *Literature and Social Reality*, Perspectives on Bhabani Bhattacharya Ed. Ramesh K. Srivastava, Vimal Prakashan, Ghaaziabad, 1982, p. 5.
7. Marlene Fisher, *The Women in Bhattacharya's Novels,* World Literature Written in English, April, 1972, p. 66.
8. Letter from Bhabani Bhattacharya Oct 1, 1971 *Perspectives on Bhabani Bhattacharya*, Ed. R. K. Srivastava, Vimal Prakashan, Ghaziabad, 1982, p. 19.
9. Harcharn Singh Boparai, *Achievement of Bhabani Bhattacharya, Perspectives on Bhabani Bhattacharya,* Vimal Prakashan, Ghaziabad, 1982, p. 209.
10. G. Rai, *Bhabani Bhattacharya: A Study of his Novels*, B. R. Publishing, Corporation, Delhi, 1995, p. 93.
11. Harish Raizada, *Symbolism in Bhabani Bhattacharya's Music for Mohini Symbolism in Indian Fiction in English* Ed, R. K. Srivastava, ABS Publications, Jalandhar, 1997, p. 72.
12. Narsingh Srivastava, *Symbol and Allegory in Bhattacharya's A Goodess Named Gold,* Symbolism in Indian Fiction in English, Ed, R. K. Srivastava, ABS Publications, Jalandhar, 1997, p. 91.
13. Balram S. Sorot, *The Novels of Bhabani Bhattacharya*, Prestige Books, New Delhi, 1991, p. 143.
14. R. S. Singh *Fictional Technique* Indian Novel in English, Arnold-Heinemann Publishers, New Delhi, 1964, p. 200.
15. K. R. Chandrasekharan, *Bhabani Bhattacharya*, Arnold-Heinemann Publishers, New Delhi, 1964, p. 170.
16. Ramesh Kumar Gupta *A Study of Bhababni Bhattacharya's* A Goddess Named Gold, The Novels of Bhabani Bhattacharya Ed. Monika Gupta, Atlantic Publishers and Distributors, New Delhi, 2002, p. 127.
17. C. D. Narasimhaiah, *The Swan and the Eagle*, Indian Institute of Advanced Study, Simla, 1969, Introduction.
18. *Op. Cit.*, 15, p. 68.
19. Bhattacharya's Letter to H. G. S. Arulandram from Calcutta Dated Feb. 29, 1980.
20. Harish Raizada *Fiction on Allegory: Novels of Bhabani Bhattacharya,* Perspectives of Bhabani Bhattacharya, Vimal Prakashan, Ghaziabad, 1982, p. 90.

21. Letters to Malta Grover, *Bhabani Bhattacharya,* Salabh Praksahan, Meerut, 1991, Appendix I, and p. 145.

22. Pritish Nandy, Literature of Protest, *Aspects of Indian Literature the Changing Pattern* Ed. Suresh Kohili, Vikash, Publishers, New Delhi, 1975, p. 83.

23. K. K. Sharma, *Points of View*, Vol. 1 No. 2, K. K. Publications, New Delhi, 1994, p. 111.

24. Gemmil, P. Janet, *An Interview with Bhabani Bhattacharya World Literature Written in English*, 14:2 Nov. 1975: 302, p. 62.

25. K. K. Sharma, *Bhabani Bhattacharaya: His Vision and Themes*, Abhinav Publications, New Delhi, 1979, p. 96.

26. Bhabani Bhattacharya, *Music for Mohini*, Orient Paperbacks, New Delhi, 1984, p. 138.

27. Bhabani Bhattacharya, *Shadow from Ladakh*, Orient Paperbacks, New Delhi, 1966, p. 215.

28. R. S. Pathak, *Modern Indian Novel in English*, Creative Books, New Delhi, 1999, p. 89.

29. Dieter Riemenschneider, *The Indo-English Novel, Indian Literature* 26/5 Sep-Oct. 1983, p. 19.

30. *Shadow from Ladakh*, p. 104.

31. T. Asoka Rani, Nationalism *in Bhabani Bhattachaya's So Many Hungers! and Shadow from Ladakh, The Novels of Bhabani Bhattacharya*, Ed. Monika Gupta, Atlantic Publishers and Distributors, New Delhi, 2002, p. 35.

32. *Op. Cit.* 25, p. 86.

33. R. Jha, *Gandhian thought and Indo. Anglian Novelists*, Chanakya Publications, New Delhi, 1983, p. 171.

34. Ramesh K. Srivastava *Colonial Consciousness in Black American, African and Indian Fiction in English*, ABS Publications, New Delhi, 1991, p. 42.

35. Mallikarjun Patil, *Bhabani Bhattacharya's So Many Hungers*! *The Novels of Bhabani Bhattacharya* Ed. Monika Gupta, Atlantic Publishers and Distributors, New Delhi, 2002, p. 11.

36. Bhabani Bhattacharya, *Literature and Social Reality The Aryan Path*, 24: 9 Sep. 1955.

37. Iqbal Bakhtiyar Ed. *The Novel in Modern India*, P. E. N. Centre: Bombay, 1964, p. 47.

38. M. K. Bhatnagar, *Political Consciousness in Indian English Writing,* Bahri Publications, New Delhi, 1991, p. 29.

39. Shaileshwar Sati Prasad, *The Insulted and the Injured*, Janaki Prakashan, Patna, 1997, p. ix
40. R. Shanti, *Tradition and Progressiveness in Bhabani Bhattacharya's* Music for Mohini, The Novels of Bhabani Bhattacharya, pp. 74-75.
41. Meenakshi Mukherjee, *The Twice Born Fiction*, Arnold-Heinemann, New Delhi, 1974, p. 103.
42. K. Venkata Reddy, *Bhabani Bhattacharya – A Writer with a Social Purpose,* Triveni, Vol. 62. No.1, Jan-March. 1993. p. 32.
43. Cromwell Crawford, *Bhabani Bhattacharya: A Mediating Man Perspectives on Bhabani Bhattacharya*, p. 11.
44. R. K. Srivastava, *Bhattacharya's Prose style, Perspectives on Bhabani Bhattacharya*, p. 117.
45. K. A. Agarwal, *Mind and Arts of Bhabani Bhattacharya, The Novels of Bhabani Bhattacharya* Ed. Monika Gupta, p. 216.
46. H. G. S. Arulandram, *Bhabani Bhattacharya's World View* Common-wealth Novel in English, Jan. 1983, p. 40.
47. Bhabani Bhattacharya *After Vietnam What?* An Unpublished Paper read at a, Conference at the East-West Centre, Hawaii, March 17, 1970.
48. *Op. Cit*, 45, p. 199.
49. Anita Myles, *Cultural Synthesis in Bhabni Bhattacharaya's* A Dream in Hawaii, The Novels of Bhabani Bhattacharya Ed. Monika Gupta, p. 150.
50. *Op. Cit*, 44, p. 235.
51. K. H. Kunjo Singh, *The Fiction of Bhabani Bhattacharya*, Atlantic Publishers and Distributors, New Delhi, 2002, p. 177.
52. E. M. Forster, *Aspects of the Novel*, Penguin Books, 1964, pp. 38-39.
53. Lewry Nelson, Jr. *The Fictive Reader and Literary Self – Reflexiveness,* The Disciplines of Criticism, New Haven, 1968, p. 174.
54. *Op. Cit.*, 51, p. 211.
55. R. S. Pathak, *Human Predicament and Bhabani Bhattacharya's Integrative Vision, Modern Indian Novel in English*, Creative Books, New Delhi, 1999, p. 62.

Bibliography

Primary Sources

1. Bhattacharya, Bhabani. *So Many Hungers!*, Hind Kitab, Bombay, 1947.
2. ——*Music for Mohini*, Orient Paperbacks, New Delhi, 1952.
3. ——*He Who Rides a Tiger*, Hind Pocket Books, New Delhi, 1955.
4. ——*A Goddess Named Gold*, Crown Publishers, New York, 1960.
5. ——*Shadow from Ladakh*, Hind Pocket Books, New Delhi, 1966.
6. ——*A Dream in Hawaii*, Macmillan India Ltd., New Delhi, 1978.
7. ——*Steel Hawk and Other Stories*, Hind Pocket Books, New Delhi, 1968.
8. ——*Gandhi The Writer: The Image As It Grew,* National Book Trust, New Delhi, 1969.
9. ——*The Golden Boat,* The Translations from Rabindranath Tagore, Jaico Publishing House, Bombay, 1955.

10. ——*Indian Cavalcade,* Nalanda Publications, Bombay, 1948.
11. ——*Contemporary Indian Short-Stories,* Sahitya Akademi, New Delhi, 1967.
12. ——*Socio-Political Currents in Bengal: A 19th Century Perspective,* Vikas Publishing House New Delhi, 1980.
13. ——*Some Memorable Yesterdays,* Pustak Bhandar, Patna, 1941.
14. ——*Towards Universal Man,* Asia Publishing House, Bombay, 1961.
15. ——*Tagore as a Novelist, Rabindranth Tagore 1861-1961: A Centenary Volume,* Sahitya Akademy, New Delhi, 1961.
16. ——*From Social Criticism to Utopianism,* Indian Novel in English. Ed. R. S. Singh, Arnold Heinemann, New Delhi, 1977.
17. ——*Women in My Stories,* Journal of Indian Writing in English. Ed. G. S. Balarama Gupta, Gulbarga, 1972.
18. ——*Literature and Social Reality,* Aryan Path, Bombay, 1939.
19. ——*Indo-Anglian,* The Novel in Modern India, P. E. N. India Centre, Bombay, 1964.
20. ——*Baseless Prejudice Against Indians Writing English,* The Statesman, New Delhi, 1968.

Secondary Sources

Books

1. Abbas, K. A. *Aspects of Indian Literature: The Changing Pattern.* Ed. Suresh Kohili, Vikas Publishers, New Delhi, 1975.
2. Agarwal, K. A. *Indian Writing in English: A Critical Study,* Atlantic Publishers and Distributors, New Delhi, 2003.
3. Albert, Edward. *History of English Literature,* OUP, London, 1923.
4. Alexander, Horace. *Gandhi Through Western Eyes,* Asia Publishing House, Bombay, 1969.

5. Andrews, C. F. *Mahatma Gandhi's Ideas*, Allen and Unwin, London, 1930.
6. Asnani, Shyam M. *Critical Response to Indian English Fiction*, Mittal Publications, New Delhi, 1985.
7. ——*New Dimensions of Indian English Novel*, Doaba House, New Delhi, 1987.
8. Aston M. Nathan. *Bhabani Bhattacharya, A Stylistic Analysis of His Novels*, Sterling Publishers Private Limited, New Delhi, 1994.
9. Badal, R. K. *Indo-Anglian Literature: An Outline*, Prakash Book Depot., Bareilly, 1975.
10. Bande, Usha. *Mothers and Mother-Figures in Indo-English Literature,* ABS Publications, Jalandhar, 1994.
11. Bari, S. A. *Gandhi's Doctrine of Civil Resistance*, Kalamkar Prakashan Pvt. Ltd., New Delhi, 1971.
12. Bhatnagar, K. C. *Realism in Major Indo-English Fiction*, Prakash Book Depot., Bareilly, 1975.
13. Bhatnagar, M. K. *Political Consciousness in Indian English Writing*, Behri Publications, New Delhi, 1991.
14. Bhattacharya, P. C. *Indo-Anglian Literature and the Works of Raja Rao*, Atma Ram and Sons, New Delhi, 1983.
15. Birla, G. D. *In the Shadow of Mahatma,* Orient Longmans Ltd., Bombay, 1953.
16. Bondurant, Joan V. *Conquest of Violence: The Gandhian Philosophy of Conflict*, Oxford University Press, Bombay, 1959.
17. Boparai, Harcharn Singh. *Bhabani Bhattacharya's Response to British Colonialism in India, Colonial Consciousness in Black American, African and Indian Fiction in English.* Ed. Srivastava, R. K., ABS Publications, Jalandhar, 1991.
18. ——*The Achievement of Bhabani Bhattacharya,* Perspectives on Bhabani Bhattacharya. Ed. Srivastava R. K., Vimal Prakashan, Ghaziabad, 1982.

19. Bose, Anima. *Mahatma Gandhi: A Contemporary Perspective*, B. R. Publishing Corporation, New Delhi, 1977.
20. Brunton, T. D. *Critical Essays on Indian Writing in English,* Macmillan, Madras, 1977.
21. Chakravarty, Joy. *Indian Writing in English: Perspectives*, Atlantic Publishers and Distributors, New Delhi, 2003.
22. Chandrasekharan, K. R. *Bhabani Bhattacharya*, Arnold Heinemann, New Delhi, 1974.
23. Cowasjee and Shahane. *Modern Indian Fiction*, Vikas Publishing House, New Delhi, 1981.
24. Crawford, Cromwell. *Bhabani Bhattacharya: A Mediating Man,* Perspectives on Bhabani Bhattacharya. Ed. Srivastava R. K., Vimal Prakashan, Ghaziabad, 1982.
25. Desai, S. K. Bhabani Bhattacharya: The Writer Who Rides a Tiger, *Perspectives on Indian Fiction in English.* Ed. M. K Naik, Abinav Publications, New Delhi, 1983.
26. Dhar, T. N. *Bhabani Bhattacharya's He Who Rides a Tiger: The Role Playing Matrix,* Studies in Indian Fiction in English. Ed. G. S. Balarama Gupta, Gulbarga, 1987.
27. Dhawan, R. K. *Bhattacharya's Narrative Technique,* Perspectives on Bhabani Bhattacharya. Ed. Srivastava R. K., Vimal Prakashan, Ghaziabad, 1982.
28. Duggal, K. S. *Modern Indian Short Stories*, Vol. I, Indian Council for Cultural Relations, New Delhi, 1975.
29. Dwivedi, A. N. *Studies in Contemporary Indian Fiction,* Kitab Mahal, Allahabad, 1987.
30. Fisher, Louis. *The Life of Mahatma Gandhi,* Tanchinty, Stuttgart, 1953.
31. Fisher, Marlene. *The Women in Bhattacharya's Novels,* Perspectives on Bhabani Bhattacharya. Ed. Srivastava R. K., Vimal Prakashan, Ghaziabad, 1982.
32. Gandhi, M. K. *An Autobiography*, Navajivan Publishing House, Ahmedabad, 1983.

33. ——*Ashram Observations in Action*, Navajivan Publishing House, Ahmedabad, 1959.

34. ——*From Yeravda Mandir*, Navajivan Publishing House Ahmedabad, 1932.

35. ——*Hind Swaraj*, Navajivan Publishing House Ahmedabad, 1982.

36. ——*Satyagraha in South Africa*, Navajivan Publishing House Ahmedabad, 1949.

37. ——*Non-Violence in Peace and War*, Navajivan Publishing House Ahmedabad, 1949.

38. ——*Truth is God*, Navajivan Publishing House Ahmedabad, 1959.

39. Ganguli, B. N. *Gandhi's Social Philosophy: Perspective and Relevance*, Vikas Publishing House Pvt. Ltd., New Delhi, 1973.

40. Gokak, V. K. *English in India: Its Present and Future*, Asia Publishing House, Bombay, 1964.

41. ——*Modern India Languages*, Publications Divisions, New Delhi, 1957.

42. Goyal, Bhagwat. S. *Culture and Commitment: Aspects of Indian Literature in English*, Shalabh Book House, Meerut, 1984.

43. Grover, Malta. *Bhabani Bhattacharya as a Novelist of Social Conscience*, Shalabh Prakashan, Meerut, 1991.

44. Grover, Verinder. *M. K. Gandhi*, Deep and Deep Publications, New Delhi, 1991.

45. Gupta, G. S. Balarama. *Bhabani Bhattacharya's So Many Hungers! – A Study*, Aspects of Indian Writing in English. Ed. M. K. Naik, The Macmillan Company, Madras, 1979.

46. Gupta, Monika. *The Novels of Bhabani Bhattacharya*, Atlantic Publishers, New Delhi, 2002.

47. Harrex, S. C. *The Fire and the Offering, The English – Language Novel of India 1935-70*, Writers Workshop, Calcutta, 1977.

48. Hasan, Z. *Gandhi and Ruskin*, Shree Publishing House, New Delhi, 1980.

49. Hemenway, Stephen. *The Novel of India,* Vol. II. The Indo-Anglian Novel, Writers Workshop, Calcutta, 1975.

50. Hewitt, Douglas. *The Approach to Fiction*, Longman Group Limited, London, 1972.

51. Holmes Heynes John. *My Gandhi*, Harper and Co., New York, 1953.

52. Holt, Henry. *Short-Stories for Study: An Anthology*, Henry Hott and Company Inc New York, C 1956.

53 Iyengar, K. R. Srinivasa. *Indian Writing in English*, Asia Publishing House, Bombay, 1974.

54. ——*Indian Contribution to English Literature*, Karnatak Publishing House, Bombay, 1945.

55. ——*Indian Literature Since Independence*, Sahitya Akadamy New Delhi, 1973.

56. Jain, Naresh. K. *Women in Indo-Anglian Fiction Tradition and Modernity*, Manohar Publishers and Distributors, New Delhi, 1998.

57. James, Henry. *The Art of Fiction,* Selected Literary Criticism. Ed. Morris Shapira, Penguin Books England, 1968.

58. Jha, Rama. *Gandhian Thought and Indo-Anglian Novelists,* Chanakya Publications, New Delhi, 1983.

59. Joshi K. N. Rao Syamala, B. *Studies in Indo-Anglian Literature,* Prakash Book Depot., Bareilly, 1964.

60. Juneja, Punim. *The East-West Theme: Some Inner Fury, The Serpent and the Rope and A Dream in Hawaii,* Indian Women Novelists set II: Vol. II. Ed. R. K. Dhawan, Prestige Books, New Delhi, 1993.

61. Kabir, Humayun. *Contemporary Indian Short-Stories*, Series-I, Sahitya Akademy New Delhi, 1976.

62. Kalinnikova, Elena J. *Some Aspects of the Contemporary Scene.* Indian English Literature: A Perspective. Ed. K. K. Sharma, Vimal Prakashan, Ghaziabad, 1982.

63 ——*The Problem of Bhabani Bhattacharya's Novels: A Study,* Perspectives on Bhabani Bhattacharya. Ed. R. K. Srivastava, Vimal Prakashan, Ghaziabad, 1982.

64. Kettle, Arnold. *An Introduction to the English Novel*, Hutchinton, London, 1969.

65. Kripalani, Krishna. *Modern Indian Literature*, Nirmala Sadanand Publishers, Bombay, 1968.

66. Lal, P. *Shadow from Ladakh: A Note, Explorations in Modern Indo-English Fiction.* Ed. R. K. Dhawan, Bahri Publications, New Delhi, 1982.

67. ——*Reviews of Fiction Writer, The Alien Insiders: Essays on Indian Writing in English*, A Writer Workshop Book, Calcutta, 1987.

68. Machewe, Prabhakar. *Modernity and Contemporary Indian Literature*, Chetna Publication, New Delhi, 1978.

69. Mathur, O. P. *The Indian Protagonist and the Western Experience,* Commonwealth Fiction, Vol. I, Ed. R. K. Dhawan, Classical Publishing Company, New Delhi, 1988.

70. Mcculloch, David. *Modern and Traditional India as Seen in Godan, Kanthapura and A Goddess Named Gold, Deep Shika*, Baring Union Christian College, Punjab, 1973.

71. Mehta, P. P. *Indo-Anglian Fiction: An Assessment*, Prakash Book Depot., Barielly, 1968.

72. Mukherjee, Meenakshi. *The Twice Born Fiction*, Arnold-Heinemann, New Delhi, 1974.

73. Munshi, K. M. *Gujarat and Its Literature*, Longmans Green and Co., Bombay, 1935.

74. Naik, M. K. *Aspects of Indian Writing in English,* Macmillan, New Delhi, 1979.

75. ——*Critical Essays on Indian Writing in English,* The Macmillan Co of India Ltd. 1977.

76. ——*Perspectives on Indian Fiction in English*, Abhinav Publications, New Delhi, 1985.

77. ——*Studies in Indian English Literature*, Sterling Publishers, New Delhi, 1987.
78. ——*The Political Novel in Indian Writing in English,* Politics and The Novel in India. Ed. Yogendra K. Malik, Orient Longman Ltd., New Delhi, 1972.
79. ——*Fiction, A History of Indian English Literature*, Sahitya Akademy New Delhi, 1989.
80. Nandy, Pritish. *Literature of Protest,* Aspect of Indian Literature the Changing Pattern. Ed. Suresh Kohili, Vikas Publishers, New Delhi, 1975.
81. Narasimhaiah, C. D. *Awakened Conscience: Studies in Commonwealth Literature*, New Delhi, 1978.
82. ——*Fiction and the Reading Public in India*, University of Mysore, 1977.
83. ——*Indian Literature of the Past Fifty Years 1917-67,* University of Mysore, 1970.
84. ——*The Swan and the Eagle*, Indian Institute of Advanced Study, Simla, 1969.
85. ——*Moving Frontiers of English Studies in India,* S. Chand, New Delhi, 1977.
86. Narasimhaiah, C. D. S. Nagarajan. *Studies in Australian and Indian Literature,* Indian Council for Cultural Relations, New Delhi, 1971.
87. Nicholson, Kai. *A Presentation of Social Problems in the Indo-Anglian and the Anglo-Indian Novel,* Jaico Publishing House, Bombay, 1971.
88. Pandeya. M. Shiva. *Studies in Modern Fiction*, Vikas, Ghaziabad, 1983.
89. Parameswaran, Uma. *A Study of Representation Indo English Novelist,* Vikas Publishing House, New Delhi, 1976.
90. Prabhakar, T. *The Indian Novel in English-Evaluations*, Phoenix Publishing House Pvt. Ltd., 1982.
91. Prabhu, R. K. Rao, U. R. *The Mind of Mahatma*, Navajivan Publishing House, Ahmedabad, 1967.

92. Prasad, Madhusudan. *Contemporary Indian – English Stories*, Sterling Publishing Pvt. Ltd., New Delhi, 1988.
93. Pyarelal. *Mahatma Gandhi: The Early Phase,* Navajivan Publishing House, Ahmedabad, 1965.
94. Radhakrishnan, S. *Mahatma Gandhi: Essays and Reflections on This Life and Thought* Kitabistan, Allabahabad, 1944.
95. Rai, G. *Bhabani Bhattacharya – A Study of his Novels*, B. R. Publishing Corporation, New Delhi, 1995.
96. Raizada, Harish. *The Lotus and the Rose: Indian Fiction in English (1850-1947)*, Aligarh Muslim University, Aligarh, 1978.
97. ——*Bhabani Bhattacharya: The Novelist of Social Ferment,* Response; Recent Revelations of Indian Fiction in English. Ed. Naikar Basavray. S. Prakash Book Depot, Bareilly, 1983.
98. ——*Fiction as Allegory: Novels of Bhabani Bhattacharya,* Perspectives on Bhabani Bhattacharya. Ed. Srivastava R. K. Vimal Prakashan, Ghaziabad, 1987.
99. Ram, Atma. *Essays on Indian English Literature*, Parimal Prakashan, Aurangabad, 1984.
100. Ramamurthi, K. S. *The Rise of the Indian Novel in English*, Madurai University, 1975.
102. Ramaswami, S. *Short-Stories in English-A Selection*, Vellayan Publishing House, Kandanur, Chennai, 1950.
103. Rao, B. Shyamala. *Bhabani Bhattacharya*, Blackie and Son Publishers Pvt. Ltd., Bombay, 1988.
104. Rao, Krishna. *The Indo-Anglian Novel and the Changing Tradition*, Rao and Raghavan, Mysore, 1970.
105. Rao, P. Mallikarjuna Rajeshwar, M. *Indian Fiction in English*, Atlantic Publishers and Distributors, New Delhi, 1999.
106. Reddy, K. Venkata. *Major Indian Novelist*, Prestige Books, New Delhi, 1990.

107. Ridout, K. Albert Jesse Stuart. *Short-Stories for Discussion*, Longman Group Limited, London, 1972.
108. Rolland, Romain. *Mahatma Gandhi: The Man Who Became One With The Universal Being*, Shiva Lal Aggarwala and Co., Ltd., Agra 1922.
109. Sethi, J. D. *Gandhi Today*, Vikas Publishing House, New Delhi, 1978.
110. Sharma, G. P. *Nationalism in Indo-Anglian Fiction*, Sterling Publishers Pvt. Ltd., New Delhi, 1978.
111. Sharma, K. K. *Bhabani Bhattacharya: His Vision and Themes,* Abhinav Publications, New Delhi, 1979.
112. ——*Points of View,* Vol. 1, No. 2, K. K. Publications, New Delhi, 1994.
113. ——*Indo-English Literature*, Vimal Prakashan, Ghaziabad, 1977.
114. ——*Four Great Indian English Novelists*, Some Points of View, Sarup and Sons, New Delhi, 2002.
115. Sharma, P. P. *A Novelist With Social Conscience Essays in Criticism,* Indian Fiction in English. Ed. O. P Bhatnagar, Rachana Prakashan, Jaipur, 1975.
116. Shimer, Dorothy Blair. *Bhabani Bhattacharya*, Twayne Publishers, New York, 1975.
117. Shirwadkar, Meena. *Image of Woman in the Indo-Anglian Novel*, Sterling Publishers, New Delhi, 1986.
118. Singh, Kh. Kunjo. *The Fiction of Bhabani Bhattacharya*, Atlantic Publishers and Distributors, New Delhi, 2002.
119. Singh, R. S. *Indian Novels in English*, Arnold Heinemann, New Delhi, 1977.
120. Sorot, S. Balram. *The Novels of Bhabani Bhattacharya*, Prestige Books, New Delhi, 1984.
121. Srivastava, Narsingh. *Symbol and Allegory in A Goddess Named Gold, Perspectives on Bhabani Bhattacharya.* Ed. Srivastava R. K., Vimal Prakashan, Ghaziabad, 1982.

122. Srivastava, Ramesh K. *Six Indian Novelists in English*, Guru Nanak Dev University, Amritsar, 1987.

123. ——*Perspectives on Bhabani Bhattacharya*, Vimal Prakashan, Ghaziabad, 1982.

124. ——*Bhabani Bhattacharya: Shadow from Ladakh, Major Indian Novels: An Evaluation.* Ed. Pradhan N. S., Arnold-Heinemann, New Delhi, 1985.

125. Subramanyam, Ka. Naa. *Modern Indian Short Stories,* Vol. III, Indian Council for Cultural Relations, New Delhi, 1977.

126. Tarinaya, M. *Bhabani Bhattacharya's So Many Hungers!, Indian Literature of the Past Fifty Years*. Ed. Narasimhaiah, C. D., University of Mysore, Mysore 1970.

127. Tendulkar, D. G. *Mahatma,* Vol. 1 to 8, Publication Division, New Delhi, 1953.

128. Venkat Reddy, K. *Major Indian Novelists,* Prestige Books, New Delhi, 1990.

129. Verghese, C. Paul. *Essays on Indian Writing in English*, N. V. Publications, New Delhi, 1975.

130. ——*Problems of the Creative Indian Writer in English*, Somaiya Publications, Bombay, 1971.

131. Verma, M. R., *Reflections on Indian English Literature*, Atlantic Publishers and Distributors, New Delhi, 2002.

132. Williams, H. M., *Studies in Modern Indian Fiction in English,* Vol. I and II, Writers Workshop, Calcutta, 1973.

133. ——*Indo-Anglian Literature 1800-1970 – A Survey,* Orient Longman Ltd., New Delhi, 1976.

Journals

1. Ameeruddin, Syed. *Social Commitment in Bhattacharya's Novels,* Littcrit, Vol. 4, No. 2, Trivandraum, Dec., 1978.

2. Arulandram, H. G. S., *Man and Religion in A Dream in Hawaii,* The Literacy Half-Yearly, Vol. 26, No. 2, July, 1985.

3. ——*Tagore's Impact on Bhabani Bhattacharya,* Indian Literature, Vol. 18 No. 4, Oct-Dec., 1975.
4. ——*Bhabani Bhattacharya: A Social Reformer, The Rajasthan Journal of English Studies,* Vol. 1, No. 2, Rajasthan, July, 1975.
5. ——*Bhabani Bhattacharya's World View,* Commonwealth Novel in English, Vol. 2, No. 1, The University of Texas at Arlington, Texas, Jan. 1983.
6. Asnani, Shyam. M. *Form Technique and Style in Bhabani Bhattacharya's Novels* Littcrit, Vol. 5, No. 1, June, 1979.
7. Aston, N. M. *Modes of Address among the Cow House Five in Bhabani Bhattacharya's* A Goddess Named Gold, The Commonwealth Review, Vol. 5, No. 2, 1993-94.
8. Bachchan, Ashok. K. R. *The Theme of Hunger in Bhabani Bhattacharya's Novels,* The Literary Voice, No. 1, Dec. 1994.
9. Badal, R. K. *Bhabani Bhattacharya and his Novel, The Literary Half-Yearly,* Vol. 12, No. 2, July 1971.
10. Bhatt, P. N. *The Impact of Gandhi on Dr. Bhabani Bhattacharya's Novel,* Triveni, Vol. 54, No. 3, Triveni Publishers, Machilipatnam, A. P., Oct-Dec, 1985.
11. Ezekiel, Nissim. *Indian Writers in Conference,* The P. E. N., All India Centre, Bombay, 1964.
12. Fisher, Marlene. *Personal and Social Change in Bhattacharya's Novels,* World Literature Writing in English, Vol. XII, No. 2, Nov. 1973.
13. ——*The Women in Bhattacharya's Novels,* World Literature Written in English, Vol. XI, No. 1, April, 1972.
14. Gandhi, M. K. *Harijan* – A Journal of Applied Gandhism, Gerland Publishing, New York and London, 1933-55.

——*Young India 1910-31 (Ganesh, Madras).*

——*Indian Opinion* (Phoenix, South Africa).

15. Gemmil, P. Janet. *An Interview with Bhabani Bhattacharya,* World Literature Written in English, Vol. 14:2, Nov., 1975.
16. Gopal, B. *Bhabani Bhattacharya and the Social Conscience,* Indian Writing in English Critical Studies, University Press, 1986.
17. Gopal, Priyamvada. *Curious Ironies; Matter and Meaning in Bhabani Bhattacharya's Novel of the 1943 Bengal Famine,* Ariel, Vol. 32, No. 3, July 2001.
18. Gowda, H. H Annaih. *Contemporary Creative Writers in English in India,* The Literary Half-Yearly, Jan., 1969.
19. Jain, Jasbir. *Contemporary Indian Fiction in English: New Directions,* Littcrit, Vol. 13, No. 1 and 2, 1987.
20. ——*The Changing Image of Gandhi In indo English Fiction* Indian Literature XII, 4, July-Aug 1979.
21. Jha, K. S. *Bhabani Bhattacharya the Humanist: A Critical Study of his Novels,* The Indian Journal of English Studies, Vol. 22, 1982-83.
22. Joshi, Sudhakar. *An Evening with Bhabani Bhattacharya,* The Sunday Standard, April, 27, 1969.
23. Kumar, Gajendra. *Bhabani Bhattacharya's He Who Rides a Tiger: Kernal of Indian Culture and Caste System,* The Commonwealth Review, Vol. 12, No. 1, 2000-01.
24. Marshal, Prema Kumari. *The Global Village in Ruby Wiebe's Peace Shall Destroy Many and Bhabani Bhattacharya's* A Dream in Hawaii, The Literary Half-Yearly, Vol. 36, No. 1, Jan 1995.
25. Mukherjee, Meenakshi. *The Poem for Mr. Bhattacharya,* The Literary Criterion, Vol. 16, No. 1, Rao and Raghavan Publishers, Mysore, 1981.
26. ——*Style in Indo-Anglian Fiction,* Indian Writing Today, IV, Jan-March, 1970.
27. Mukherjee, Sujit. *India's Entry in English Fiction,* Quest, XL VII, Antumn 1965.

28. Nandakumar, Prema. *The Achievement of the Indo-Anglian Novelist,* The Literacy Criterion, Vol. VI, No. 1, Winter 1961.
29. ——*The Amulet Gandhi Gave, Review of* A Goddess Named Gold, Swarojya, July 28, 1962.
30. Narasimhaiah, S. D., *Indian Writing in English-An Introduction,* Journal of Commonwealth Literature, No. 5, July 1968.
31. Narayana, A. Syamala. *Indian English Novel: Steady Growth,* Littcrit, Vol. 5, No. 2, Kerala University, Kerala, 1979.
32. Pandia, Mahendra N., *Relevance of Bhattacharya's Fiction,* The Indian P. E. N Vol. 50, No. 10-12, Oct-Dec., 1989.
33. Rajan, B. *The Indian Virtue, Journal of Common wealth Literature,* No.1, Sep. 1965.
34. Rajiva, Stanley F., *Contemporary India Writing in English,* Quest, LX, Jan-Mar., 1969.
35. Ramachandraiah, P., *The Short Stories of Bhabani Bhattacharya's,* The Literary Endeavor, Vol. 6, No. 1 to 4, Mysore Printing and Publishing House, 1984.
36. Ramakrishna, D. *Academics and Yogis: Reflections on the Recent Indo-English Fiction,* The Journal of Indian Writing in English, VII, 2, JIWE Publications, Gulbarga, July, 1979.
37. ——*Bhabani Bhattacharya's* A Dream in Hawaii: *A Study in Post Colonial Spirituality,* Kakatiya Journal of English Studies, Vol. 18, Kakatiya University, Warangal, 1998.
38. Rani, T. Asoka. *Nationalism in Bhabani Bhattacharya's* So Many Hungers and Shadow from Ladakh, Commonwealth Literature Special, Vol. 1, No. 3, Autumn 1995.
39. Rao, A. V. Krishna. *Shadow from Ladakh: A Critical View Point,* The Literary Endeavor, Vol. 1, No. 2, April 1986.

40. Rao, B. Shyamala. *Bhabani Bhattacharya as a Novelist,* Triveni, Vol. XL, April 1971.

41. Roy, Lila. *Bhabani Bhattacharya: A Profile,* Indian Literature, Vol. II, No. 2, Apr-Jul., 1968.

42. Reddy, K. Venkata. *An Approach to Bhabani Bhattacharya's So Many Hungers!,* Journal of South Asian Literature, Vol. 22, No. 2, East Lansing, Michingan, Sum-1987.

43. ——*Towards Indian English,* Triveni, Vol. 52 No. 2, Jul-Sep. 1983.

44. ——*Bhabani Bhattacharya: A Writer With a Social Purpose,* Triveni, Vol. 62, No. 1, Jan-March 1993.

45. Reddy, T. Vasudeva. *Microscope Versus Horoscope in Bhattacharya's* Music for Mohini, Indian Scholar, Vol. II, No. 1, Raipur, M. P, Jan 1989.

46. Roy, Ashutosh. *Bhabani Bhattacharya's A Goddess Named Gold*, The Quest, Vol. 9 and 10, No. 2 and 1, Dec-June 1995-96.

47. Sharma, Susheel Kumar. *Bhabani Bhattacharya's* Shadow from Ladakh *A Plea for Syntagmatic Relationship,* Punjab Journal of English Studies, Vol. II, 1996.

48. Shimer, Dorothy Blair. *Bhabani Bhattacharya – Gandhi Biographer,* The Journal of Indian Writing in English, Vol. 2, No. 2, Gulbarga Jul 1974.

49. Singh, Ajay Kumar. *The Individual and Society in the Two Early Novels of Bhabani Bhattacharya,* The Quest, Vol. II, No. 1, June 1997.

50. Singh, R. S. *Bhabani Bhattacharya: A Novelist of Dreamy Wisdom,* The Banasthali Patrika, No. 13, Banasthali Vidyapeth, W. B., 1969.

51. Singh, Shashikala. *The Image of Modern Indian Women in Bhattacharya's* Music for Mohini, The Journal of Indian Writing in English, Vol. 28, No. 1, Jan 2000.

52. Ray, Lila. *Bhabani Bhattacharya: A Profile* Indian Litera2ture, Vol. XL, 1971.

53. Reddy, T. Vasudeva. *Tradition Versions Modernity in Bhattacharya's Music for Mohini,* The Rajasthan Journal of English Studies, Vol. 9, Rajasthan, 1988.

54. Sircar, Arjya. *Duplicity in Saffrom Robes: A Contrastive Study of the Guide, He Who Rides a Tiger and Putul Nacher Itikathu,* The Quest, No. 33, May-Jun. 1982.

55. Srivastava, R. K., *Perspectives on Commonwealth Literature,* Alien Voice, Lucknow, 1981.

56 Swain, S. P. *Self and Society: A Study of Bhabani Bhattacharya's So Many Hungers!,* The Journal of Indian Writing in English, Vol. 25, No. 1 and 2, Gulbarga, Jan-Jul 1997.

57. Tamilarasan, C. *Bhattacharya's Music for Mohini: A Study, The Literary Endeavor,* Vol. 2, No. 2, Mysore Printing and Publishing House, 1982.

58. Tarinayya, M. *Two Novels, Indian Literature,* Vol. 13, No. 1, Mar. 1970.

59 Tripathi, Bimalesh. K. *Bhabani Bhattacharya's He Who Rides a Tiger: A Socio-Economic Study, The Quest,* Vol. 1, No. 1, Mar 1987.

60 Verghese, C. Paul. *Indian English and Man in Indo-Anglian Fiction, Indian Literature,* Vol. 13, No. 1, Mar 1970.

61. ——*Problems of the Indian Novelist in English,* Banasthali Patrika, Banasthali Vidyapeeth, IV, 12 Jan. 1969.

62. ——*Modern Indian Novel in English,* Quest, 58, July-Sep. 1968.

63. Vinoda, T. Music for Mohini: *A Classic of Flawed Perspective,* Kakatiya Journal of English Studies, Vol, 13, Kakatiya University, Warangal, 1993.

Index

T